Democracy
as a neocon trick

Democracy
as a neocon trick

Alexander Boot

RoperPenberthy Publishing

Copyright © 2014 Alexander Boot

RoperPenberthy Publishing Limited
23 Oatlands Drive
Weybridge
KT13 9LZ
United Kingdom

All rights reserved. No part of this publication may be reproduced,
stored in a retrieval system or transmitted in any form or by any means,
electronic, mechanical, photocopying or otherwise, without the prior
written consent of the publisher.
Short extracts may be used for review purposes.

ISBN 978 1 903905 85 2

Typeset by Avocet Typeset, Somerton, Somerset TA11 6RT
Printed and bound in the UK by PublishPoint from
KnowledgePoint Limited, Reading

Dedicated to the memory of Ken Minogue
– thinker, scholar, friend

"For we wrestle not against flesh and blood, but against principalities, against powers, against the rulers of the darkness of this world, against spiritual wickedness in high *places*."
St Paul

"But what is liberty without wisdom, and without virtue? It is the greatest of all possible evils; for it is folly, vice, and madness, without tuition or restraint."
Edmund Burke

CONTENTS

Preface	9
Setting the stall	11
Why the neocons?	15
Hellenes, Christians and the state	21
The organic state	49
The first modern state: a tragicomedy in three acts	63
The American religion	93
The American religion gets its St Paul	109
Democracy as a battle cry	129
'A deviant constitution'	145
The last nail in the coffin of Christendom	173
Conservatism and the Babel of politics	189
Defining and refining conservatism	201
Reality mugged by 'liberals'	229
History ends, then restarts	249
Russia and the reign of error	259
2001 and all that	201
An epilogue without an end	315
A brief bibliography	326
Index	??

Preface

Alexander Boot is a master of language. As even in the title, he works by hyperbole, metaphor and image. The book is full of pithy expression and a dry humour. The subject, however, is very serious. He deplores the loss of a Judaeo-Christian world view in the West and its replacing either by anti-Christian ideas drawn from the radical Enlightenment, culminating in ideologies like Marxism and Nazism, or by empty values like 'democracy' without important safeguards regarding conscience or freedom.

It is important, for him, that civilisations have a moral and spiritual framework but he is also well aware that intellectual totalitarianism results in its political version. He is equally scathing about a reductionist politics that downsizes our common life to 'bread and circuses' for the masses.

Christianity's great contribution has been the discovery of the human person, not just as a number to be counted but in terms of the interior life from which come the building blocks of a free and just society.

He is right to see equality as a spiritual value, equality before God, and then its authentic social working out in terms of dignity, freedom and opportunity.

If there is to be a genuinely free society, we need critics like Boot to be ruthless in their analyses of conventional wisdom and its seers. Only then will our societies be built on solid foundations.

Bishop Michael Nazir-Ali

Setting the stall

In pursuit of notoriety, Herostratus burned a temple down to cinders. In pursuit of evil, Robespierre and Lenin went the Greek one better by also murdering everybody inside, starting with the priest. On any legal scale they are more culpable than the attention-seeking firebug. But culturally there is no difference, for in both instances the temple was no more.

In parallel, a motley assortment of Western 'useful idiots', useless intellectuals and *bien pensant* masses, while generally refraining from physical violence towards the temple, perpetrated the crime of its vulgarisation. The methods were different, the result the same: the temple was no more.

The temple of Artemis at Ephesus, the one Herostratus torched, was considered the most beautiful building in the world. Likewise, I regard the metaphorical temple of Western civilisation as the most beautiful of God's and man's creations. That is why it pains me to watch the edifice being brought down by carnivore and vegetarian alike, those who perpetrate this crime consciously or negligently, with much bloodshed or none, with their faces distorted by ugly scowls or lit up by beatific smiles. In the end it makes no difference: the temple is no more.

It took me about 10 years of examining the scene of the crime, the West, to arrive at this melancholy observation, and another 10 or so to make enough sense of it to start writing. But once I got going, I could write about nothing else. Most books I have published since, though perfectly capable of standing on their own, are chapters in an ongoing attempt to ponder the shattered temple, to understand why it was destroyed and by whom, to pull together its scattered fragments to see how they

DEMOCRACY AS A NEOCON TRICK

add together, while hoping, perhaps forlornly, that one day they would again become whole. Each of my books focused on one aspect of modernity, be it culture, religion or economics. This one is about politics, which in today's West is dominated by totemistic worship of a mythological ideal that is misleadingly called liberal democracy.

The frequent fusion of the two words implies that there is no contradiction between them. Yet often there is. For example, if a predominantly Muslim community in Britain (and there are many of those) votes to legalise forced marriage, this will be democracy served but liberalism abused. Actually the very existence of predominantly Muslim communities in Britain and throughout Western Europe is an affront to liberalism, what with Islamic law and everyday practices generally representing a pre-Enlightenment, which is to say pre-liberal, frame of mind and set of practices. But democracy, which depends on actuarial calculations of majority views, disarms those who maintain that Islamic immigration has turned into Islamic colonisation. You have voted for your MPs, have you not? And have they not voted for admitting practically unlimited numbers of Muslim immigrants? Well then, what we see is democracy in action, something impossible to complain about.

As with many other totems, the myth of liberal democracy is based on a groundless superstition deployed by its shamans to distract people from reality. If reality were laid bare by using real words to describe real things, mass apostasy would follow and the totem would be brought down. That is why the shaman caste vigilantly protects its toxic myth behind a smokescreen of vague cant, allowing the contagion to spread and infect areas that traditionally were beyond its reach. Just as Darwinism was encouraged to leave its original domain of biology to penetrate political and social thought, so is democracy no longer just a way of organising political life. It has become a versatile stencil, and everything that sticks out is supposed to be cut away.

This can be *observed* by anyone who has opened a few books, read a few newspapers and talked to a few people in university halls, offices or, if such is one's wont, public bars. But it can be *understood* only by those who realise that a political phenomenon never exists in isolation from all others. One can learn much about modern politics by going to a concert, opening the business section of a broadsheet, ringing a doctor for an appointment or joining the crowd at a football match. In fact I would suggest that no serious understanding of modern politics is possible without detecting the common thread running through all those, and many other, aspects of our daily lives.

Hence no analysis will ultimately succeed without a synthesis, and this is the task I have set myself. Moreover, the synthesis cannot just be a hoop of ratiocination rotating around the horizontal axis of the present – it must also turn on the vertical axis of history. What we see around us today is largely the work of generations past; what we do is our legacy for the generations to come. Though I shall touch upon the future only tangentially, the past will make frequent appearances throughout this narrative for, as George Santayana said, "Those who cannot remember the past are condemned to repeat it." Or, as he would doubtless rephrase if he were alive today, "to falsify and thus destroy it".

But it is the present that is the principal theme of this essay. I shall try to strip away the veil shrouding modern democracy and show what hides underneath. My argument will be that, if acted upon, the belief in universal suffrage as the sole possible alternative to despotism is in itself intellectually despotic. And if we have learned anything from history, when intellectual despotism reigns supreme the political variety is just round the corner.

Why the neocons?

The unquestioning worship of liberal democracy, or rather of the political superstition that goes by that misnomer, is the dominant feature of today's political thought in the West. By itself, as an academic preference, this bias is unobjectionable. One may consider it intellectually unsound, historically and philosophically ignorant or even morally questionable, but people are entitled to hold whatever views help them to get through the day – provided, and nowadays this is an important proviso, they do not deny the same freedom to others.

Unfortunately, however, this particular attitude has now been transformed into an ill-advised messianic policy aggressively followed by many Western nations, but mostly by the USA and her closest allies, especially Britain. The political movement largely, though not solely, responsible for this amalgamation of thought and action tends to call itself neoconservative, though some of its most prominent proponents coyly deny their affiliation with any such movement.

This brings us back to the question posed in the title to this chapter. Why should a British writer, or for that matter his readers, be interested in neoconservatism, which is still mainly an American phenomenon? Some highly respected conservative scholars, including the man to whose memory this book is dedicated, have asked me this question and, since I do respect them highly, they deserve an answer. Or rather several answers, to be exact. Here they are, in ascending order of importance:

1) In America, neoconservatism supplies much human, and even more intellectual, material for the shaman caste preaching at the totem of democracy. Considering America's

status in the world, this makes neoconservatism influential globally, especially in the Anglophone sphere.

2) Thus, though neoconservatism is still mostly an American trend, it is no longer strictly that. It has crossed the Atlantic and is rapidly gaining in influence here. As a reliable sign of this tendency, the magazines and think tanks of British neoconservatism are more generously financed than their conservative counterparts.

3) Partly because real conservatism seems to be going out of fashion, neoconservatism may come across as a dynamic movement capable of offering a viable alternative to socialism. I shall discuss the differences (and the dearth thereof) between neoconservatism and socialism later, but for the time being I am talking about perception, not reality. Alas, the distinction between the two is these days slight; according to Marshall 'the-medium-is-the-message' McLuhan, for all practical purposes they are one and the same.

3) Neoconservatism is not just a misguided academic trend contained within the proverbial groves. As I have mentioned earlier, it animates much of the policy-making in the West, especially in the Anglophone West, which renders it influential quite out of proportion to its feeble cerebral content and its still limited representation in Western governments.

4) Most important, neoconservatism is a cauldron in which the more objectionable traits of modern political thought are boiled together to produce a stew that intensifies the rancid taste of each ingredient. Prime among them is a clean break with the two millennia of Western civilisation, accompanied by ignorance of the religious, cultural and intellectual heritage of that civilisation, and often hostility to it.

This is garnished with disregard for reason, the faculty in the name of which modern politics was concocted to begin with; semantic mendacity, with few words used in their true meaning; emotional afflatus that is neither new nor conservative; eagerness to do concrete murder on behalf of abstract principles, which are in any case misconceived; lust for power; arrogance and conceit.

WHY THE NEOCONS?

Neoconservatism is an eerie mishmash of Trotskyist temperament, infantile bellicosity, American chauvinism (not exclusively on the part of Americans), expansionism masked by pseudo-messianic verbiage on exporting democracy to every tribal society on earth, Keynesian economics, Fabian socialism, welfarism and statism run riot – all mixed together with a spoonful of vaguely conservative phrases purloined from the rightful owners to trick the neocons' way to broader electoral support.

Hence an argument against neoconservatism constitutes a battle against everything that is unsound, dishonest and destructive in modern Western politics. As such, it is a battle worth fighting, and one I shall attempt to engage, but only as a corollary to my main theme. Towards the end I shall show how the philosophical paucity of neoconservatism has led to appalling errors of judgment in practical politics, specifically in relation to Russia and the Middle East.

When this project was still in its embryonic stage, I set out to do proper research. Since my intention was to use neoconservatism for illustration only, and the main theme of this essay is so-called liberal democracy, the first step was to organise everything I had ever read on political theory. This had to involve getting reacquainted with thinkers who have influenced me over the years, either positively or negatively. The first category spans two and a half millennia of thought, a timeline densely dotted with, in no particular order of either chronology or importance, Aristotle and Machiavelli, Augustine and Aquinas, Burke and de Maistre, Voegelin and Burnham, Chateaubriand and Kirk, Coleridge and Ortega y Gasset, Santayana and Hayek, Canning and Oakeshott, Collingwood and von Mises – well, if you can put together a complete list of your intellectual influences, you are a better man than I am.

The second list, that of negative influences, those that elucidated for me the political concepts to shun and oppose, would begin with Plato, then jump over a couple of millennia to Hobbes and Locke. From there it is only a short hop to the Enlightenment, which blanket term I tuck loosely around such diverse thinkers as Voltaire and Rousseau, Hegel and

17

Kant, Fichte and Montesquieu (who, along with Plato, overlaps somewhat with the first category), Hume and Smith (ditto), half a dozen of the American Founders and also such Enlightenment offshoots as Mill, Bentham, Marx, Lenin and Trotsky. This being a polemical rather than scholarly essay, I do not feel duty-bound to quote any of my sources from either category chapter and verse. Whenever I use a direct citation, I shall identify its author but not always the publication, an economy measure that will not be unduly restrictive to the reader, what with the universal availability of the Internet. At the end I shall provide a short bibliography of books I had close at hand while writing.

Though neoconservatism acts only in an auxiliary capacity here, it is still important to my argument as it channels the polemic into a reasonably straight conduit. Over the years I have read probably hundreds of articles churned out by the founding fathers of this movement, mainly Irving Kristol and Norman Podhoretz, but also Nathan Glazer, Daniel Patrick Moynihan and Jeanne Kirkpatrick, along with their dynastic and ideological heirs in the next generation. But journalism is by its nature transient, moth-like, while books are the rocks that define the intellectual landscape enduringly if not eternally.

In search of such rocks I set out to read at least a dozen books by contemporary neoconservative authors. Standing apart from other works are Irving Kristol's *Reflections of a Neoconservative: Looking Back, Looking Ahead* and *Neoconservatism: The Autobiography of an Idea*, which at least have the advantage of being written cogently, in places brilliantly.

The next batch included *The End of History and the Last Man* by Francis Fukuyama, and half a dozen other books by both American and British neoconservatives (I shall explain shortly why I am not being more precise here). Since most neoconservative authors defer to Leo Strauss and Alan Bloom, I reread *Natural Right and History* by the former and *The Closing of the American Mind* by the latter – the first without any pleasure, the second with some. That, I have to confess, was as far as I got: the second batch also turned out to be the last.

One does not have to drink a whole bottle of corked wine

WHY THE NEOCONS?

to know it has turned to vinegar. Nor does one need to watch more than six horses bolting out of the neocon stable to realise they are all identical clones. Contrary to any claims of individualism explicit or implicit in their prose, one could never guess, reading their books unattributed, that they came from different authors. Their underlying emotions, arguments, conclusions, sources, treatment of facts are as identical as those of the party apparatchiks from my Soviet childhood. Even the British authors, whom I know to be nice gentlemen sporting bespoke suits and expensive accents, are indistinguishable from their American *Parteigenossen*. Never once in their books do they hint at any British relevance of their ideas, and their 'we' typically refers to Americans, not Englishmen. But then neoconservatism is nothing if not universalist, or at least aspiring to be.

Amazingly, even the style of the books I read looks as if it came from some manual bearing the party's approval stamp (Irving Kristol's work is an exception). For example, none of the authors I read can see an infinitive without aching to split it, and they all show a perverse affection for such unsightly neologisms as 'equivalencing'. This cavalier treatment of stylistic convention may be the neocons' way of establishing their group identity, which is a time-honoured function of any argot. Or else it might simply be testimony to the lamentable failure of the educational system. One way or the other, today's neocons, with perhaps one or two exceptions, make Mrs Malaprop look good.

My mind hopelessly numbed by the outpourings by this uniform entity, I lost, along with the will to live, any ability to distinguish among the principal constituents. Therefore, when citing their works I shall refer to them only as the Collective Neocon, COLLENE for short. I would have included Fukuyama into this rubric, but in his case no subterfuge is possible: everybody knows which neocon talked about the end of history.

You need not feel deprived: just as the by-line did not matter in the identical *Pravda* and *Izvestia* articles of my childhood, exact attribution would serve no purpose in this instance. It is not the dummy man who speaks but the ventriloquist *apparat*. Whether it makes its wishes known directly or osmotically is immaterial as long as it is crystal-clear that it does indeed make them known. Even worse, as a characteristic of our time, is the distinct likelihood that no such collusive *apparat* exists, and the discipline binding the neocons is self-imposed. If they pick their identical ideas out of ambient air, then the air is poisoned, and we are all in trouble.

Neoconservatism, along with most other brooks flowing into the political mainstream, has inscribed democracy on its banners. The whole world, writes COLLENE, is ready for Democracy (capitalisation implied), even if most parts of the world may still be unaware of this. Hence democracy has to acquire a didactic extension, laser-guided to make the recalcitrant see the light and presumably hear the bang. Spare the bomb and spoil the world seems to be the underlying wisdom.

But before we get down to the nitty-gritty of modern politics, I shall take a few chapters to argue the fallacy of the absolute democratic presupposition even within the Western world itself. Historically, democracy has never been, and certainly is not now, either the only or indeed the most viable alternative to despotism. Quite the opposite, its modern, one-man-one-vote, version has always had the seeds of tyranny within itself.

These seeds have now sprouted, growing into a new despotism made so much worse for not generally being perceived as such. As this is impossible to comprehend without plunging into history, I propose to do that first. The plunge will not be too deep – we shall swim close to the surface and fast, arriving as soon as possible at our present-day destination.

Hellenes, Christians and the state

1

"Man is by nature a political animal," said Aristotle, undoubtedly an extremely intelligent thinker. Two thousand-odd years later Dr Johnson, another extremely intelligent thinker, begged to differ: "Public affairs," he wrote, "vex no man." Yet the Greeks had a word for someone who could not be 'vexed' by public affairs. This word came down to us as 'idiot', an epithet we would hardly apply in its current meaning to the distinguished author of our first dictionary.

These two thinkers thereby expressed mutually exclusive views. If one is right, then the other is wrong; no compromise is possible. Either man is above all a political animal, rather than, say, a thinking or artistic one, or he cannot be bothered about public affairs in general and politics in particular.

Which of those two extremely intelligent men was right? The answer is, they both were. It is just that the Greek spoke of one kind of man and the Englishman of another. Aristotle commented on the man of his time, the pagan Hellene, and celebrated his public spirit. Samuel Johnson commented on the man of *his* time, the Christian Westerner, and lamented his impending demise.

A quick empirical observation is in order, one you can make for yourself at any place where people chat about things that 'vex' them. You will notice that once gossip, sex, sports and home decoration have been covered, politics invariably comes up. Prime Minister Jones or President Smith will be described as either decent or [expletive deleted] useless, or else honest or [expletive deleted] corrupt. You will get the impression that the toings and froings of Messrs Jones and Smith matter almost as much to the interlocutors' lives as gossip, sex, sports and home decoration. For some, those tagged disparagingly as 'political junkies', they may matter even more.

If we agree that both Aristotle and Dr Johnson were right and that they only differed on that score because their times did, then we have to conclude that perhaps life has come full circle. It will seem to us that we have jumped backwards, leapfrogging Dr Johnson's time and landing smack in the middle of Aristotle's, at least as far as interest in politics is concerned.

Our approximate contemporary Thomas Mann concurs: "All intellectual attitudes are latently political." In other words, just as in times classical, man has again become a political animal. Irving Kristol, one of the first neoconservatives, and the proud wielder of the term, liked to stress this similarity so much that one is surprised he did not call this movement 'neoclassicism' instead. Perhaps he thought that the term had been pre-empted by architecture. Or else he decided that his frame would look less incongruous wrapped in a Brooks Brothers suit than in a toga.

Yet one does not have to possess a degree in classics to know that in every other respect our double-breasted post-Christians are the chalk to the cheese of the toga-draped pre-Christians. In fact one needs little education to know that the differences go far beyond matters sartorial. Once we have realised this, the neocons' attempts to legitimise themselves by fulsome claims to classical heritage will be revealed for the humbug they really are.

I suggest that unless we get to the bottom of this we shall understand next to nothing about modern politics. The differences among modern democratic, totalitarian and authoritarian regimes will be lost upon us; the distinctions among real conservatives, neoconservatives, libertarians and so forth will mean nothing. We shall have not an understanding, but a compendium of slogans.

2

For all their obvious differences, the pre- and post-Christian worlds converge in their assessment of the relative importance of politics. But politics never exists in a vacuum. Rather it is a reflection of the numerous religious, social, cultural, legal and intuitive attitudes that go by the name of civilisation. To rise up to the level of a civilisation, rather than languishing as mere personal idiosyncrasies, such attitudes have to be collective – and *dominantly* collective, shared by most and accepted by all. Using Aristotle's own inductive method, we can understand much of his civilisation – or of ours, come to that – by just looking at the artistic residue it left in the world. "Ye shall know them by their fruits," taught that famous proto-conservative, and this lesson applies to civilisations, not just to individuals.

We judge an apple tree not mainly by its height, the colour of its leaves or the beauty of its blossoms but by the fruit it produces. Human societies also bear fruit, each testifying either to the greatness or folly of the human race in general and each society in particular. Much can be inferred about their respective civilisations – including their politics – from comparing the Hellene's temple, the Christian's cathedral and the modern man's skyscraper.

Admiring, say, the Parthenon, we are captivated by its streamlined beauty. The harmony of straight lines intersecting at just the right angles, the symmetrical proportion of shapes and sizes, the measured rhythm of the building all contribute to the feeling that we are in the presence of noble, restrained perfection – *sancta simplicitas*, or whatever the Greeks used to call it before Latin took over in the West.

By contrast, if we look at the outside of, say, Rouen Cathedral, we shall find much that is sacred but nothing that is simple. The structure was clearly put together by many men over many centuries, which shows in the mishmash of architectural styles and ornamentation springing from the eclectic tastes of the architects, builders and stonemasons. Though vaguely symmetrical, the front towers look like distant cousins rather than siblings, much less twins; the ornate façade is overloaded with the exorcised spirits of gargoyles and the statues of saints (some of them headless, reflecting modernity's favoured style of art criticism).

It is only when we step inside that we discover exactly what sanctified the saints and exorcised the spirits. The message then becomes not merely sacred but also simple – and sacred in its simplicity. We understand then that, unlike the Parthenon, Rouen Cathedral was built from the inside out. What matters there is the content, not so much the form. And it is the content that dictates the form. While the façade of the Greek temple is the whole book, the façade of the Gothic cathedral is but the table of contents.

Extrapolating from there we reach the conclusion that Hellenic civilisation was vectored outwards, not inwards. That is why the quintessential art of the Greeks, one that expressed the core of their culture (much as music expresses the core of ours), was sculpture, that most external of arts. Unlike painting, which uses a broad gamut of techniques (composition, different perspectives, shadows, variously distinct lines, shades and intensity of colours and so on) to guide the eye towards the focal and away from the incidental, sculpture is more or less free of subtext.

Moreover, while great Christian artists were able to put every nuance of human expression on the faces of their statues, Greek sculpture is all glorious surface and no inner content. Praxiteles's marble faces are impersonally, coldly beautiful, but that is all they are. By contrast, working in the same medium and ostensibly similar style, Michelangelo animated his Moses with so much humanity that one expects the prophet to rise from his chair at any moment and unleash his wrath on the impious Hebrews.

The same outwardness of the Hellenes is noticeable in their religion. We know much about their glorious rites, noisy processions and solemn sacrifices – and yet precious few prayers have come down to us, hardly any individual appeals to God's mercy. As the Hellenes did not perceive themselves as autonomous individuals, they could not routinely conduct one-to-one dialogues with their gods. Their religious self-expression was more or less reduced to pomp and circumstance, displaying the same cold perfection of form as their art did. No inner warmth of the human soul was in evidence. It was not just that the Hellenes' art was an expression of their religion; it was also the other way around.

The Greeks obviously had a concept of the individual, and it was a cherished concept at that. They just did not see an individual as something self-contained. He was valuable in as much as he expressed himself outwardly, and his value, rather than being intrinsic, depended on how well he did so. It was his public life that provided a respectable arena for self-expression. That is why the Greeks are not known for psychological insights. What lay at the core of the Hellenic world and therefore its philosophy was ethics, the Socratic belief refined by Plato and Aristotle that virtue is the source of happiness (*eudemonia*), joyous life in this world. Happiness was one reward for virtue; health and physical perfection another. Hence all those eyeless discus throwers whose sound bodies bespoke their sound minds.

This points at one critical distinction between the Hellenic and Western cultures, one that goes far beyond aesthetics. For the Greeks the form was its own meaning. For us the form is only a shell that contains the real meaning. Hellenic body that held no secrets was replaced by Western soul, everything about which, apart from the fact of its existence, was not only a mystery but an unsolvable one at that.

3

It is such observations that lead to the conclusion that for the Hellenes life was indeed vectored outwards. In politics, that vector was like an invisible hand grabbing the good citizen of Athens – or for that matter Rome – by the scruff of the neck and dragging him out of his house and into the public square, the agora. Even as the Hellene sought outward perfection in his art, he strove for harmony in his politics. Achieving it in the agora was more important to him than finding happiness at home.

Plato described this pecking order with helpful honesty and unmatched mastery in his *Republic* and especially in *Laws*. The *polis* was everything; the individual qua individual, next to nothing. The same went for that extension of the individual, his family, which was to be reduced to more or less the state's breeding farm. For example, according to Plato, who can be credited with the invention of eugenics, it was up to the *polis* to pair off couples on the basis of the potential usefulness of their offspring to the common good.

Before Cleisthene's reforms created the *polis* around 500 BC, such views would have been unthinkable to the Greeks. Their society had revolved around the family, clan, kinship and other personal ties. But by Plato's time the variably democratic *polis* had made the family redundant in every sense other than the good of the *polis*. This is the first intimation in history of the relationship since then amply proved: democracy and family are at odds. They are not friends, nor even allies, but competitors: the stronger the one, the weaker the other.

Sensing this, John Locke, who laid out the groundwork for the liberal democratic state, countenanced not only divorce but even polygamy: "He that is already married may marry another woman with his left hand..." It is reassuring to see how solicitously our Lockean modernity is trying to make sure his prophesy can come true – if in Locke's time hostility to marriage was still inchoate, by now it has grown to full maturity.

Because the idea of personal freedom, indeed of a *person*, was alien to him, Plato did not recognise the self-significance of the individual. Hence in his *Timaeus* and *Critias* dialogues he hailed the laudable subjugation of the individual to the collective achieved in Atlantis, Plato's imaginary island organised along primeval lines. Atlantis was his ultimate, primordial society where the tribe was everything and the individuals nothing. Rousseau later found a similar ideal in his fictitious *noble sauvage*, the originally perfect creature later to be corrupted by Western institutions, especially the church.

But what if people refused to act in a subservient capacity? Well, they had to be taught the true facts of life. And if they would not learn, they had to be coerced into toeing the line. Hence, in the absence of any metaphysical concept of individual freedom, the Platonic order could only be imposed by coercion. And considering the kind of order it was, such imposition necessitated the amount of force that only a totalitarian state could bring to bear.

4

Any modern reader this side of Soviet Russia or Nazi Germany would find such notions not just abhorrent but insane. However, the Athenians were suspicious not so much of Plato's ideas as of his personality, too outstanding for Hellenic tastes. Their tendency to seek outward, evenly spread perfection made them uneasy about too much individual brilliance. Considering that the fifth century BC in Greece boasted as much of such brilliance as any other presumptive golden age in history, this will seem odd – but only until we have considered the vital political implications.

Because brilliant people tend to have their own take on things, they ask awkward questions, something a culture of collective harmony cannot countenance. A boat rocked is one that may capsize, the Greeks feared. It was more because of this than for any specific transgressions that Plato's teacher Socrates was killed and Plato's disciple Aristotle had to flee Athens a step ahead of the hemlock cup. (As he was running away, Aristotle quipped that he wanted to spare Athenians the folly of wronging philosophy twice, in clear reference to Socrates's fate).

For any Greek, be that Athenian, Spartan or Syracusan, his home was not his castle. Nor was it really his home either, only his bedroom. His true home was the *polis*, its *agora* his drawing room. This was where he rushed first thing in the morning, to discuss the issues of the day with his real family, fellow citizens. Spartans would often not even go home at meal times; communal feasts rid them of any necessity to rush back to their families, thus interrupting what to them was real life. (It is instructive to observe how modern urban life has begun to resemble the Greek model – people again use their homes as merely bedrooms. Their day's work done, they spend some time chatting or drinking with their colleagues, then go out to eat and only get home at beddy-bye time. Even young married people rush out at every opportunity, especially if there is nothing interesting on TV.)

Citizenship was to the Hellenes the ultimate kinship; it

represented firmer and more binding ties than those springing from biological incidentals. Hence the easy familiarity with which they addressed one another: the ultimate equality rooted in citizenship trumped any inequality of age, status or wisdom. They were all offspring of the same parent: the *polis*. In fact, Aristotle defined a just society as one in which the people accept such inequalities as a necessary factor of the common good.[1]

From there it is easy to deduce the Hellenes' political preferences and the kind of institutions that satisfied those preferences. Since the state was their common love, family, vehicle for self-expression, depository of virtue and sum total of aspirations, the Hellenes felt it was their right, nay duty, to play an active role in state affairs, not just to argue about them in the agora. Any infringement of that right was to them so abhorrent that they would never have submitted to it regardless of any potential gains in wealth.

If, for example, in Russia a great culture could be created in the nineteenth century under a regime rightly regarded as despotic, the brief periods of tyrannical rule in Athens (as, say, during the oligarchic revolutions at the time of the Peloponnesian War or the rule of the Thirty Tyrants after it) rendered her society temporarily barren. It was as if the Greeks did the Galatea in reverse by calcifying into their own statues. Any murmur in the political heart cut off the circulation of cultural blood. All life stopped. Culture lay fallow.

Hence the suspicion the Hellenic world felt for its outstanding men and especially politicians, including such titans as Pericles and Caesar. Neither man was a tyrant, both topped their contemporaneous statesmen by an intellectual head. Largely because of this, the ensuing desire to chop Pericles down to size was barely contained in Athens; in Rome, Caesar was not so lucky.

Democracy, with power divided among all citizens,

---

1 A Western conservative may take exception to the route Aristotle took to this conclusion, but not to the conclusion itself: accepting our ultimate equality before God precludes too much acrimony towards inequalities of physical life.

was therefore the most organic political setup for Greece and Rome – any other systems could have been installed by coercion only. The Romans came up with a different but comparable term 'republic', *res publica*, public matter. There was no *res privata* worth speaking of; all interests were supposed to be subsumed in Roman republicanism or Athenian democracy. Since the people, *demos*, were the heart, brain and sinews of the Hellenic body politic, it was up to them to decide how various limbs of the body moved. And that body was as beautiful as the body of Venus de Milo: all parts belonged together, everything was coldly perfect, nothing looked like an alien implant.

Athenian democracy had no need for any system of representation. The 30,000 or so fully enfranchised citizens (out of the population of about a quarter of a million in Athens at her peak) could all vote for every piece of legislation direct, with 5,000–6,000 constituting the quorum. In fact, Plato suggested that this was not only the minimum acceptable but also the maximum desirable number of active participants in a democracy. Going over that cut-off point, he warned, would result in mob rule.

The Athenian Assembly was a precursor of our parliaments, a legislative body to which all enfranchised citizens had a right to belong. Unlike in modern parliaments, members were often chosen by drawing lots, as if to emphasise the equality of citizenship (looking at our today's legislators, it is hard to escape the conclusion that a blind draw might indeed produce better results than those delivered by modern elections).

However, someone had to be entrusted with the actual administration of the *polis*, and such officials could never be excessively numerous. Yet in Athens the executive body was still larger than in most modern democracies: its Council was about 500-strong. Members were changed every year, and no one could serve consecutive terms, or more than two over a lifetime.

Given the prevailing political culture of the time, the job was easy, if ultimately never free of potential pitfalls. The officials themselves recognised that their position was precarious because in some ways it ran against the very ethos of society. It was inevitable that they would assume a somewhat greater power than the rest of the citizens – which is to say they would appropriate to themselves a particle of the political capital rightfully belonging to all. Being entrusted with such communal property was a high honour, and one that had to be not only merited but also bought.

Hence all citizens occupying public office had to pay for the privilege, and not just in the monetary value of each post. Greek statesmen also had to assume most of the burden of voluntary taxation and much of the onus of serving in the army. The idea of public officials being paid for their services would have been not so much repugnant as incomprehensible to the Greeks until the late fifth century[2] – even the Sophist philosophers were condemned by Socrates and practically run out of town when they dared to charge tuition fees. Hence victorious Roman generals were paid in wreaths and triumphs, not so much in coin (by way of *res privata*, they might have helped themselves to sizeable booty, but this was a matter of little public concern).

Athenian democracy was not without its fault lines. These eventually turned into clefts because democracy naturally promotes egalitarianism, which runs contrary to human nature. Whenever societies try to arrange themselves horizontally rather than vertically, a certain element of artificiality has to be present. In time this can prove destructive. That is partly why Lycurgus's hierarchical constitution of Sparta eventually proved more stable and long-lived than Solon's egalitarian constitution of Athens – the former was more consonant with human nature. But certain assumptions were nevertheless held throughout the Hellenic world.

Athenians may have elected their rulers and even their generals by either voting or drawing lots, but running the *polis* or its army was a fulltime job. As the leaders were supposed not only to work without pay but also to subsidise liturgies and festivals, they had to have independent means to begin with.

---

2   Even then Council members were paid only small daily allowances.

HELLENES, CHRISTIANS AND THE STATE

Hence in effect they had to be drawn from aristocracy, the only group that could be confidently expected not to depend on wages. Thus Greek-style democracy (or for that matter any other) carries oligarchic seeds within it: the class that consistently supplies most leaders will inevitably try to separate itself from others and lord it over them.

Even the Roman Empire was more similar to our presidential republics than to the absolute or even somewhat limited monarchies of Christendom. In fact, throughout much of their imperial period Romans continued to refer to their state as *res publica*. A paid bureaucratic class did not exist there for most of Rome's history and only began to appear as a recognisable caste under Constantine, when *Pax Romana* was on the way out and Christendom on the way in.

Family mattered to Rome, but only as an economic, political and legal institution. It was usually for such reasons rather than romantic and spiritual attraction that couples came together. Utility, not love, was the magnet.

As a result, emotional bonds akin to those tying together both pre- and post-Hellenic families hardly ever existed. Divorce, remarriage and adoption were encouraged by the Roman state, with no legal distinction made among the children adopted or produced in, or outside, multiple marriages. Nor was there any distinction made between the conjugal practices of men and women: both were expected to float about from one marriage to the next and implicitly from one liaison to the next. The more the merrier was the prevailing attitude to families. That way the state, especially during its imperial phase, could procure more building blocks for its army and administration, the need for which increased with geographical expansion, unknown to the pre-Alexander Greeks.

As a predictable fallout from that utilitarian ethos, unwanted children, mostly girls, were often dumped to die by the roadside – or else handed over to the state for safekeeping. In one of the earliest letters to survive from ancient Greece, a husband writes to his pregnant wife, "if it is male let it live, if it is female get rid of it". Wild beasts delivered the services these days delegated to abortion clinics, while Rome became the first provider state in

31

history, with up to a quarter of the city's population[3] subsisting on what today we call welfare. Decadence, which is widely credited with being a contributing factor in Rome's downfall, was of course another by-product of her family policy.

It was the good of the state, rather than love for one's fellow man, that was at the heart of Rome's social provisions, and in this sense our modern governments are the wind that "returneth again according to his circuits". The forms adopted by rampant statism in Rome changed somewhat compared to Athens or Sparta. The essence remained the same.

5

Christianity changed all that by privatising the spirit and internalising man, thereby altering his idea of himself – and consequently of the desired interaction between himself and the state. The spiritual revolution that caused the change was by far the most sweeping in history – and the only one in which the very nature of man seemed to have undergone real changes, rather than the trumped-up ones to be claimed by all subsequent revolutions.

Indeed back in the 1960s it was fashionable to portray Jesus Christ as a political revolutionary, a sort of Che Guevara of Galilee. That was of course nonsense, as any reader of the Gospels can find out for himself in a lazy afternoon. Yet at a level much deeper than politics, Jesus of Nazareth indeed was a revolutionary, the greatest of all time. What he overthrew was not a government or political system but rather the edifice of man's erstwhile self-understanding. It was that temple, not just the physical one in Jerusalem, in which not a stone was left standing upon a stone. The Christian revolution exploded not in city squares but in people's minds.

Every person was to be regarded as an autonomous human being, to be cherished not because of any towering achievement or superior character but simply because he was indeed human.

---

3 On the basis of the scarce demographic data available, this is variously estimated at about 200,000 on either side of a million.

HELLENES, CHRISTIANS AND THE STATE

In fact, people short of achievement or incapable of it, like those frail boys routinely drowned by the Spartans or those unwanted baby girls left to die in the woods by the Romans, began to be seen as God's creatures to be loved before all others. Though some people may have been wicked, some weak and some moribund, none was useless. They all had redeeming qualities because they had all been redeemed.

Hence the institutions for the care of the old and infirm, widows and orphans, lepers and cripples that rapidly spread already during Constantine's reign. In fact, the emperor Julian the Apostate, who had switched from Arian Christianity back to his beloved paganism, reluctantly praised the 'Galileans' for looking after the weak and needy, "not only theirs, but ours as well," so much better than the pagans did. Moreover, rather than being regarded as merely chattels of their fathers and then their husbands, women began to play an important, often decisive, role in society. It was women who founded and ran most hospitals and schools, and in many European countries it was Christian queens who made their pagan husbands convert.

As a result of the about-face in society's understanding of the nature of man, the Christian, while still keeping on his chiton or toga for the time being, gradually shed other vestments and vestiges of Hellenic life – especially its outwardness, its orientation towards the collective entity of the state. Just as the Christian content determined the outer form of a Gothic cathedral, so it defined the political forms of the new world. Like the cathedral, Christendom was built from the inside out. This sequence of the construction project guaranteed a diminished role of the state.

This could not have been otherwise: what we do largely depends on what we think, and what we think largely depends on what we believe. A materialist who believes that his purposeless life will end at death will always attach a great importance to the trappings and artefacts of his outer life; someone who knows he is immortal will pay less attention to the stage set within which the drama of his life is being played out. That was true 2,000 years ago and it is just as true today.

The same applies to the complex interaction between the

state and the individual. The Christian believes his life is eternal. He also knows from history books that the life of a state is not: even extremely successful ones only ever lasted between 1,000 and 1,500 years, and others considerably less time than that.

Compared to eternity, this stretch seems tinier than a speck of dust would appear next to the universe. The individual will therefore perceive himself as more significant than the state and for that reason alone will never accept its tyranny. Because he sees his worldly life as merely a finite particle of an infinite life, a Christian will obey the state, however grudgingly – but only for as long as it does not encroach upon his soul. Thus Christians obeyed Julian the Apostate and even served in his army – while resisting to the death any demands incompatible with their faith.

Etched into a Christian's soul is the innate conviction that he is transcendent but the state is transient. Hence in everything that matters he can only regard the state not as his master but as his servant. If the state's actions suggest that it is assuming the role of spiritual master, then the believer may either resist it or pretend at a moment of weakness to be going along to protect himself from persecution. But inwardly he will never acquiesce.

At the same time the materialist may well accept the spiritual tyranny of a powerful state more readily. After all, his lifespan is much shorter than that of the state. The state had existed before his birth and will happily survive his death. That is why when it is communicated to him, overtly or otherwise, that he is but the material out of which the state is built, then, no matter how much he may loathe the idea, he will find it hard to come up with a strong argument against it while at the same time remaining a staunch materialist. Appeals to individual sovereignty ring hollow outside Judaeo-Christianity.

When Europe was still only inching her way to Christianity, and the religion was outlawed in the Roman Empire, the communicants' tendency was to follow literally Jesus's teaching on the primacy of the devotional commune over the family: "If any man come to me, and hate not his father, and mother, and wife, and children, and brethren, and sisters, yea, and his life also, he cannot be my disciple."

Answering this call, strapping young men and fertile young women, some of them already parents, would abandon their families and join Christian communes growing all over the Mediterranean world. Pre-Benedictine monasticism and hermeticism were also beginning to claim souls and bodies. This deprived the Roman state of some of its human sustenance, consequently making it more hostile to Christianity than to any other creed. Nor could it accept the Christians' refusal to deify the emperor – their own concept of man-God was in direct conflict with such worship. As a result, the proverbial lions dined on 'Galileans' more regularly than, for example, on Jews, who were tossed into the cages only sporadically.

However, once Christianity became Christendom the sacred and secular realms had to come together to some extent. An accommodation had to be found between religious and everyday life, between soul and body whose unity was both taught and personified by Christ. After all, had mankind turned into one contiguous celibate community, it would not have survived beyond one generation.

That clearly was not what Jesus had in mind: according to him, the end of the world would come when God, not man, willed it. Life on earth might have been seen as only the ladder to the heavenly kingdom, but without such a ladder no one would be able to climb there. The conflict between religious man and *pater familias* had to be resolved, and so it was with the development of feudalism, which defined Western politics for about a thousand years, roughly from 500 to 1500 AD.

Such accommodation was found in an alliance between the church and the state, which by definition had to limit the state's role. It was Christendom, not modernity, that practised limited government in a real, as opposed to bogus, sense. And it was feudalism that left the legacy of small government to conservative thinking on modern politics.

6

The early mediaeval world began to take on a new social and political shape. Just as God and man had come together in Christ, they now united in a world reflecting him, which curiously gave it a character we instantly recognise. Suddenly the protagonists of the contemporaneous chronicles become familiar to us in the sense in which, say, Homer's or Euripides's heroes were not. Rather than being symbols representing various virtues and vices, they become recognisable men and women. Rather than being heroes whose traits we could worship or deplore, they become persons we could love or hate. After all, love is at least partly recognition of a kindred soul, while hate is largely failure to detect one.

Socially and culturally, the individual ousted the state from its formerly central position. Private life crowded out much of public life. Instead of rushing outdoors to rub shoulders with fellow citizens, the Christian would rather spend his time at home, trying to come to terms with himself and his God. Yet this did not mean society became atomised: on the contrary, people saw themselves as individuals not only autonomous but also interdependent – not just in their physical life but above all on a much higher level, where they were all in communion. Prayer, either collective or private, became a way of life for all, and for some it spilled over into artistic, literary and philosophical exploits.

Inevitably the family had to be reinstated to its pre-*polis* status of society's core institution; it is for the family that the Christian reserved the same intimacy and warmth the Hellene could spare only for the state. The family became sacred, second only to God. And just as love for and by God was seen as the essence of religious life, so did love for and by one's family became the defining feature of secular life.

Because Christianity is a teleological religion, with life seen as a progression to the ultimate goal, the mediaeval Christian perceived his family in three tenses: past, present and future. It represented a linear, uninterrupted progression from Creation to the Kingdom of God. Hence the respect the Christian felt for the generations past, the duty of care he assumed for the generation present and the concern he genuinely felt for the generations to come. The Christian's life was more or less circumscribed by incessant striving for his own salvation after

HELLENES, CHRISTIANS AND THE STATE

death and for the well-being, both spiritual and material, of his family in this life.

Where did that leave the central state? What role could it play in the individual's life? Precious little. In fact, Christianity separated society and state, the personal and collective, so sharply that for all spiritual, if not practical, purposes a central state became redundant. Few of a man's nobler aspirations could any longer be realised through the state – and most could be jeopardised by it. If for the Hellene state and society overlapped spiritually, for the Christian they not only went their separate ways but often found themselves on a collision course. A conflict between the two, something unthinkable in the Hellenic world, became a defining feature of the West. Such a conflict came to a head when the state and the church regrettably went their separate ways in day-to-day life, with the latter no longer able to mitigate the excesses of the former.

"Render unto Caesar the things which are Caesar's, and unto God the things that are God's" was not a doctrine of separation between the state and the church; it was one of separation between the state and the individual. *Res privata* triumphed over *res publica*. Augustine's city of God and city of man were a literary expression of that separation and, though Christ achieved the eternal unity of the two in his own person, the unity was never that of two equals. When Jesus stated that his kingdom was not of this world, he left the listeners in no doubt that his kingdom was higher than this world. Hence he claimed priority of allegiance in case of any conflict.

While laying the foundations for the doctrine of the transcendent origin of state power, which later was somewhat inaccurately turned into the divine right of kings, St Paul reiterated that this antinomy resolved into a unity of two unequals: "Let every soul be subject unto the higher powers. For there is no power but of God: the powers that be are ordained by God." Possibly the subtlest thinker ever, Paul of course knew that some of 'the powers that be' were far from benign; he himself suffered from the ill will of earthly rulers and he knew they would eventually kill him. But though they could claim dominion over his body, his soul was beyond their reach. His power was therefore greater than theirs for theirs, though derived from heaven, stayed on the ground.

To Paul the unity between the sacred and the secular was achieved at a higher level than the rights and wrongs of this life. The power vested by God in human institutions could be abused by men, but it would serve the higher purpose nonetheless. Divine ordination of secular power was not a guarantee of virtue – Archangel Lucifer, after all, had been ordained to a much higher office than that of any king and yet we all know what happened to him. It was, however, a hint at the higher purpose of life and a restatement of its pecking order. If the secular realm derived its power from God, then it worked under God and was held accountable to him. In practical terms this meant that the state was morally accountable to the church, God's representative on earth.

However, while newly made redundant at this spiritual level, the state could not have been made redundant physically, for personal security depended upon it – as did the continuing survival of the church. A family could protect itself by itself from neither foreign invaders nor internal criminals; this function had to be delegated to the state, thereby vindicating its existence. People needed protection from those threatening their persons or their faith; the state was there to provide it. The word 'only' was never stated, but for the Christian it was presumed: because war and strife could jeopardise the church, and therefore its communicants, the state was needed to maintain peace – but only for that purpose. It was understood that, as security was not easy to guarantee, the state had to be strong enough to keep its implicit promise.

Hence the need for private citizens to relinquish some of their individual liberties and pool them together under the aegis of the state. Hence also the need for a certain number of public administrators empowered to assemble, finance and command bodies of armed men for both external and internal use, and consequently also to collect whatever taxes were needed to achieve that purpose. A strong central state came to be regarded as an unfortunate necessity, but a necessity nonetheless.

It thus had to acquire considerable power, with society, led by the church, keeping a vigilant eye on its activities to make sure the state did not overstep the limits of its usefulness. As both society and the state were united in their faith and therefore understanding of morality, it was only natural that the church assumed the role of arbiter in any conflict between the two. More than that, it offered itself as the crucible in which society and state could be melted into one if they so wished. Barring that, they could at least remain allies, with neither encroaching on the other's role in life.

In practical terms, the church had to conscript many ground-level institutional recruits, both religious and secular, to act on its behalf as agents of social cohesion based on virtue. Such smaller institutions were sorely needed, if only to allow the church to concentrate on its core business, leaving the people to protect themselves from any possible excesses of government officials. Having of necessity relinquished some of his less important liberties, the individual was so much more vigilant in protecting those that remained. He had to insulate himself and his family from the state, and this was achieved by putting in place a thick gasket of family-like groups: clan, parish, village commune, cooperative, trade guild, kindred, monastery.

Those groups were held together by personal ties, and the central state hardly ever infringed on their autonomy. Even had it tried to do so, the church would have used its authority to nip any such attempt in the bud. Consequently the demographics of life shifted from big to small, from city to town to village. The idiocy of rural life, as Marx described it, was in fact idiocy only in the Greek sense of the word: indifference to public affairs, especially those conducted in the capital.

Occupying a public office stopped being merely an honour and became a chore: a man had to tear himself away from things that were important to him and attend to tasks that society regarded as at best a necessary evil. Consequently a man engaged in public service felt he had to get paid, and wreaths were no longer good enough. Society, in its turn, did not mind paying him out of gratitude – he after all had agreed to perform tasks others found distasteful.

Thus the embryonic bureaucratic class that first appeared

in the latter stages of the Roman Empire began growing to adulthood under Christendom, mostly at the courts of the more powerful princes. As government was becoming a lucrative career and a pathway to power, those pursuing it began to separate themselves from others.

That was only a hint at things to come in modern times, and for the time being the hint was too subtle to be taken. Yet had it been taken, the danger would have become apparent: being fallen and therefore fallible, people tend to look at any professional career as a vehicle to drive them towards greater prosperity and higher social status. Once government became a career like any other, it came to be treated the same way and eventually only the same way. That is why, in direct contradiction to Christian beliefs, the weight of taxation and military service was gradually shifted from wealthy government officials down, towards small landowners, peasants and townsmen. The embryo of the inchoate ruling class was already displaying facial features so familiar to us now.

Working for the state may be called public service, but this is usually a misnomer. People tend to serve above all others themselves and those who pay them. Illustrious exceptions notwithstanding, this is a tendency that springs from human nature. Of course one could argue that in a democracy it is the public and not the state that pays government officials. I shall discuss the fallacy of this assumption later. For now let us just say that, with the demise of the Hellenic world, words like democracy and republic began to disappear from the general vocabulary. For the time being, *res privata* triumphed over *res publica*.

7

A populace keenly interested, and eager to participate, in public affairs is a prerequisite for any democracy or republic. Since such a human base no longer existed, nor indeed could exist, by the middle of the first millennium AD these terms had lost any other than antiquarian meaning. Nor was it just democracy and republic: given the ethos of the time, no absolute, territorial and national state, which is such an ever-present fixture of modern history, could have possibly appeared. For that to happen the ethos had to change. While a central state has to be impersonal, the mediaeval world thrived on personal bonds in public as well as private life. Even royal power, resident as it was within a family, was in fact denationalised and privatised, to use modern terms. When the disintegration of the Western Roman Empire made strong central government impossible, it was on such familial bonds that people relied to hold their society together. But the bonds at first proved too ill-defined and consequently too fragile to do what was expected of them. That plunged political and social life into chaos, threatening the very existence of the new civilisation.

It was the church that provided not only a spiritual and cultural adhesive, but also a political one. *Pax Romana* effectively became *Pax Christiana*, with the church assuming a multitude of secular and even political functions. That held the fort for a while, but such versatility ultimately proved detrimental to the church's health. Its dignitaries of the time were of course aware of the perils, but there was little they could do about it in the absence of proper secular institutions, subject to the church's moral guidance but not direct control.

Because such institutions were still in their infancy, it was the church that had to act as the mature adult. Somebody had to step in to prevent the individual atoms of society from spinning out of control. And until feudal relationships began to take shape, mainly in the Carolingian empire, the church had been the only body capable of keeping the atoms within the social molecule.

In broad strokes, feudal bonds were personal and in fact quasi-familial: the lord, while staying filial to the emperor or prince, was a father figure to his vassals, who in turn had a paternalistic relationship with the peasants. The arrangements were reciprocal: the prince undertook to protect the lords, who in return assumed the son's obligation of helping out the prince in time of need. Unless severely provoked, the prince would treat the lords' land as sacrosanct, while they in turn treated their vassals' property the same way. The vassals and the peasants had a similar father-son relationship (usually called manorial), and in each case protection was exchanged for services or else paid for in kind.

This is a most schematic representation of the intricate lattice of political forms being developed in the mediaeval world. By and large, the forms sprang from the content of pluralism and decentralisation, which in turn owed its origin to Christian social morality with its emphasis on individual autonomy and responsibility.

A Western Christian enunciates the idea of pluralism, if only subliminally, every time he recites the Apostles' Creed, reaffirming his belief that the Spirit proceeds both from the Father and the Son. He thus develops an intuitive predisposition towards an even balance of authority that is harder for an Eastern Christian to welcome. That is partly why, when Western Christendom was making its first tentative steps towards a workable political dispensation, local pluralism was fighting centralism every practical step of the way. In Eastern Christendom, this fight, if it was put up at all, was weak and half-hearted, which goes a long way towards explaining much of subsequent history.

I have already likened the process of creating Christendom to the building of a Gothic cathedral, and perhaps the simile can be made to work harder. For, though many manifestations of what later was to be called feudalism ran contrary to Christian morality, this system could have appeared only in Christendom. (The same, incidentally, can be said about modern politics.) It is deeply rooted in the new concept of man first enunciated in Galilee during the reign of Tiberius.

That is why the chaotic political forms of the early Middle Ages so faithfully reflect the eclectic mélange one admires on the façade of Rouen cathedral (or rather they both reflect the same inspiration). One has to get inside to embrace the content that dictates and animates the forms. Similarly, for as long as the content of society was indisputable, the mishmash of political forms did not really matter. No one was likely to find anything much wrong with them, just as no one would have

HELLENES, CHRISTIANS AND THE STATE

taken aesthetic exception to the absence of perfect symmetry in a cathedral's structure. That was not what really mattered. These days the words 'feudal' and 'mediaeval' are in the main used pejoratively. We talk, for example, about 'mediaeval tortures' practised by modern tyrants. The logical incongruity escapes us: if wanton cruelty was the property of the feudal Middle Ages, then how is it that the first democratic century, the twentieth, with its two murderous world wars and countless smaller ones, as well as its Kolyma and Auschwitz, Lubianka and Treblinka, Cheka and the SS, outdid almost two millennia of Christendom a hundred times over? Suffice it to say for now that the Middle Ages, while displaying their fair share of wickedness, did not possess priority rights to it. Nor were they so bad as modern ideologues like to depict them.

It was not only great cathedrals but also great universities that owe their existence to the men of the Holy Roman Empire and their contemporaries. The uncompromising war supposedly waged against learning and science by the mediaeval church is a figment of modernity's morbid imagination. In fact, during the Middle Ages it was the church that provided not only all institutions of learning, but also all encouragement to it.

After Augustine attempted to bring together the God of his faith with the God of his philosophy, the two remained inseparable. They stayed together not only in Western thought but also in its bearers. Until Descartes (d. 1650), all major philosophers had been either monks or priests who used Christianity as their sole, and solely possible, frame of reference. Yet the influence of the church went deeper, or at least wider, than just philosophy.

Science in particular drew its animus from the biblical injunction to subdue the earth and have dominion over everything on it. One cannot subdue what one does not understand, and Judaeo-Christianity made rational understanding possible. Nature was now seen as a single creation of a single rational God and not, as it was in the Hellenic world, an agglomerate of unconnected realms, each controlled by a separate deity. The greatest of the Greeks sensed the unity of the physical world, but they could not make it intelligible because they could not reconcile it with their epistemology. In his *Essay on Metaphysics*, R.G. Collingwood explained why natural science in any modern sense could only have appeared within Christendom:

> "Aristotle thought, and he was not the only Greek philosopher to think it, that by merely using our senses we learn a natural world exists. He did not realise that the use of our senses can never inform us that what we perceive by using them is a world of things that happen of themselves, and are not subject to control by our own art or anyone else's. I have already pointed out that the existence of such a world is... the first and fundamental presupposition, *on which alone any science of nature can arise*... This metaphysical error was corrected by Christianity."

Once mediaeval scientists had corrected the Greeks' metaphysical error, they could be certain that nature obeyed universal laws – it was after all created by a universal law-giver. Moreover, these laws and indeed the world itself existed objectively, outside man's senses. The scientists' job was understood to be finding out what those laws were, and this understanding lies at the heart of every presupposition of modern research. (This regardless of whether the scientist has lost or preserved the original faith.) That is why science eventually became incomparably greater in the West than in any other civilisation – only Christendom possessed and cultivated the essential prerequisites.

Yet it is neither science nor culture that is the subject of this essay, but politics, and many political realities we take for granted today also spring from the Middle Ages. That the rulers as well as the ruled are to be subject to legal and moral restraints is one such reality, and probably the most important one. While in the Hellenic world every new official document expanded the public domain at the expense of the individual, the great legal charters of the mediaeval world aimed to protect the individual from the despotism of the rulers. The Charter of Liberties, Magna Carta and the Bill of Rights were only the culmination

HELLENES, CHRISTIANS AND THE STATE

of this development; its beginnings go back centuries earlier. Tracing them back step by step, we shall arrive at their ultimate provenance in the Christian doctrine of the autonomous individual as the focus of earthly life. While early Christians did not use the term 'human rights', duty being the spine of the Christian body politic, they would not have been unduly bothered had an intrepid stranger mentioned it to them, provided he could explain what he meant. By contrast, Plato or Aristotle would have thought the stranger not so much intrepid as mad. People to them had rights as citizens, not as mere human beings.

As it was from barons' councils that our modern parliaments have evolved, the post-Hellenic system of representation has ancient roots as well. For example, in England before the Norman conquest it was the Witenagemot, the assembly of the kingdom's leading nobles, that would convene after a king's death to select a successor. That was, to name one instance, how Harold Godwinson took the throne, which he then lost to a Norman arrow in 1066.

The same can be said about the system of adjudication and property protection, whose historical precedence goes back to the Old Testament but whose political embodiment was mediaeval. Above all, it was during the Middle Ages that the individual could feel relatively secure behind the wall of intermediate, familial institutions I mentioned earlier. Parish, village, guild, monastery, cooperative, neighbourhood and the family itself – all as anchored in the church as the latter was in faith – had their autonomy generally respected.

Originally created mostly for the purpose of keeping people safe from encroachment by central government, in time those institutions assumed the role of the formulator, educator and custodian of the social and moral order. It was such institutions that gave physical shape to the three pillars on which, according to Burke, government should rest: prejudice, which is intuitive knowledge; prescription, which is truth passed on by previous generations; and presumption, which is inference from the common experience of mankind.

The social and moral order maintained by familial institutions was by definition conservative – its origin was assumed to have been derived from the word of God, and that word was not subject to change. For the same reason, the church is (or rather ought to be) *ipso facto* a conservative institution – its function is to preserve the tradition that is not only two millennia old but is also based on eternal and immutable truths. Politically too, the church either has to eschew progressivism or betray its own function in earthly life, that of acting as social adhesive, moral judge and mediator of salvation. The first meant staying intertwined with secular society; the second, rising above it; the third, eventually leaving it behind.

While the second and third are self-explanatory, the first in the mediaeval world meant mainly ensuring that the patchwork quilt of numerous, and often competing, familial groups would not threaten social cohesion. The danger was inherent: it could be assumed with certainty that various groups would at times pursue diverging, and possibly conflicting, ends. Whenever their secular interests were pulling them apart, the church would step in to remind, say, the warring clans that at the highest possible level they had more to bring them together than to tear them apart. Without this moderating, conservative role played by the church, familial institutions would never have added up to cohesive society.

The political realm outside that familial order was always fluid and more tactical than strategic in its *modus operandi*. Rooted not in dogma but in expedience and custom, it was not so much chiselled in stone as drawn on quicksand. While personal relationships within the family clan were constant, the political relationships among various elements of the feudal political order changed all the time.

Without running too far ahead of this narrative, one ought to stress that such fluidity was not then, nor is now, contrary to real conservatism – it is in fact its essential characteristic. Burke said as much when commenting that "a state *without* the means of some *change* is *without* the means of its conservation". Change was aplenty in feudal times: a vassal could become stronger than his lord, or the latter richer and more powerful than his prince. The formal bonds among them might have survived the shifts, but the vessels would be empty – the contents were no longer there. Geographic demarcation was equally fluid: a lord could switch his allegiance from one prince to another, taking his land into another domain. Or else he could become a prince himself, claiming new lands and rearranging the political geography of his region.

Thus no nation, or rather nationhood, could have appeared, at any rate not in our modern sense of territorial, political, economical, legal, cultural, ethnic and linguistic unity. The genitive designation of the Holy Roman Empire as that 'of the German Peoples' referred to religious and cultural commonality only, not to an entity definable in clearly drawn geographical terms. Even England, whose geographic limits are defined naturally, remained an agglomerate of independent provinces throughout the Middle Ages.

Weak or at least limited central government had neither the strength nor the inclination to encroach upon the autonomy of local institutions. Though it sometimes had to regard them as competitors and act accordingly, an all-out attack was unthinkable until a mighty absolute state appeared and began to put its foot down. The triad of state, church and family (along with family-like institutions), with the last two at least holding their own against the first, was then destroyed. The state emerged victorious. And once the protective wall of inter-mediate institutions was swept out of the way, the state's power over the individual could be reliably predicted to gravitate towards becoming absolute at some point.

The conclusion is clear: the social and moral order of Christianity is incompatible with a political triumph of the central state over local, familial institutions.[4] As such a triumph is always tantamount to the subjugation of the personal to the collective, and therefore some enslavement of the individual, it could only be achieved at a cost to such institutions. The cost was their diminution and ultimate demise, which was the levy

---

4   Pope Pius IX (d. 1878) provides an interesting illustration. He fought the 1870 unification of Italy under secular authority tooth and nail, correctly perceiving it as detrimental to the church's health. Eventually he banned all Catholics from voting in parliamentary elections, effectively boycotting Italy's democracy.

no traditional state was prepared to pay.

For the modern state, however, it was cheap at the price. Modern democracy is so inseparable from central government riding roughshod over local pluralism that for all intents and purposes they are one and the same. Strip the word 'democracy', as it is used today, of its armoured shell of demagoguery, and it becomes synonymous with limitless centralisation, leaving people unprotected from the encroachments of an impersonal, omnipotent state administered by an increasingly corrupt bureaucracy. If only for this reason, an uncontested democracy exclusive of competing forms of government is incompatible with the essence of the traditional moral and social order in the West. But there are many other reasons as well.

The organic state

1

Many different modifiers have been attached to the type of state emerging towards the end of the feudal order. Historians have called it monarchic, absolutist, theocratic, tyrannical, primitive and many other things, except the one that really matters: organic.[5]

Rather than being a contrivance resting on abstract (and typically wrong) principles, it was an organic development of the Christian ethos as refracted onto secular life. There were no savants getting their heads together to sort out an elaborate constitution with all its riders and amendments. The state appeared so seamlessly, and without any visible involvement of any human agency, that it was tempting to take a cue from St Paul and believe it was indeed willed by God – in fact both Burke and Joseph de Maistre interpreted it that way. According to Burke, the same God "who gave our nature to be perfected by our virtue, willed also the necessary means of its perfection. – He willed therefore the state."

This sounds like a rhetorical flourish on the philosophy of natural law going back to Aquinas and other scholastics, or Aristotle before them. It shows, among other things, the dangers inherent in any attempt to apply theology to politics directly. From there it is an easy transition to the idea of theocracy: after

---

5 Nothing I say about times past should be taken as uncritical adulation. They had their fair share of wickedness, as will any society of fallible people. However, my contention is that societies of old were more conducive to suppressing the bad side of human nature and encouraging the good than today's societies are. The organic nature of the pre-modern state had much to do with this.

all, 'perfecting human nature' for future salvation is the institutional domain of the church, not of the state. If, as Burke suggested, the state has the same purpose, then it is either redundant or else can act only as an adjunct to the church. Rather than merely keeping an eye on the state's behaviour and judging it on the basis of Christian tenets, the church would then in effect have to run it. That is neither its natural function nor even its doctrine: salvation is individual, not collective. It is as individuals, not as citizens, that people will be saved.

No state, including theocracy, can be included in the kingdom of God. That kingdom has to remain stateless, for the state is by definition coercive. It is a gigantic whip-around enabling citizens to chip in some of their liberty in exchange for security. Once bartered away, that part of liberty is irredeemable, and the state will not give it back even if this involves violent suppression.

On the other hand, faith is by definition a free union between two entities. A man born to a faith usually has the option of not espousing it; the same man born within the realm of a state has no option but to follow its laws on pain of punishment. A theocracy by its very nature cannot accept freedom of conscience to the same extent as theology must. As freedom of conscience is not just essential to Christendom but is in fact its only valid definition of freedom, the notion of Christian theocracy is oxymoronic.

To what extent the state of any type can be seen as God's tool of perfecting human nature is thus open to debate. And so it will remain because few of us have a two-way line of communication to God, and only he would be able to clarify the matter. Until then we can safely assume that it is not the state's function to create paradise on earth. Its purpose is only to prevent hell on earth. De Maistre was perhaps more accurate than Burke in his phrasing when arguing that traditional institutions go so far back that they disappear in the haze of time – we cannot trace them back to their historical origin. Therefore we might as well assume they come from God.

One also wonders if Burke still would have persisted in his belief that *any* state was divinely ordained had he come back

THE ORGANIC STATE

in the twentieth century and seen Bolshevik Russia and Nazi Germany in action. Perhaps he would then have been inclined to trace the provenance of at least some states back to the odious creature described in the Bible as 'the prince of this world'. But if we choose to interpret Burke's thought figuratively (which is probably not how he meant it), it sounds nearer to the truth than Locke's idea that the state was brought into existence merely to protect private property.

The post-mediaeval state was an extension of the Christian moral and social order, which had for a thousand years found its political expression in feudalism. Localism had stood fast against centralism then, and property had been adequately protected by the insulating wall of decentralised familial institutions.[6] Moreover, property ownership was in the Middle Ages as diffused among small holdings and manufacturing shops as political power was diffused among local bodies. It is unclear how growing centralisation could protect property much better than that – in fact, it is easier to see how private property would become less rather than more secure in the tender care of a powerful central state.

One cannot, for example, imagine any reasonable mediaeval prince trying to confiscate half or more of the people's income – an outrage we these days accept meekly as a natural prerogative of the state. Both this prerogative and our meekness derive from the unchecked and unmediated power of the central state, which is a distinctly modern, post-Enlightenment development. Indeed the modern political state is by its nature expropriatory: its very existence depends on purloining both wealth and political power. In fact, when the Reformation heralded the arrival of the modern state in England, one of the first measures undertaken by Henry VIII was expropriating monasteries and, while he was at it, many small property owners as well.

What is undeniable is that, compared to the traditional

---

6 'Adequately' should not be taken to mean 'perfectly'. We are not in this world blessed with perfect institutions, and any attempt to hold them down to that standard is usually animated by underlying hostility. 'Adequately' is the best we can do.

51

Western institutions, a strong central state is better equipped to wage acquisitive wars, both external and internal, aimed at looting property that belongs to others. In fact acquisitive expansionism is an ever-present feature of a centralised state, regardless of its internal politics or proclaimed principles. Only a greater force can keep this inner imperative in check.

The pre-modern territorial state that existed roughly – very roughly – from the beginning of the sixteenth century to the end of the eighteenth was not qualitatively different in that respect, though quantitatively it was rather vegetarian compared to its modern counterpart. The difference lay in its organic nature: it rearranged the practical manifestations of Christendom without abandoning its underlying ethos. This is not, nor ever was, the case with post-Christian states.

Looking at Western states in their present form, we see some that are more or less organic and some that are more or less contrived. None has retained the same form it had centuries ago, all have developed. But while some are to a large extent evolutionary, some others are primarily revolutionary. Most had their organic development violently interrupted in the past; but some more than others. To see which is which we can apply a simple test that would work in most cases: unlike the origin of a contrived state, the origin of an organic one cannot be pinpointed to a single historical event or, for that matter, any precise moment in time.

We can say with certainty that the American republic started in 1776, the French one in 1789, the unified German state in 1871, the Soviet one in 1917 (or more accurately in 1923, when the Soviet Union officially came into being), Israel in 1948 and so forth. But when did the English state begin? We cannot be sure.

All we can do is suggest any number of milestones on the road to its present form, such as its baptism, the Norman conquest, Magna Carta, the Civil War, the Restoration or the Glorious Revolution. Advocates of the primacy of any such event will present their arguments; we may agree with some and dismiss others. But the very fact that there are many such events vying for the honour, and that they are scattered all over

THE ORGANIC STATE

the historical continuum, points at the organic nature of the English state.

The same can be said, *mutatis mutandis*, about the states of Holland, Sweden, Denmark, Norway and to a large extent Spain. They have all developed organically over the turbulent, meandering, violently swerving pathways of history, and where exactly those pathways began is not much clearer than where they will end.

Aware of this continuity, the people of all these organic realms have preserved their monarchies (with minor hiatuses here and there), even though they may have divested them of any real executive power. However, they understand intuitively that dispensing with even the seemingly powerless monarchs would represent an irreplaceable loss. Contrary to what Walter Bagehot (d. 1877) thought, they know that monarchy is so much more than just 'the decorative aspect' of the constitution.

As all those countries are now enthusiastically secular and ideologically democratic, few people there would be able to identify what it is that they would be reluctant to lose. If pressed, they are likely to refer obliquely to 'tradition', without fully realising what that means. Many would resent the thought that monarchies link their secular present with their Christian past, yet this is precisely what monarchies do. They are Christendom's envoys to modernity, and even those people who would throw up their arms in horror at this suggestion will still hear vague, intuitive echoes in their souls.

Royal families remind them of the origin of their own families – kings and queens are their link to the past they ostensibly no longer cherish and to God in whom they ostensibly no longer believe. This is whence they derive their sense of organic continuity, something they desperately, if often unwittingly, crave – and something that is denied to nations where monarchies no longer exist or have never existed. They may not know exactly what they are missing, but rest assured that deep down they all know they are missing something vital, something they will not get from any secular creed.

Christian families, royal or otherwise, are organic and therefore cherished institutions because they are patterned after the universal family sharing one divine father. That all-inclusive family is strictly hierarchical, headed by the father whose authority is unequivocal and unquestionable. Divine authority is transmitted downwards through ministers of the church – just as royal authority is communicated through ministers of the government. It is on this familial basis that Christianity and monarchy converge. It is on this basis that both parishioners and subjects are mutually dependent, an interdependence akin to that of children of the same father.

Democracy, on the other hand, by definition rejects a father figure at its head. Therefore it is inherently and institutionally hostile to all familial arrangements, starting with monarchy and ending with ordinary families. The present disintegration of the core family, much bemoaned yet seldom understood, is a direct consequence of the disappearing metaphysical foundations on which the family used to rest. The present debauchment of monarchy has the same roots.

Secular creeds, or rather their absence, can also act as telltale signs of an organic state. Though fundamentally based on a metaphysical premise, no such state draws its historical legitimacy from a founding secular myth. What is the founding mythology at the conception of the state in Holland? England? Norway? There is none – these are organic states whose genesis can no more be pinpointed to a particular idea than to a specific event.

Ask a Dutchman or a Swede what idea gave birth to his state and he will shrug his shoulders. His state just is. Not so, say, with the USA, Israel or Russia, or even France. An American, assuming, and this is an unsafe assumption these days, that he is literate, will have no problem naming 'manifest destiny' as his state's *fiat lux*, nor will an Israeli or a Russian hesitate to identify their own formative mythology.

2

In its content if not necessarily form, the state emerging out of the Middle Ages was as similar to the previous political order as it was different from the subsequent one. This in spite of its

THE ORGANIC STATE

tendency towards benign and limited centralisation.

It was centralisation because the monarch gradually acquired an indisputable, though hardly ever unchecked, executive power. It was benign and limited because the familial institutions at the heart of the mediaeval order were largely left in place, and thus the relationship between the princes and the paupers remained essentially as it had been in the past. Some local institutions had to transfer some of their power to the central state; but, though they bled, they did not bleed white. For the time being centralism and localism were at peace.

In other words, the new territorial state was not so much a radically different entity as simply an organic development of the ancient one. The development was multifarious, and it is not my intention here to comment on it in detail. As both the political and economic factors contributing to the appearance of the post-mediaeval state have been analysed to death, I shall only mention one aspect that has not received quite as much attention: culture. Just as politics, cultural life seems to have a built-in tendency to centralisation, and in that sense politics and culture may be pulling in the same direction.

One could argue that a loose, scattered network of local communities in the Middle Ages was less conducive to cultural expression than it was to protecting people's physical and spiritual autonomy. When the need for such expression became uncontainable, cultural fault lines appeared in the feudal order, adding one last crack to those already created by other tensions.

Taking a leaf out of Augustine's book, St Anselm (d. 1109) defined culture as faith seeking understanding. A purely empirical observation, however, would show that the cultural road to understanding is not open to everybody. In fact, at the risk of sounding unfashionably elitist, one could suggest that the urgent desire to approach God through culture is the lot of the few. Even fewer are those who have the spiritual, intellectual and creative wherewithal to travel this road to any productive destination. But for those who have this ability, the need to develop it tends to take over their whole being — they jump on a rollercoaster that never stops, and they cannot jump off without risking spiritual life and limb. Such people can never be

55

enslaved by others, but they have to become slaves to their own minds and talents – to their own destiny.

Now for the sake of argument imagine one such man, still a youngster, living in a village somewhere in central Italy. Let us, arbitrarily of course, call it Aquino. The time is the thirteenth century, both the cultural peak and the political finale of the Middle Ages.

His faith is pure and strong and, as he possesses an original and fecund mind, his piety demands intellectual understanding. He studies at the nearby Abbey of Monte Cassino and is talked about as its abbot in the making. But the Abbey is not big enough to contain the youngster. He craves daily contact with his intellectual superiors and equals; he fears that without access to responsive sounding boards his mind will for ever remain a clean slate.

What he seeks can be found only at international centres of learning instituted during the Middle Ages. Great universities of Bologna and Padua are not far north, and he could easily go there. But destiny takes him to Paris whose university is basking in the reflected light of Abélard, Peter Lombard, William of Champeaux and other illustrious minds of the previous centuries. Moreover, Albert the Great, the giant of natural philosophy, an Aristotelian who has fused faith and science, is there now, willing to take the youngster on as his student. Unlike most of the boy's classmates, Albert does not mistake his taciturnity for obtuseness. This young man, he says, has a great future.

What follows is a saintly life of intellectual achievement seldom if ever equalled in history. Now what would have happened to the youngster had he stayed at Monte Cassino, never mind Aquino? In due course he would probably have become an abbot known in the area as a true savant. Conceivably, he would perhaps even have become a saint. But would he have become the Thomas Aquinas we know? One doubts it.

The saplings of inquisitive minds and creative talents need a proper soil in which to grow. Rather than stealing the nutrients and juices from other saplings, they share them, nurturing and fertilising one another so that all will grow tall. Some will grow taller than others, but no giant trees grow in a desert. They grow in a forest of many other, shorter trees. That is why seekers and practitioners of culture flock together and, when enough of them gather in the same place at the same time, they create what their descendants will call a Golden Age.

It was not by accident that, from Haydn and Mozart to Beethoven, Schubert and Brahms, Vienna could boast so much musical genius within a relatively short period. This would have been impossible without the profusion of Picchinis, Salieris, Hummels, Clementis, Eyblers, Süsmayrs and Stamitzes lying thick on Vienna's ground at the same time.

Thus intellectual and artistic culture tends to centralisation, and this is true of political culture as well. Just as a savant seeks greater knowledge only to be found at cultural centres, so does a gifted statesman seek greater, meaning more centralised, power. The two are in fact indivisible, for cultural exploits need to be both properly financed and duly appreciated. History shows that this is possible only when money, political power and cultural refinement are all more or less monopolised by the same people. A society where this was the case is usually called aristocratic, though it could be simply called Western (as opposed to modern).

Culture was only one force behind the great shift towards the centre that characterised, and ended, the late Middle Ages. There were many others, all similarly vectored. The difficulty lay in maintaining the right balance between centralism and localism and, like any balance, this one relied on the strength and immobility of its fulcrum – the Christian order.

3

This order depended on the sustained strength of the faith whence it had come. For a variety of reasons that strength began to attenuate as the world emerged out of the Middle Ages. Yet what matters in the context of this essay is that the new political forms not only negated their predecessors, but also reaffirmed them. There was destruction involved, but it was indeed creative, to borrow Joseph Schumpeter's term.

When the princes turned into kings, the lords into courtiers and the vassals into landed gentry, central government began to acquire new powers. Mostly this came at a cost to the institutions that formed the feudal order, especially the church. However, the cost was not exorbitant: as political power radiated from the centre towards the periphery it would be losing much of its impetus. Thus the absolute monarchs of the immediate pre-modern era had practically unlimited, indeed absolute, power over their loftiest courtiers, but precious little over the lowliest peasants.

Localism may have ceded some of its positions to centralism, but it had been an organised retreat, not a rout. Hence, when Louis XIV declared that he was the state, he was not boasting absolute powers, as Marxist or liberal historians try to make us believe. The Sun King was in fact bemoaning the limited nature of his state, which throughout the pre-modern period could flex its muscles mostly at the court or perhaps in the capital.

However, that period lasted only from the beginning of the sixteenth century to the last quarter of the eighteenth. As humanism gathered strength, people increasingly saw themselves fit to play a hands-on role in government affairs. Superficially this resembled similar sentiments prevalent in the Hellenic world, but in fact the motivation was more opposite than the same. If the Hellene's desire to participate in politics was driven by affection for the collective entity of the state, the early modern man was mostly animated by animosity towards the traditional order based on Christianity.

To understand why that was the case we must try to put ourselves in the shoes of those who lived at the time, and that is a notoriously hard task whenever human behaviour is the object of analysis. A certain amount of guesswork is inevitable, especially since each subsequent scientific discovery in behavioural sciences seems not so much to elucidate as to darken the issue. When Socrates said "the more I know, the less I know" he must have presciently had modern neuroscience in mind.

When we try to understand people of centuries ago, the task becomes so much harder: inevitably we shall be applying the

THE ORGANIC STATE

standards of our own time, and times change, as do people. However, people do not change so much that we can never fathom why they acted in some ways and not in others. When all is said and done, human nature is immutable; it just manifests itself in different ways in different eras.

Until the advent of humanism it had been assumed, not always justifiably, that most people would have their behaviour governed by Christian morality. Hence the relatively low-key legislative activity at the time: when people could be expected to obey higher laws, few human laws were needed to restrain their behaviour. Obviously, it would have been impossible to build a society wholly on the Sermon on the Mount – only an obtuse fundamentalist would fail to see the inevitable need for some amount of elasticity that could only come from human interpretation of divine laws. But as long as the centre of the civilisation held together, minor concessions at the flanks did not matter all that much.

Renaissance humanism struck at the centre by secularising Christian morality, removing it from its source while trying half-heartedly to preserve its tenets, or rather their shells. That created a simulacrum of traditional order, a growing shadow of the diminishing real thing. Defying physics, the shadow eventually separated from the object and began to acquire a life all its own. For many people found the simulacrum more palatable than the original.

This is not hard to understand, for to most people the demands of Christianity began to feel too onerous. Most rejected the freedom offered by Christ because, like any freedom, it came with concomitant responsibility. This, many felt, was a yoke around their necks. Anyhow it was not the freedom to pursue salvation they craved but the liberty to pursue bread. That is why, as Chesterton once put it, "The Christian idea has not been tried and found wanting. It has been found difficult – and left untried." But until an easier alternative presented itself, people had been trying to comply with the commandment to shape their lives and personalities in the mould of love and charity. Alas, loving not only one's neighbour but even one's enemy does not come easily. A conscious effort has to be made

59

all the time and, given our nature, such efforts are at least as likely to fail as they are to succeed.

The failure has to be blamed on someone or something, and few of us are prepared to blame ourselves – again, this is not in our nature. Hence it was logical that, when people realised they were failing to live up to Christian ideals, it was not themselves they tended to blame but Christianity. When humanists came in, first whispering into their ear, then shouting off the rooftops that every man was uniquely important not because he was created in the image of God but of his own accord, people sat up and listened. They liked what they heard.

All they needed was a good pretext to move away from the church, making it easier for them to blame religion for their own failings. Such pretexts were never in short supply: though the church was divinely ordained, it was a human and therefore imperfect institution. Some of its high officials, including the Popes, were downright unsavoury. For example, in 955 the throne, and the title of John XII, was assumed by a 16-year-old youngster who turned the Vatican into a place of ill repute. Not only did he drink, gamble and fornicate but – much worse – the Holy Father celebrated mass without taking communion, gave banquets in honour of pagan gods and even offered toasts to Satan. This was rather an exception but, when we rake history in search of excuses for our own wickedness, in our minds exceptions effortlessly turn into rules. When militant atheists wish to attack the church, it is the Borgias they talk about, not Augustine or Gregory the Great.

Some reasons for diminishing piety at the exit from the Middle Ages were undeniably the church's own fault. Others were not, and the Black Death pandemic of 1348–1350 was prime among them. The same questions were asked before, by and after Hume: if God is omnipotent, omniscient and good, then how come we have [insert your own disaster or anything else you do not like very much]. This is not the place to tackle this issue, but one can imagine how fourteenth-century people, most of them unburdened by doctorates in divinity or even basic literacy, responded to a pandemic claiming 30 to 60 percent of Europe's population. And always in the background

THE ORGANIC STATE

were the humanist Iagos, whispering in the ear of suspicious Othellos that it was all the fault of God who, illogically, might not even exist. That did not make Europeans become agnostic overnight, but they began to move in that direction.

Step by step, the Christian ideal of autonomous man striving with God's grace towards his own salvation was turned into yet another simulacrum: man seeing himself as independent not only of ecclesiastical authority but also of God. Instead of worshipping God, people were beginning to worship themselves, which is always easier. But a millennium and a half of Christendom had left an indelible imprint on people's psyche, and they had to feel guilty about their apostasy. Guilt often manifests itself in hostility: you will see many naughty children (of all ages, often reaching well into biological maturity) claim they hate their parents because deep down they blame them for their own naughtiness. One could surmise that when hostility, or at least antagonism, towards the church became widespread, it was a result, rather than the cause, of diminishing piety.

Since Christianity lay at the foundation of all traditional institutions, this hostility was bound to spill over onto those institutions and indeed tradition. For such destructive sentiments to find a practical outlet, people had to engage in political activity at every level, from cultivating certain attitudes in private to expressing them through specific deeds in public.

Jumping over the head of the traditional local bodies, Europeans began to look to the central state as a deliverer from the familial institutions now seen as being oppressive. They did not realise that the state, as it then was, was organically intertwined with those institutions: just like them it had walked out of the Christian order, by a different but parallel path. As the state could not, in that form, plausibly provide an outlet for iconoclasm, in due course it had to become its target.

For the time being, the kings were held to be above suspicion: the monarchs basked in the reflected warmth of the residual affection people still felt for the old order, even as they were prepared to rebel against it. But the monarchs were living on borrowed time.

The first modern state: a tragicomedy in three acts

1

Unlike a common-or-garden rebellion that can be triggered off by a passing resentment, a revolution worthy of the name has to be launched from some philosophical platform. For while rebellions merely try to unseat the old government and create a new dispensation, revolutions try to unravel the old tradition and create a new man. This has to proceed from some sort of understanding of what the new man ought to be like – from a philosophy, in other words.

However, once the revolutionary ball starts rolling, its philosophical actuator usually becomes an antique full of sentimental value but no other. Even that value will in time be discounted, although lip service to the original ideas may still be paid. One way or the other, a rocket has to shoot off from somewhere, even if the launch platform will then be dismantled and sold for scrap.

The West's journey from the organic to the modern state started with the small step of philosophy too, but a philosophy more physical than metaphysical. It was science that provided the starting point. By the eighteenth century scientific advances had produced a radically new concept of the world. Copernicus, Galileo, Newton and Leibniz had changed the way people viewed the universe, and in an odd sort of way the heliocentric notion of the cosmos put forth by the scientists catered to the egocentric view of man put forth by the humanists.

The earth was no longer seen as a unique stage created by God for the drama of man to be played out. The universe was now perceived as a mechanical entity wholly describable in mathematical terms. It took another three centuries of scientific progress for mystery to make a comeback, but for the time being all seemed to be crystal-clear: the divine clock-winder did his bit at the beginning, and then Copernicus, Descartes and Newton, assisted by Hobbes, Locke and Smith, took over. The world was no longer a stage, with people as the actors. It was a machine, with people as its cogs.

But as the cogs were sentient and sapient they decided they could do more than just turn within the machine. They thought they could run it by the simple expedient of learning more about the mechanism and seeing how different parts of it fit together. Since the only tangible workings of the machine, those that had a direct impact on people's lives, were political and economic, the square peg of politics and economics had to be forced into the round hole previously occupied by religion. Just dumping faith was never good enough – politics and economics were supposed not only to oust religion but also to imitate it. The rule by simulacrum was upon us.

The modern state, forged by the Enlightenment and annealed by the fire of three revolutions, English, American and French, had to find its own eschatology – the memory of Christendom was still too vivid in people's minds for them to have settled for anything less. Again the techniques of replacing traditional certitudes with their simulacra came in handy: people weaned on the expectation of the kingdom in heaven were now fed the illusion of one on earth. Since God had been removed as the central figure of any realm, man himself had to fill the vacancy thus formed. At issue was not just a new object of worship, but a new reality. The French *philosophes* of the misnamed Enlightenment hoped that this new reality would effortlessly slot into the empty groove of the old one. But the fit turned out to be imperfect.

From the very start of this project, man proved his unsuitability for such a lofty role. Having abandoned the Creation and the Salvation, the beginning and the end, man found himself imprisoned in the middle ground dominated by the Fall. For a while the perpetrators of the French Revolution managed to convince the world that martial law was liberty, a cull of the upper classes (and anyone else the revolutionaries disliked) was equality, and dressing most of the eligible population in uniforms of the same design was brotherhood. But the ruse could not last indefinitely; people may be gullible enough to fall for short cons, but given time they can usually figure out the long ones for what they are. Pointed questions began to be asked: What is it all for? What comes in the end? *Quo vadis*, you poor man?

In common with most secular revolutionaries in history, the Enlightenment brigade realised that the threadbare fabric of empty phrases would soon be torn to shreds. Violence could only keep it stitched together for so long. And anyhow, the sense of balance demanded that the thesis of a stick had to be counterbalanced with the antithesis of a carrot, hoping that a successful synthesis would somehow emerge.

A tangible promise was urgently needed, some material, palpable replacement for the reward people had been taught to expect in heaven. The self-appointed Enlighteners took stock of their puny bag of tricks and found only one item that could possibly qualify in any meaningful sense: money. Economics was bound to assume new significance as a result, and a new political dispensation had to be built around it. Economics and politics had to come together to form the quasi-religion of modernity. Or rather they were to provide the simulacrum of the body, with jingoism typically filling the vacancy of the soul. For old times' sake, the new antinomy had to resemble the old one, if only in the same way in which a spoof resembles the original.

The shift was everywhere revolutionary, and violently so, but it manifested itself in a variety of forms in various places. However, if in the good tradition of our civilisation we peek beyond the different forms, we shall find that their content was not so different as commonly believed.

For example, much has been made of the fundamental differences between the American and French revolutions, or indeed between the Anglo-American ('rightwing') and the French ('leftwing') Enlightenment. Yet even though Burke and other respectable thinkers argued in favour of this demarcation, if not in so many words, their arguments were not as immediately persuasive as Coleridge found them, to name one conservative scribe. Both the philosophical and religious sources of the putative two types of the Enlightenment were the same, owing much to humanism and its intellectual spawns Hobbes and Locke. This debt was acknowledged as gratefully by the American Founders as by Montesquieu or Voltaire. Hysterical hatred of monarchy as the political manifestation of Christendom and of Trinitarian Christianity as its base, egalitarianism, deism, pluralism understood in a most mechanical sense and divorced from localism – all these were shared equally by the *philosophes* of both the Old and the New World. If one lot arrived at their deism, in effect atheism, from a heretical-Catholic starting point and the other from a sectarian Protestant one, they all got there in the end.

Allowing for local peculiarities, Jefferson and Franklin were Enlightenment *philosophes* in the same sense in which Diderot and Helvétius were. The qualifying clause reflects the temperamental differences between the Latins and the Anglo-Americans, and also the necessary tactical adjustments they had to make in order to realise their vision. But the vision was exactly the same.

At the positive end, the *philosophes* on either side of the Atlantic set their sights on empowering the common man or, to be exact, the radical intellectual elite acting in his name. At the negative end, their vision was focused on destroying or at least emasculating Christendom and marginalising the religion that had begotten it. It was immaterial whether this involved, as a first step, the cull of aristocrats sporting the powdered wigs of French nobility or of soldiers wearing the red coats of British infantry (along, in both instances, with those who sympathised with the hated group). Whatever it took.

Americans, taking their cue from Burke, like to portray their revolution as somehow being conservative, distinct from the French radical one. Only blind faith and fundamental dishonesty can prevent anyone from realising that a 'conservative revolution' is a contradiction in terms. The neocons of course have the requisite qualities to overlook oxymorons and other rhetorical fallacies. Thus COLLENE, my collective neocon: "Because the status quo... is no longer conservative, conservatives must seek to change the status quo. In so doing they must become new conservatives, radical conservatives – revolutionary conservatives. They should become neoconservatives." Or else, with refreshing candour, "We're closer to being revolutionaries than conservatives, and the title 'revolutionary conservatives' certainly fits the movement well..." Yes, but it does not fit any reasonable definition of conservatism. In fact, the American revolution, the first in Western history to create a purely secular state, had nothing to do with conservatism: it overturned the existing order as radically and irrevocably as any other such event.

Presumably to merit grateful emulation by all subsequent revolutionaries, it also laid out the groundwork for criminalising not just deed but also word – and even thought. Those expressing the mildest sympathy for British rule, or even merely suspected of being likely to harbour such feelings, were routinely attacked both by the new-fangled law and the extra-judicial mob. The law hit suspected infidels with confiscation, fines, imprisonment, deportation from any area threatened by a British advance, confinement to internment camps. The mob would attack, rob and torture suspected Tories by tarring and feathering. The infidels would be made to recant publicly and forced, often at gun point, to take an oath of allegiance to the new republic.

Burke was sage on most political matters, specifically when he ripped the French Revolution to shreds in his *Reflections*. But he was sorely misguided when describing the earlier similar event in America as "a revolution not made but prevented." One suspects this temporary myopia was brought on by the intensity of the Irishman's abhorrence of the French mayhem – for polemical reasons he simply had to contrast it to some other revolution, even if the contrast was illusory. Commenting on the opposite polarity of Burke's passionate reaction to the two revolutions, Coleridge insisted that in both cases the great Whig proceeded from the same principles. That may be, but he certainly did not display the same prescience.

While the French revolution proved every bit as hideous as Burke's prophetic vision of it, the American one was far from being as benign as he believed (with some reservations). Not only was it as unlawful and radical as the French version, but it caused comparable long-term damage by wreaking destruction on the last vestiges of Christendom. With the benefit of hindsight one can argue that the perennial effect of the self-evidently inalienable right to the pursuit of happiness has been as harmful, and perhaps as sanguinary, as that of liberty and fraternity, underpinned by equality. The very term 'pursuit of happiness' appropriately comes from Locke who, armed with the Cartesian method and Hobbesian agnosticism (masquerading as deism), was the principal prophet of the new order.

Historically, the nihilist equality of all before the guillotine needed to be counterbalanced with the philistine equality of physical comfort to complete the destruction of Christendom. The two ends, nihilist and philistine, had to be in equilibrium. Both the American and French revolutions sought to provide that balance, minor differences between the two notwithstanding. In that they are much closer together than the popular doctrine has it. Even the amount of blood spilled in the two upheavals is similar if we justifiably regard the American Civil War as the third act of the revolution, with the Declaration of Independence and the Constitution having signposted the first two.

Unlike the revolution in France that destroyed the country's old order to create a new one, the American counterpart had to create not just a new order but a new country. This was to be populated by a new man, the American. That ambitious undertaking could not have been carried out in one fell swoop: the play had to have more than one act. After all, the Founders were uncertain about the possibility, or indeed desirability, of retaining some old-world values when creating a new world.

Politically, pluralism vested in localism was the fundamental political principle and practice of Christendom, and at least some of the signatories to the Declaration of Independence, those less sullied by modish humanism, felt vestigial affection for it. And even those who did not still had to proceed with caution in the face of opposition at home: trying to effect a cosmic break from England, they could hardly risk too many internal rifts at the same time. The potential for such rifts was large: many newly 'liberated' Americans still regarded themselves as loyal subjects of George III.

The centralisers among the Founders were incongruously called Federalists, semantic larceny being a sure telltale sign of modern politics from its very beginning. But although the Federalists were stronger than the opposition, they were still not dominant, and the opposing forces far from feeble. Unity was of the essence though – the external threat was too great for the colonists to afford too much internal bickering. Compromise was the order of the day.

That is why for the time being their explicit intent was to create a republic that would be a loose federation of independent states, with each retaining the right to secede from the Union. The right to secession was far from trivial, as subsequent history has shown. In general, the liberty to cut loose, be it a country leaving a federation or an individual leaving a country, is perhaps the most fundamental liberty of all.

Yet the issue is not as straightforward as it may appear, and the operative word in the previous sentences is 'federation'. Most setups described by this word rely on a constitutional arrangement that stipulates a great deal of self-government and the right to secede. Hence a province in a federation does not have the same legal status as that of a region in a state constituted differently. In practical terms this means that, say, Texas has the option to secede while, say, Essex does not. Forcibly preventing Texas from seceding would therefore ride roughshod over the constitution, at least its spirit – it would be borderline despotic. Conversely, preventing Essex from following suit would merely mean enforcing the law of the land.

The Federalists intended to use the republic as but the first step on the road to rampant centralism, but they wisely kept that intention under their stovepipe hats. The ruse worked: their opponents took the early pronouncements at face value, failing to realise that revolutions have their own inner logic that may be quite different from the revolutionaries' intentions, whether real or merely stated.

In this instance, by enunciating their rather facile grievances against the putative tyranny of King George, the least tyrannical monarch one can think of, the Americans did something irreversible. They opened the floodgates and modernity rushed in, sweeping aside even what was worth keeping and marring the landscape with the flotsam of petty ideas and puny aspirations. Sooner or later the flood was bound to sweep away every political expression of Christendom, emphatically including its localism.

Democracy, which this side of its sloganeering means imposing central and ever-increasing power in circumvention of any traditional localism, had to follow inexorably, even if this was not the Founders' original design. Many of them, John Adams specifically, were horrified when observing the chicken hatched by the egg they had laid. In 1806 Adams wrote, "I once thought our Constitution was a quasi or mixed government, but they had made it… a democracy."

This, by his correct if belated judgment, had a disastrous effect not only on America but on the whole world. In 1811 Adams rued, "Did not the American Revolution produce the French Revolution? And did not the French Revolution produce all the calamities and desolation of the human race and the whole globe ever since?" Laudable hindsight, but only hindsight nonetheless.

Though some of the colonists may not have realised this, they were rebelling not just against England specifically but against the traditional order in general. Wittingly or unwittingly, they had problems not so much with George III as with Christendom. Most of the Founders were deists; they believed in the divine clock-winder but not in a living God. They could bandy liberal phrases on freedom with the best of them, but the ultimate meaning of freedom, one that comes from the ultimate truth, escaped them.

2

American Founding Fathers, apart from such rare exceptions as Fisher Ames, came from the line of cultural descent that led from Hobbes and Locke to Condorcet and Helvétius, Smith and Hume. Local colour came from the nature of American society formed as it was by immigrants from diverse cultural backgrounds who had all drifted to America for their own reasons.

Most of the reasons, however, fell into two broad categories: religious and economic. Many of the early Americans were sectarian Protestant dissenters of a fundamentalist type, such as the English Puritans, Dutch Calvinists or German Mennonites, who had fallen foul of authorities in their native lands. Many others fled to the New World simply to escape poverty; they were attracted by the promise of a vast continent awaiting colonisers. Free enterprise was thus particularly important to the Americans, as aggressive economic activity was a common element on which all the disparate groups overlapped.

That is why Locke's political philosophy with its emphasis on property rights struck such a resonant chord with Americans – the vacuum left by apostolic religion had to be filled with a simulacrum, however puny. Yet the rhetoric of the American Revolution could ignore neither the religious nor the economic animus, which is why the radical ingredients of it had to be spiced up with dollops of deism, a generous handful of Turgot and Smith and dashes of 'manifest destiny'. But these rhetorical spices could not mask the decidedly Enlightenment taste of the dish.

We do not need to be aware of the personal ties linking the likes of Jefferson and Franklin with the *philosophes*; just reading the Declaration of Independence tells us all we need to know. This document is the first of its kind, the original statement of intent coming from a near-triumphant modernity. Almost every word in the Declaration can yield a rich crop if analysed within the framework of this essay, especially in the first two paragraphs where the moral justification for independence is established.

The colonists insist on their right to "assume among the Powers of the earth, the separate and equal station to which the Laws of Nature and of Nature's God entitle them..." They go on to say that they "hold these truths to be self-evident, that all men are created equal, that they are endowed by their Creator with certain unalienable [*sic*] rights, that among these are Life, Liberty and the pursuit of Happiness." People are entitled to organise their government on such principles that "to them seem most likely to effect their Safety and Happiness." This is all Enlightenment talk. No political thinker of Christendom could have written that or indeed signed his name to any of it. He would have objected that:

a) Regardless of what Locke and Paine (and their intellectual descendant Leo Strauss, the neocons' idol) had to say on the subject, 'separate and equal station' for either individuals or countries cannot be derived from 'Laws of Nature'. There is no law of nature that says a colony is entitled to independence from the metropolis. There exists, however, a tendency among modern revolutionaries to pass their aspirations as rights. A 'separate and equal station', desirable though it may be to some, can only be achieved either by agreement or by force. No group has equality built into its reclaimable biological make-up. Portraying independence as a right that somehow supersedes the law was modern demagoguery at its most soaring.

b) Pantheistic 'Nature's God' is clearly there to mollify believers of a more primitive type, those who react to the word 'God' by reflex and for whose benefit wise people (who were, of course, above such nonsense themselves) had to put the word in.

The author of the Declaration himself illustrates the pitfalls of a cavalier treatment of God. Thomas Jefferson had a selective approach to the Scripture: some of it was acceptable to him, some was not. So he clipped the acceptable passages out of the Bible and pasted them into a notebook, thus creating his own Scripture and turning himself into the fifth evangelist. One can argue that possibly all Protestants and certainly all deists go through the same exercise in their minds, if not literally. Atheism is the ineluctable result, even if it is masked, as in America, by fulsome protestations of piety.

c) God is the only truth that can be regarded as self-evident in that, by definition, it is either taken on faith or not at all. Any other truth, before it can be accepted as such, needs to be forensically proved.

d) That 'all men are created equal' is, self-evidently, rather the opposite of truth. Again this is an attempt to pass wishful thinking for a fact. All men are created unequal physically, intellectually, morally, socially. The political (and for that matter any other) culture of Christendom is a direct product of this inequality, and its very survival depends on it. Rather than striving to expunge earthly inequalities, a Christian accepts them with equanimity.

Apart from displaying intimate familiarity with the works of Thomas Paine, the use of this phrase echoes Rousseau's theories of the *noble sauvage* beautiful in his state of primitive grace, a *tabula rasa* on which modernity can scribble its message to the world. It was this 'created equal' business that adumbrated the eventual slide of republicanism into democracy and of the latter into egalitarianism of the most vulgar kind in the most inappropriate areas: statesmanship, aesthetics, morality, culture, religion.

Not just the traditional order but any sensible one must be based on a hierarchy of realms, people, beliefs, ideas. Also self-evident here is the sleight of hand typical of modernity: people used to be taught to believe they were equal before God. That heavenly equality trumped any worldly inequality of status, wealth or intelligence. The advent of the rule by simulacrum shifted this indisputable notion from the divine to the secular realm, at once turning it into little more than the battering ram of modernity.

e) It is questionable whether the term 'rights' has any value in serious discourse on political matters. Today we are served up any number of rights: to marriage, education, health, development of personality, leisure time, orgasms, warm and loving family or – barring that – warm and loving social services, employment, paternity leave and so forth. These 'rights' are bogus as they fail the test of not presupposing a concomitant obligation on somebody else's part. When a 'right' does presuppose such an obligation, it is no longer a right but a matter of consensus, or else an aspiration.

Thus one's right to employment would mean something tangible only if someone consented or were obligated by law to give one a job. One's right to a developed personality (guaranteed by the 1948 UN Declaration of Human Rights, which was signed by such authorities on human rights as Stalin's Russia) presupposes an obligation on somebody else's part to assist such development. One's right to a fulfilling sex life… well, this is getting too silly for words. Far from being natural, all these rights become tangible only if they are granted by others; and anything given can be taken away, so there go all those pseudo-rights alienated right out of the window.

f) The right to political liberty, as opposed to spiritual freedom, is also a pseudo-right, since it has to be derived from consensus. An individual's political liberty, understood as the state placing no unreasonable restraints on human behaviour, depends on society accepting the individual's definition of an unreasonable restraint. This right is therefore bogus, for its exercise involves an obligation accepted by others. In general, 'liberty', along with all its cognates (liberal, liberation, libertarian and so forth), is a word fraught with semantic danger: one man's liberty is another man's licence and yet another's anarchy.

For example, is the absence of anti-homosexuality laws a factor of liberty or licence? If the answer is the former, as it has to be in our PC times, then we ought to ponder the fact that the first modern country without such laws was Soviet Russia between 1917 and 1934, a place and period not otherwise known for a *laissez-faire* attitude to life.

g) The right to life mentioned in the Declaration is legitimate as its enforcement does not pre-suppose an obligation on anyone else's part. The question it raises, however, is not

"Is it legitimate?", but "Is it terminologically useful?" The English Common Law, operating in the colonies at the time, provided adequate provisions for the protection of life, which would seem to have rendered any invocation of this right redundant. If the law was being abused or not enforced properly, then the practice of it needed to be revised. This could hardly have been helped by dragging in a new theoretical construct that was always more likely to confuse than elucidate the issue.

Moreover, as with all redundant terms, this one is not without some potential for casuistic abuse either. Is the death penalty a violation of the right to life? Is abortion? How is it that the proponents of the latter are almost always opponents of the former and vice versa, with this redundant right invoked in each case? The more pronouncements on rights it makes, and the more laws it passes in support, the more does the state prove it is a contrivance, not an organic development. The traditional, organic state was based on something that did not require constant reiteration and reassurance.

h) 'Happiness' was at the time a vogue term denoting a secular substitute for virtue as the purpose of life. Whatever meaning one chooses to assign to it, and there are endless possibilities, the word is either extraneous or even alien to the principal desideratum of Christendom: the pursuit of truth, virtue, inner freedom and ultimately salvation. That pursuit was more likely to result in suffering than happiness.

Suffering lay at the foundation of Christendom – it was understood that man's salvation was bought at the price of Jesus's excruciating death on the cross. Christian eschatology, man reaching out for the kingdom of God anointed by Christ's blood, presupposes the redemptive value of suffering. Hence in Christendom happiness was devoid of any autonomous meaning or value – it was understood only as a by-product of unity with Christ. Lockean *pursuit* of happiness would have been impossible; happiness could only have resulted from other pursuits.

Perching happiness on top of their totem pole, the authors of the Declaration committed either a gross metaphysical error or, more likely, conscious metaphysical subversion. And they even went further than wielding that meaningless word: as Alexander Hamilton explained in *Federalist*, they used 'happiness' in the same sense in which Locke used 'property' or 'estate'. The word 'happiness' in the Declaration was thus the birth cry of our soulless, rudderless, materialistic modernity: for the first time in history happiness was openly equated with money.

True enough, much of the language used in the Declaration of Independence can be found in John Locke, the shining light for both American and French Enlighteners. In an often quoted statement Locke mentioned 'life, liberty and estate' in the context of 'natural rights', a concept of his that can only charitably be described as dubious, especially when used widely and indiscriminately (as it tends to be by the Straussians among the neocons).

Otherwise Locke's full statement is unobjectionable. What he talked about was *preserving* a man's "life, liberty and estate against the injuries and attempts of other men" – the rule of law, in other words. But this was not how it came out in the Declaration. Its statement was snappy, a quality essential to slogans but sometimes detrimental to truth. The Founding Fathers chose a less precise term 'happiness', preceded by 'the pursuit of', a combination they declared to be a natural ('unalienable', as they put it) right. That semantic preference stemmed from either too little understanding of Christendom or too much distaste for it.

This was more than a matter of metaphysics only: Locke's underlying idea was stood on its head. The *pursuit* of property, rather than the Lockean legal *protection* of property already amassed, was a *de facto* declaration of money-based eudemonia. The teleological nature of acquisitiveness, beatified by the Reformation, was thus canonised by the Anglo-American Enlightenment.

In purely moral terms, the pursuit of money, assuming that it does not involve arbitrary or fraudulent separation of other people from theirs, does pass the no-obligation test, but it runs

The first modern state

head-on into the same objection raised earlier. This right is not spurious; it is redundant. Laws against theft, burglary, robbery, fraud and the rest derive from the Decalogue and do not need a modern term to bail them out. On the contrary, it was precisely the separation of such laws from their true source and their shift into the modern, secular area of 'rights' that made their enforcement so difficult in the West.

The right to property, one of the few real rights, is a case in point. Born out of the ethos of 'rights', the modern political state, while continuing to assert 'the pursuit of happiness' or versions thereof as canonical law, has elevated judicial confiscation of people's money to a level unthinkable in either the Hellenic world or Christendom. For example, Caracalla who, according to Gibbon, "crushed every part of the empire under the weight of his iron sceptre" by increasing the inheritance tax from five to ten percent (thankfully, "the ancient proportion was restored after his death"), was a babe in the woods compared to a modern democratic parliament that will hit one for forty percent faster than one can say 'judicial expropriation'.

While property rights are more valid than almost any others claimed by various demagogues, they are not without an offensive potential either. This is manifested when they are raised to an absolute, as they tend to be wherever post-Enlightenment liberalism has triumphed, especially in the Anglophone world. Anglo-American *philosophes*, from Locke to Friedman, have to accentuate property acquisition and protection as the cornerstone of liberty. However, in a stark demonstration of the self-refuting nature of all purely secular constructs, property rights can also act as the cornerstone of slavery.

In fact, it was these rights that were invoked by Southern confederates in listing their grievances against the North – just as they had been by the Founders in listing their grievances against George III. The rebels had ironclad logic on their side: the status of a slave in the South was that of chattel property whose legal standing was on a par with that of livestock, which is to say nonexistent. Therefore an attempt to emancipate the slaves was indisputably a gross violation of Lockean property rights. On its own terms the South was thus as justified to secede from the Union as the Founders had been to declare their independence from England. Those terms, however, were invalid on a level deeper than that plumbed by the Enlightenment apostles of secular liberty.

The American revolt was triggered by Britain trying to extract from the thirteen colonies a tax in the overall amount of £78,000. To put this in perspective, it cost Britain more than £200,000 a year to maintain her troops in North America after the French and Indian wars. The colonists allowed that the sum in question, though large, was not exorbitant. However, they refused to part with even such a trivial amount without what they saw as proper representation. In that they faithfully followed the ideas of Locke, who regarded representation as the only legitimising factor of taxation. Neither Locke nor his followers, such as Jefferson, realised that this insistence was in direct contradiction to protecting property rights, supposedly the *raison d'être* of liberal democracy.

For by transferring all sovereignty to a representative body, the people will eventually make its power absolute – to a degree that the 'absolute' monarchies of Christendom never even approached. When unchecked, this power extends to confiscating as much of personal income as the representatives see fit – in effect trampling over property rights so cherished by Locke and the Founders. In fact, at the time of their revolutionary outburst, American colonists were paying lower taxes than residents of Britain proper, many of whom were not represented either. Bostonians even got their British tea at half the price Londoners paid – this in spite of the tea tax that inspired the Boston Tea Party.

In due course this vindicated the old saw about being careful what you wish for – you may just get it. Americans, along with the rest of us, would eventually discover that they dislike taxation even *with* representation. Taking a wild stab in the dark, one would guess that, given the choice of being taxed at half their income with representation or at 10 percent without, a landslide majority would opt for the latter. But the expensive toothpaste of centralising statism (otherwise known as modern democracy) cannot be squeezed back into its tube.

The pursuit of fiscal happiness was more important for the nascent American state than for Europe, where at the time ancient title to land was indeed still regarded as self-evident and therefore needing no reiteration. The pursuit of money was, after all, an important part of what brought most Americans together. It was thus more crucial than almost any other founding tenet of the new state.

However, what made the States united was not just acquisitiveness but also an earnest commitment to the eradication of Old World survivals, grudges against which were part of the baggage many settlers had brought from Europe (this hostile intent was passed as the creation of a new type of man, the American). That particular chip was grafted onto their shoulders, and there it has remained to this day. "Repudiation of Europe," the novelist John Dos Passos once wrote, "is, after all, America's main excuse for being." Sectarian Protestant hostility to Trinitarian Christianity was – and remains – an essential, some will say the main, part of the animosity the settlers felt towards the Old World. For them, orthodox Christianity, the church and episcopalianism were worse oppressors than even European kings. Hence the Americans' concerted effort to marginalise apostolic Christianity – this was a *sine qua non* for expurgating the old order.

Money was useful to that end too, for it could function as the stick, not just the carrot. When all is said and done, the human qualities required for making money, especially in the modern world, are often diametrically opposite to those that went into the foundations of Christendom. The moment money became the universal yardstick with which human worth was measured, the death knell sounded for the traditional order.

Even these days, with the battle against Christendom long since won, American political scientists emphasise protection of property more than do even conservatives in Europe who still, for old times' sake, tend to regard it as only one of many prerequisites for civilised society. However, Americans usually manage to seduce Europeans into accepting the transatlantic pecking order of virtues.

3

Earlier I argued that the erstwhile organic states within Christendom trace their origin back to a metaphysical premise, not a secular idea. The American republic was founded on both, for it too proceeded from a metaphysical presupposition. Theirs, however, was a simulacrum. Unlike that of the organic states, the premise was wholly mythological: its accent was on the redemptive value of happiness, which is to say money. As far as metaphysical premises go, this one was both petty and wrong.

As is always the case, wrong metaphysics led to wrong practices: for example, the Founders' liberal theories could happily coexist, for many of them, with slave ownership. They were not Lockean for nothing: in drafting his peculiar *Fundamental Constitution of Carolina*, Locke stipulated that "every freeman of Carolina *shall have absolute power and authority over his Negro slaves* of what opinion or religion whatever." In other words, the slaves were to be deprived not only of outer liberty but also of inner freedom.

Acting in that spirit, Enlightenment demagogues like Jefferson, Washington and Madison saw no incongruity between their liberal rhetoric and owning (in Jefferson's case also procreating) chattel human beings. It was slavery, which in England had been out of fashion since at least Elizabethan times (even though slave trade was legally banned only in 1807), that was an important factor in England's intransigence during the American Revolution, although this is seldom mentioned. Another fact often ignored by historians is that American black slaves greeted advancing British troops as deliverers and often volunteered to fight on their side.

Small wonder. For slavery had been deemed abhorrent in England for at least 200 years before the Americans saw the light. A report of a case as far back as 1569 states that: "... one Cartwright brought a slave from Russia and would scourge him; for which he was questioned; and it was resolved, that England was too pure an air for a slave to breathe, and so everyone who breathes it becomes free. Everyone who comes to this island is entitled to the protection of English law, whatever oppression

THE FIRST MODERN STATE

he may have suffered and whatever may be the colour of his skin." In 1772, ruling on the 'Somersett's case' of a slave suing for his freedom when brought to Britain, Lord Chief Justice Mansfield declared that "no court could compel a slave to obey an order depriving him of his liberty."

Dr Johnson, who unlike Burke was a Tory and therefore less susceptible to serpentine liberal seduction, expressed this in his typical epigrammatic fashion: "How is it that we hear the loudest yelps for liberty among the drivers of negroes?" The simple answer was that the yelps for liberty were hot air designed to suffocate Christendom, while slave ownership was wealth, which is to say happiness, which is to say real life. Dr Johnson with his dignified poverty was an old-order survival; Jefferson with his 5,000-acre Monticello estate, on which he bred slaves using the same agricultural principles as those applied to breeding farm animals, was the new order personified.

As Christianity was the essence of the old order, it had to be shoved aside. In deference to the sectarian part of the American population, this had to be sold as protecting religion from encroachments by the state. But the real purpose was to protect the newly hatched radical state both from the church's moral opprobrium and its efforts to safeguard the last vestiges of Christendom. Jefferson, the fifth evangelist of his patchwork scripture, was quite clear on this point.

The US Constitution, the second act in the revolutionary drama, coyly eschews the phrase 'separation of church and state'. Instead the First Amendment states only that "Congress shall make no law respecting an establishment of religion, or prohibiting the free exercise thereof." But in his comments both before and after the ratification Jefferson was unequivocal: this amendment, he gloated, built "a wall of separation between Church and State".[7]

Implicitly, this was a dig at England, which Jefferson and

---

7 Jefferson was at the time in France, as Minister Plenipotentiary. However, though he could play no active role in the drafting of the Constitution, he was still a major power behind the scenes and also Madison's close friend.

most of his colleagues cordially loathed. They wanted to transplant onto the American soil the trees of the English Common Law, while severing their roots nourished by England's Trinitarian faith. Jefferson's views on religion were greatly informed by Locke's *A Letter Concerning Toleration*, ostensibly preaching equanimity towards all creeds, except naturally Trinitarian Christianity.

Yet treating all religions with equal respect has the same effect on a Western society as treating them all with equal disdain. In either case, Christianity is no longer seen as the transcendent authority conferring legitimacy on the temporal one. In other words, it becomes irrelevant to everyday life, which was precisely the intent.

There is nothing wrong with tolerance, properly understood. However it must not be allowed to undermine the spiritual foundations of society – tolerance is not a suicide pact. The organic states of Christendom saw their duty in protecting not only the physical property of the citizens but also their spiritual health, which in those days was tantamount to guarding Christianity from heresy. Locke and the Founders viscerally hated the traditional order, and they correctly identified Protestant sectarianism as an effective weapon to use against it. Hence tolerance, which in the inchoate tradition of liberal lexicology got to mean intolerance, its exact opposite.

Animated by Enlightenment values, the Americans aspired, perhaps unwittingly, to create a new order that would be a simulacrum of the one they had overthrown, not its development. Politically, removing the moral and spiritual authority of the church presupposed also dispensing with familial localism inherent to the political tradition of Christendom. Hence the Constitution, claiming overriding political power for the central state, or rather usurping it from the 13 colonies.

The US Constitution was adopted in 1787, 11 years after the Declaration of Independence, and many scholars regard it as a conservative counterbalance to the radical rhetoric of the Declaration. Yet a written constitution cannot be conservative by definition – the very fact that it has to be put down on paper points at its being a contrivance, rather than an organic development. Joseph de Maistre wrote in practically every book of his that, unless a constitution is already written in the people's hearts, any written document will be wanting. Conversely, if a constitution is indeed written there, any written document will be redundant.

A common objection to this line of thought as applied to America is that de Maistre's maxims may work for old and established countries, but not for those starting from constitutional scratch. However, though sounding plausible at first airing, this argument does not quite work. For in that sense the United States was not started from scratch: it had in place the English Common Law, lovingly developed over centuries to protect the legal autonomy of the individual before the state, as embodied by the monarch.

All the colonists had to do was retain this proven guarantor of civil liberties, merely specifying the divergences inevitable in the switch from monarchy to republic. They would then have had to put down on paper only the technical aspects of government, such as the length of terms in political offices, the quantitative make-up of Congress and so forth. Beyond that, redundant reiteration could only undermine the law already in place.

To be fair, many elements of the Common Law did go into the legal makeup of the new state. For example, the Supreme Court (as originally intended, not as it operates today) was constituted along common-law principles stemming from legal precedents. And even the government structure created by the colonists was a simulacrum of England's constitutional arrangement: for monarch, read president; for the Lords, the Senate; for the Commons, the House of Representatives.

Yet this was merely a parody used to serve the new hierarchy: while mimicking the form of the old dispensation, it lacked the critical aspect of its substance – it did not reach all the way up to heaven. Transcendent derivation, expressed as divine right or otherwise, is the soul of traditional or even constitutional monarchy. It is the essence of the political aspect of Christendom. No secular equivalent will suffice.

As the English Common Law was the only organic aspect

of the new republic, the law had to assume functions that in its original habitat were performed by other institutions. As a result, the law gradually turned into legalism, overstepping the fine line separating the two. It is conceivable that America's litigiousness stems from that shift, as does her unique approach to politics and the preponderance of lawyers in her governing bodies. This is a useful lesson to us all: when legality is equated with morality there is always the danger that the former will oust the latter – to the detriment of both.

Even Tocqueville, generally well-disposed towards American democracy, noticed as early as in the 1830s that sooner or later all political problems became legal in America. The Founders overplayed their legal hand probably because they felt they had to press on as fast as possible: any slowdown in the tempo of their revolution could lead to its demise. Had they truly understood (or rather accepted) the metaphysical underpinnings of the organic state, constitutional differences between America and England might not have gone any further than the differences in the English language spoken by the two nations: essentially the same thing, but with slightly diverging accents and phrasing.

There is, however, one fundamental difference between American English and the American state: the language has developed more or less organically; the state was an ideological contrivance. The first is evolutionary, the second revolutionary. And the formative animus of all revolutions is mostly destructive – any creative intent, if it exists at all, is secondary. Unlike some European revolutionaries, the Founders and the Framers unquestionably wanted to create, but only a naïve analyst would fail to notice the ever-present concomitant desire to destroy. The US Constitution served both purposes.

It is quite possible that the Framers realised that their revolution was not a one-act play. Before the curtain fell, the plot had to be primed to accommodate sequels. It was for this realisation above everything else that the Framers deserve their reputation for sagacity. They knew that the document they were drafting had to be sufficiently open-ended to set up subsequent twists in the plot, especially since popular support for it was at the time practically nonexistent.

THE FIRST MODERN STATE

The Constitution is a curious document, showing traces of various – and one would think mutually exclusive – inputs. Unlike the Declaration of Independence, which is a straightforward statement of Enlightenment principles, most of them lifted from Locke and the *philosophes*, the Constitution has various sources. This starts with the Preamble: "We the People of the United States, in Order to form a more perfect Union, establish Justice, insure domestic Tranquillity, provide for the common defence, promote the general Welfare, and secure the Blessings of Liberty to ourselves and our Posterity, do ordain and establish this Constitution for the United States of America..."

The wording bears an uncanny resemblance to the constitution of the Iroquois nations: "We, the people, to form a union, to establish peace, equity, and order..." Considering that the colonists had been busily slaughtering Indians for the best part of two centuries, and were to continue to do so for much of a third, this choice of idiom was odd. Psychoanalysts could have a field day with this Stockholm syndrome in reverse: it was not just the practice of scalping that the colonists borrowed from the aboriginal population they had conquered. Or else they were so prescient as to anticipate the advent of multiculturalism.

Typical of all revolutions is that their perpetrators invariably assume the right to speak for 'the people'. In this instance this was as mendacious as in all others. The 54 delegates to the convention were not mandated to represent 'the people', only the states. Sixteen of those delegates, disgusted by what they saw as abrogation of the states' autonomy, refused to sign the document, and less than three percent of 'the people' actually voted for its ratification.

The Federalists, who mostly drafted the Constitution, were in favour of strong central government (though they would not have dared to use the adjective 'omnipotent', it was implicitly inscribed on the margins), but they had to fight off stubborn opposition from such prominent revolutionaries as Samuel Adams, Patrick Henry and James Monroe. Though the anti-federalists did not, perhaps could not, delve into the philosophy of localism versus centralism, much less of Christendom versus modernity, they understood the practical problems involved: federalism, as conceived by Messrs Adams, Madison, Jay, Hamilton *et al.*, spelled slow death for states' rights – especially the right to secede.

That was exactly the end Jefferson saw in his mind's eye too, but for the time being he had to settle on a palliative. "Half a loaf is better than none," was how he put it. As a result, a constitution inspired by modern centralism had to include various, and variously empty, nods towards traditional localism.

Another problem was one that the Framers wisely foresaw: no constitution put down on paper in one go, rather than evolved over centuries, could possibly accommodate every future development. To a conservative that would be a ringing argument against the very idea of a written constitution: if, as it must, it leaves room for future embellishment, it also leaves room for future invalidation.

Such a constitution also leaves too much leeway for interpretations reflecting the *Zeitgeist* rather than any immutable principles. For instance, putting down freedom of speech is all fine and well, but what if later generations interpret it as freedom to riot? Moreover, what if some right, say that to same-sex marriage or free healthcare, unspecified in the constitution, would come to be regarded as inalienable in a century or two?

Alexander Hamilton who, along with James Madison, was to the Constitution what Jefferson had been to the Declaration, understood the problem. Hence he felt it would be better not to mention any rights at all, just to be on the safe side: "I go further, and affirm that bills of rights, in the sense and in the extent in which they are contended for, are not only unnecessary in the proposed constitution, but would even be dangerous. They would contain various exceptions to powers which are not granted; and on this very account, would afford a colourable pretext to claim more than were granted." Also less, one is tempted to add with the benefit of hindsight.

Hamilton gets top marks for prescience, but those who eventually overruled him and added the Bill of Rights to the

Constitution were clever too. Do let us specify some rights as we understand them today, they argued. But at the same time let us leave the door ajar for the arrival of any subsequent rights, those of which we are unaware at present, but which our descendants might wish to stipulate. Thus a most amazing rider was attached to the Bill of Rights, the Ninth Amendment: "The enumeration in the Constitution, of certain rights, shall not be construed to deny or disparage others retained by the people."

In other words, the rights we mention are inalienable, but then others, those we cannot even imagine, will be inalienable too if at some time down the road the people come to regard them as such. Opportunism joins simulacrum to form a ruling duopoly.

The simple logical corollary unfortunately escaped the framers: the Ninth Amendment implies the likelihood of not only addition but also subtraction. Some rights considered vital might in future not only be augmented but also devalued or even discarded. For example, the Eighteenth Amendment of 1917 enshrined prohibition of alcohol as a constitutional principle, while in 1933 the Twenty-First Amendment smashed the shrine by repealing the Eighteenth and confusing the issue. Obviously 16 years was a lot of bootleg whisky under the belt, but what does any of this have to do with constitutional rectitude?

The potential for confusion was huge from the very beginning, and it could only be reduced by yet another constitutional amendment, one written not in ink but in blood. It has no number, but it has a name: the American Civil War.

4

America suffered heavier casualties in the Civil War than in all her previous and subsequent wars combined. Such gushing bloodshed was to be expected: that was the decisive war in which modernity fought tradition, or rather faint echoes of it. For it was to the South that Christendom's holdouts had drifted. Perhaps they were attracted by an economy that revolved around agriculture and was therefore conducive to localism, with its corresponding institutions and even some version of aristocracy – the nature of agricultural economy precludes any great centralisation of the populace in vast urban metropolises.

It is also likely that French and Spanish, which is to say Catholic, influences in that area added a tinge of traditional civility for which settlers with such inclinations reached, realising that modernity would reign supreme in the mercantile North. In any case, an oasis of tradition, or rather its simulacrum, flourished in the South, and it was only marred by the institution of slavery that was the bedrock of its economy.

This is one of the countless contradictions in which history abounds. In Christendom slavery is an unacceptable institution for, unlike the way it was seen in Hellenic times, modern slavery has to be based on the metaphysical assumption that some men are more human than others. The Negro had to be dehumanised and reduced to the level of cattle for Southern planters to feel justified in running their economy that way.

Actually, the conviction that the blacks were less than human was held by most Founders and Framers – especially those who, like Jefferson, Washington and Madison, had Southern roots. Yet we are all, regardless of race, created in the image and likeness of God, a belief that is impossible to reconcile with slavery. (No Greek philosopher, including Plato and Aristotle, could have a similarly decisive objection to slavery, even though one or two opposed it on different grounds. But the status of a slave was different then, mainly because slaves typically shared their race and often ethnicity with their owners.) Treating human beings as livestock has therefore always been abhorrent to the church, and it objected to it with varying fervour from the days of the Roman Empire.

Yet at the same time the manorial setup of the South, though resting on a repulsive institution, was a semblance of the traditional order – at least until secession wafted through the air. At that point the Confederacy quickly acquired the same centralising tastes as those of the government in the North. But until then the predominantly agricultural, decentralised economy of the South had nourished a closer proximity to Western culture than the North could achieve. The odds, however, remained stacked against the South, and the aroma of tradition had to be drowned by the smoky stench of modernity.

Both sides displayed an all-out commitment to the Civil War, sensing that no conflict between the two orders could ever end without one side scoring a decisive victory and the other suffering total annihilation. The North realised that nothing short of a 'scorched earth' policy would do. The South knew that the North did not just desire the end of slavery – it craved wiping out its habitat, the South. In the process, certain iconic personages behaved in a way that belied their subsequent reputation.

Abraham Lincoln, for example, closed down 300 pro-Southern newspapers (and had their presses smashed), suppressed the writ of habeas corpus and, according to the Commissary General of Prisoners, had 13,535 Northern citizens arrested for political crimes from February 1862 to April 1865. Comparing his record with that of Mussolini, who only managed 1,624 political convictions in 20 years and yet is universally and justly reviled, one begins to see modern hagiography in a different light.

Interestingly, many Northern commanders, such as Grant and McClellan, were themselves slave owners, while many Southern generals, such as Robert E. Lee (who had freed his slaves two years before the shooting began) were not. This emphasises what has to be obvious to any unbiased observer: the war was not just about slavery.

True enough, the eleven Southern states seceded largely because the federal government had put obstacles in the way of spreading slavery into the newly acquired territories. However, Lincoln and his colleagues explicitly stated on numerous occasions that they had no quarrel with slavery in the *original* Southern states. Their bellicose reaction to the secession was caused not by slavery but by their in-built imperative to retain and expand the power of the central government. "If that would preserve the Union, I'd agree not to liberate a single slave," Lincoln once said. Note also that his Gettysburg Address includes not a single anti-slavery word – and in fact Lincoln dreaded the possibility that he himself might be portrayed as an abolitionist.

In launching its rebellion against the North, the South proclaimed exactly the same Enlightenment principles as those that had driven them both to the insurrection against England. Most of the principles were originally enunciated by John Locke, and prime among them was the implicit endorsement of revolution as the only realistic way for the people to withdraw their consent to be governed.

I shall discuss this in greater detail later, but suffice it to say for now that, if self-determination is held to be sacrosanct, then the Confederate states served that particular deity with greater consistency than the North did. Jefferson Davis and Robert E. Lee had exactly the same 'right' to lead the rebellion against central authority as Thomas Jefferson and George Washington had had to lead the rebellion against the Crown. To deny the validity of such rights one has to revise the Enlightenment principles whence they sprang.

Such were the central issues over which the Civil War was fought. Where does this leave slavery? Certainly not in the niche it occupies in popular mythology, that of the principal *casus belli*. Slavery ran against the grain of both orders, old and new. Both Christian morality and modern pragmatism would soon have squeezed it out anyway – it simply could not survive. Massive violence was redundant: even an authoritarian Russia managed to find a bloodless way of eliminating serfdom, her *de facto* version of slavery, and she did so two years before the Emancipation Proclamation was issued in America.

What slavery could do, however, was to act as a pretext camouflaging the real animus for the war: hostility to Christendom in general and its political expression in particular. Centralism had to ride roughshod over localism, even its half-hearted Southern version. Typically the human cost was not even a consideration for the newfangled 'liberals'. Did Thomas Jefferson not reassure the doubting Thomas, aka John Adams, that it was perfectly acceptable to spill "rivers of blood" as long as it was in the cause of advancing whatever it was that the revolutionaries wished to advance?[8] Of course he did. A civil war was thus a small price to pay for chiselling central power in stone.

Just as the Ninth Amendment provided for future pseudo-constitutional shenanigans, so did the Civil War lay out the groundwork for future *ad infinitum* expansion of the central secular state. The seeds of such expansion were planted by the Revolution and cultivated by the Constitution, but they only blossomed into a luxuriant tree after the Civil War. Those who desired a strong central state eventually got more than they bargained for: a state omnipotent to a point where it could turn many constitutional liberties into their empty shells. Coupled with a populace viscerally committed to economic 'happiness', with no checks applied by religion, an omnipotent central state would turn the USA into a land bursting with testosteronal aggression tinged with the oestrogenal propensity for admiring itself in the mirror.

Ever since then America has been trying to convey to the outside world and also, by way of self-reassurance, to herself the impression that she has solved all the little problems of life. She is the provincial autodidact who, having studied a subject for a fortnight, not only regards himself the ultimate authority on it but also feels the urge to bring the folk in the capital round to his way of thinking.

The term that America came up with to sanctify this odd impulse is 'manifest destiny.' This was more than just a figure of neo-messianic speech. It was a tacit admission that, having eliminated the old order based on Christianity, the new state urgently needed its simulacrum.

---

8   This sentiment was shared by quite a few other political figures of history, with Robespierre, Lenin and Hitler immediately springing to mind. Unlike Jefferson, however, none of them is widely regarded as the paragon of goodness and the distillation of political virtue.

The American religion

1

The word 'simulacrum' keeps popping up in this narrative and it will continue to do so. For the essence of modernity is in replacing everything real (these days, paradoxically, even money, that mother's milk of 'happiness') with virtual caricatures. The Founders realised that any state probably, and any Western state certainly, is a physical expression of a metaphysical fact. A weakness in the original metaphysics could eventually spell a physical collapse, and Rome provides far from the only example of this.

The Old World from which the settlers escaped was founded on historical Christianity. The Christian synthesis of body and soul, physical and metaphysical, God and man, was reflected in every traditional European institution – not just religious, but also cultural, legal and political. One would think that, having been weaned on Christendom, the American settlers had a working model on which they could build their new country. However, we have already seen that every aspiration of the new republic ran contrary to Christian tradition. The settlers had to choose between God and man, much as some of them were reluctant to do so.

Any republican democracy[9] is partly founded on the philo-sophical, political and moral ethos of pagan antiquity – it has to

---

9 The distinction between republicanism and democracy was valid at the time of Lepanto and perhaps even at the time of the American Revolution, but not in modern times. A political state built on Enlightenment principles, even if it starts out as a republic, cannot help turning into a democracy, as it did in America much to the chagrin of most Founders.

presuppose the primacy of the collective over the individual. It therefore presupposes the primacy of centralism over localism, of innovation over custom, of a big state over a small man whose political self-expression traditionally relied on familial institutions. Christianity, on the other hand, *ipso facto* cultivates in its adherents an aversion to the big state, what with its innately totalitarian tendency to override private spiritual pursuits. The old religion simply could not be twisted enough to accommodate the new ethos.

Yet the American colonies were founded by people who practised what they thought was Christianity, even though much of it was seen as heresy in the countries they had left behind. It was therefore essential that the new secular state should create a new secular religion that would be sufficiently close to the original to mollify the residually Christian conscience of all those pursuers of happiness. Moreover, the new religion had to resemble the old one in as many respects as possible, for too much divergence could have rung too many alarm bells. Structurally it had to mimic the Christian synthesis of body and soul.

The pursuit of happiness worked nicely as the body of the new creed, but it was too monistic and materialistic to function as the soul as well. The new religion had to mimic the duality of Christ to look legitimate. Hence, much as the new Americans felt self-righteous in their eudemonic pursuits sanctified by their founding documents, the material thesis of money had to be offset by a dematerialised antithesis to create a quasi-metaphysical synthesis. Happiness was to be pursued, but it could not also be worshipped, not by itself at any rate. The totem pole begged for another bull's head to share its top with happiness.

It was soon found, and one has to admire the logic behind the discovery: since every old object of worship had been found wanting, the new nation decided to worship itself instead. And since this *amour propre* could sound a bit too secular for the tastes of sectarian Protestant settlers, it somehow had to be linked to God.

If we put ourselves in the moccasins of the first Americans, we shall see that they could hardly avoid a certain amount of pantheistic mysticism when finding themselves face to face with a vast, promising and yet hostile expanse. Much as they prayed for riches in the future, they knew that the present was more likely to greet them with the fangs and claws of wild beasts or else the arrows and tomahawks of aboriginal scalpers. The only way to keep going was to lay some groundwork for optimistic fatalism: they had to deify their exploits. God had to be on their side because no one else was. To find enough resolve to build a new country they had to strive to build a new Jerusalem.

But there is only one real Jerusalem – everything else, including England's green and pleasant land, can only be its simulacrum. This was demonstrated by the first batch of English settlers who colonised the Massachusetts Bay colony. As early as 1630 their leader, the Puritan lawyer John Winthrop, delivered an oration in which he alluded to Matthew 5: 14 by describing the new community as a 'city upon a hill'. Let us for a brief moment consider the contextual implications of this scriptural verse, delivered in Jesus's Sermon on the Mount: "Ye are the light of this world. A city that is set on an hill cannot be hid."

This proselytising verse issues both a promise to the world and an entreaty to the listeners: by following Christ they would light a lantern illuminating the righteous path for the rest of mankind. Not only would they acquire an ability to do so, but they would also acquire the duty. "Let your light so shine before men, that they may see your good works…," continued Jesus. Thus when Winthrop likened the new colony to a city on a hill, he implicitly equated it to the beacon that shone the word of God onto the rest of the world. And since he did so in a secular context, the religion based on this premise could only be secular. Hence it was not really a religion but an ideology pretending to be a religion: mimicry gone sanctimonious, the transient pretending to be transcendent.

It actually went further than that. For all European monarchies of the time based their legitimacy on the doctrine of divine right or something similar. A king was usually neither elected[10]

---

10   The Polish-Lithuanian Commonwealth with its elective monarchy was an exception.

nor imposed on the people by any secular pressures – his power derived from God. The apostolic succession of popes and dynastic succession of kings could be traced back in parallel lines, only converging at the original starting point: God's will. Whatever we think of this doctrine, it ran unopposed in the organic states of Christendom. Winthrop's 'city on a hill' was thus a battle cry: it was not a monarchy but a republic that was divinely ordained. It was also a statement of intent: the New World being built on the ruins of the Old would be no more than its simulacrum.

The Biblical phrase immediately entered the American lore and there it remains to this day. The underlying spirit cuts across party lines: the phrase 'a city [shining or otherwise] upon a hill' was used by both the arch-Democrat John Kennedy and the arch-Republican Ronald Reagan. America is not just different from all other countries; it is saintlier and therefore better.

While other lands amble aimlessly through life, it is America's right and duty to carry out a messianic mission, to give 'light unto all that are in the house' by spreading the ideals of liberalism, democracy, democratic liberalism, liberal democracy, republicanism or any other voguish political term denoting the underlying virtue. The tactics for dealing with those who refused to be guided by the light shining from the top of the hill were left out for the time being, but they were strongly implied.

In 1809 Jefferson expressed the principle of America as a beacon without relying on biblical references: "Trusted with the destinies of this solitary republic of the world, the only monument of human rights, and the sole depository of the sacred fire of freedom and self-government, from hence it is to be lighted up in other regions of the earth, if other regions of the earth shall ever become susceptible of its benign influence."

Tastes differ but facts should not: America was not "the only monument... and the sole depository... of freedom and self-government". Britain, to name one other country, had form in those areas too. But then the puffery of political pietism knows no bounds.

In due course the 'city upon a hill' was helped along by other words from the lexicon of American exceptionalism.

THE AMERICAN RELIGION

In the 1840s the journalist John L. O'Sullivan coined the term 'manifest destiny' to describe America's messianic mission in the world. Said manifest destiny was according to him 'divine': it was incumbent upon America "to establish on earth the moral dignity and salvation of man".

As Tocqueville's *Democracy in America* had already laid bare for the natives the salient feature of their society, it was understood, though not universally stated, that both the dignity and the salvation could only come from broad, if not yet universal, suffrage. This had to be coupled with the worldwide enforcement of all those supposedly natural rights enshrined in the Declaration of Independence. Already at that early date the impression was conveyed, for the time being obliquely, that America's founding documents were binding not just for the country that had adopted them but also for the unsuspecting outside world. If all those countries did not realise what was good for them, it was up to America to teach them – and chastise them if they proved recalcitrant.

Never in the history of the world, at least not since the collapse of Rome, had there existed another nation so bursting with such refreshingly sanctimonious arrogance. The world had to wait until the twentieth century for the American antithetical *doppelgänger* to appear: Soviet Russia on her own messianic crusade. The differences between the two are obvious enough, but the similarities are just as telling, if less commented upon.

Interestingly, Tocqueville prophesied that America and Russia would one day rule the world: "There are now two great nations in the world which, starting from different points, seem to be advancing towards the same goal: the Russians and the Anglo-Americans." Like many of Tocqueville's prophesies, this one was only half-right. It was based on the two countries' potential for demographic growth, not on their messianic desiderata. But who says prophets are ever driven by reason alone? And surely America and Russia have indeed advanced towards one shared goal, that of doing away with Christendom. In that sense they are two jaws of the same vice.

The two messianic countries tucked away at the periphery of Christendom had both a positive and a negative constituent

DEMOCRACY AS A NEOCON TRICK

to their aspirations. The first came from what they wished to create, the second from what they desired to destroy. While their positive aspirations differed, as did their definitions of happiness, their negative desiderata were identical: the destruction of the old order, otherwise known as Christendom. America was more successful in achieving both her positive aims (they were more achievable to begin with, for being more pragmatic) – and definitely the negative ones. In that she was nothing short of subversive, and her success nothing short of predictable. A seducer, after all, is likely to run up a higher amatory score than a rapist.

To reinforce the quasi-religious aspects of their self-worship both countries borrowed their iconography from various creeds, either pagan or *faux* Christian. In ghoulish mimicry of Christian relics, for example, the 'uncorrupted' body of Lenin still lies in its mausoleum, minus the erstwhile mile-long queues of worshippers. Rumours used to be spread that Soviet scientists were working on ways to bring Lenin's body back to life, and every Soviet city, town or village was adorned with posters screaming "Lenin lived, Lenin lives, Lenin will always live!". Lenin and until 1956 Stalin were (in a more limited way still are) worshipped as saints and their pronouncements heeded as gospel.

Many have commented on the perverse references to religion in Bolshevik iconography, but few have noticed that the same mimicry is just as robust in America. Hardly any speech by American leaders from the eighteenth century onwards has omitted quasi-religious references to canonised historical figures, whose deeds are routinely described in Biblical terms. "Fellow citizens, the ark of *your* covenant is the Declaration of Independence," pronounced John Quincy Adams, and he meant it exactly as it sounded.

Sacral visual imagery also abounds, as do the mock-religious shrines to past leaders. Mount Rushmore with its 60-foot likenesses of George Washington, Thomas Jefferson, Theodore Roosevelt and Abraham Lincoln carved in granite is an obligatory site for American pilgrimages. George Washington in particular is worshipped in a religious manner

98

as 'Great Father of the Country'. The interior of the Capitol dome in Washington displays a fresco entitled *The Apotheosis of Washington* where the sainted Father is surrounded by Baroque angels and also representations of other Founders in contact with various pagan gods, such as Neptune, Vulcan and Minerva.

In the same vein, the Lincoln Memorial is designed as a Greek temple and is actually identified as such in marble: "In this temple, as in the hearts of the people, for whom he saved the Union, the memory of Abraham Lincoln is enshrined forever." The Jefferson Memorial, not far away, is also a replica of a pagan shrine, with various quasi-religious references inscribed. Cited, for example, is a quotation from Jefferson's letter to Washington preaching "God who gave us life gave us liberty. Can the liberties of a nation be secure when we have removed a conviction that these liberties are the gift of God? ... Commerce between master and slave is despotism."

It is useful to remember that these ringing words were uttered by a man who had his chattel slaves flogged to mincemeat for trying to escape. Jefferson also openly despised every Christian dogma and sacrament. The statement would therefore be either hypocritical or downright cynical if we were to forget that by then 'God' had become the shorthand for 'America'. Thus the sacred shrines in Washington's Tidal Basin attract millions of secular pilgrims every year, those eager to worship at the altar of Democracy.

To emulate the God of the Scriptures, the American deity had to claim creative powers. God Mark I may or may not have created the world, but it is definitely up to God Mark II to recreate it. In that sense, one has to agree that America fulfilled the prophesy of one of her spiritual fathers, Thomas Paine. In his revolutionary gospel *Common Sense* Paine thundered off his pulpit that, "We have it in our power to begin the world over again. A situation, similar to the present, hath not happened since the days of Noah until now. The birthday of a new world is at hand..."

Where one would disagree with Burke's opponent is in his rating of the new world: while he welcomed it as an unqualified paradise, a stubborn holdout from Christendom is more likely to regard it as a comfy cultural hell for the whole family. Neither description is entirely accurate, yet both are equally valid in that they reflect two opposite concepts of life. (Note to neocons: other concepts of life do exist, and they have an 'unalienable' right to continue to do so.) But you will notice the similarity between Paine's language and that, say, of Lenin or Trotsky. They too talked about the birth of a new world. They too knew this meant the death of the old one.

Thus from the beginning American patriotism took on certain characteristics that until then had been more commonly associated with love of God, not of one's country. New patriotism began to claim precedence over old morality. This is not to say that no true religious spirit existed in America – it did, and at the time it was still rather virile. But that residual piety had practically no role to play in the day-to-day running of the new republic. For America's politicians the Bible was not so much a guide to their activities as an inexhaustible source of spiffy phrases, a precursor to the *Roget's Thesaurus of Quotations*. Real life was driven by the unreal religion, one based not on a God worshipped but on a country deified.

Obviously Americans were not the first people to love their birthplace. Patriotism may have been the last refuge of a scoundrel to Dr Johnson, and indeed many a scoundrel has used it as such. But there is nothing wrong with loving one's country, especially if it is lovable. ("For a country to be loved it ought to be lovely" was how Burke put it.) However, patriotism elevated to the perch previously occupied by religion is always pernicious. Here it would be useful to consider various levels of patriotism as expressed through everyday phrases uttered to describe them. This is best imagined as a ladder, with degrees of patriotism forming descending rungs.

"I love my country" sits at the top. This is a laudable statement. The country in which one is born and grows up does not have to be ideal any more than a woman has to be ideal to be loved. Whether it is perceived as perfect or flawed, one's own country offers the degree of intimacy, warmth and shared historical memory that is keenly felt and cherished. Like two siblings who possess a knowledge inaccessible to a stranger, countrymen – regardless of their individual differences – are united by a bond as strong as it may be invisible to outsiders.

This bond does not need expressing in words: two strangers from the same country visiting, for example, Italy may exchange knowing smiles at the sight of some local shenanigans, say people using their hands when talking or a woman dressed to the nines just to pop across the street for a loaf of bread. Such smiles or other semiotic exchanges would take a few sentences to explain on paper, but for the two countrymen there is no need for even a few words – they understand each other anyway.

To expand on this observation, earlier I pointed out the intellectual weakness of the phrase "We hold these truths to be self-evident…" But the phrase is unassailable on a sub-intellectual level: a nation truly becomes one when most people in it regard most of the same truths as self-evident. In that sense the American states had been united even before the Declaration – that is, united in what most of their denizens accepted as axiomatic. Such shared knowledge and mutual understanding indeed come close to the feelings of two siblings: in that sense, brotherly love and love of one's country are similar.

Nor is there anything wrong with regarding one's country as unlike any other. All countries are different; if they were not, we would not have so many different countries. This is so obvious that one would think it hardly needs saying. But of course what matters here is not the text but the subtext: when people insist that their country is exceptional, they usually do not mean 'different from…', they mean 'better than…'. They are entitled even to that opinion, as long as they recognise that tastes may differ.

Moving down a step, "I love my country, right or wrong" begins to be problematic. However, the problem is not insurmountable: after all, though we like *for* something, we love *in spite of* everything. A normal son cannot always stop loving his mother just because she is a compulsive shoplifter. Nor will a normal mother stop loving her son even if he boasts a string of juvenile convictions before his sixteenth birthday. So perhaps Burke's aphorism quoted above ought to be ever so slightly modified. A country has to be lovely to be liked – loving it is a slightly different matter.

Another step down, and we overhear the statement "I love my country because it is always right." Between this step and the previous one a line was crossed separating patriotism from jingoism. No country is always right. The belief that one can be is as false as it is widespread at the American grassroots.

When such sentiments are translated into action, we begin to leave behind the rivers supposedly flowing with milk and honey and approach a swamp fuming with putrid emanations. Implicit in this statement is tribal, what before the advent of political correctness used to be called Hottentot, morality: if I steal his cow, that is good; if he steals my cow, that is bad. It took several millennia of civilisation to overcome such tribalism, and by the looks of it the job has never been finished.

Another step down, and the morass sucks us in waist-high. Here one hears "My country is always right because it is guided by God in everything it does." Typically this has nothing to do with any true religious faith: after all, Christ was unequivocal in stating that his kingdom was not of this world. America or any other country is 'under God' because everything is – but only for that reason.

At this level 'manifest destiny' and 'a city on a hill' are joined by the 'Third Rome' of Russia (replaced for a few decades by a more aggressive communist messianism) and the '*Gott mit uns*' of the SS. The underlying assumption is that our actions cannot be judged by infidels, only by God, and he has given us an open-ended endorsement. Thus anything we do is justified simply because we do it.

The lowest rung reaches to the bottom of the swamp, where real creepy-crawlies take refuge. Here the sentiment is "Because our country is guided by God, it is our duty to impose our ways on others, whether they want it or not. Others may be either seduced or coerced, it does not matter which, as long as they join the fold." Since no real faith in God underlines this feeling, the explanatory clause at the beginning of the sentence may at some point be dropped for being superfluous.

Only Americans and Russians ever descend this ladder below

THE AMERICAN RELIGION

the top two rungs in noticeable numbers, and only Americans hardly ever stumble along the way. Also unique to America is the heavy representation of this genre of patriotism in the political mainstream. In other countries it is usually relegated to the lunatic fringe, an area inhabited, say, by France's *Front National*, German neo-Nazis or our own dear BNP. Other places also have individuals prepared to dive headlong into the swamp of sanctimonious jingoism, except that in those places such willing divers do not represent the dominant, nor even influential, ethos.

It is the bottom rungs on our imaginary ladder that have provided the historical and psychological springboard for modern neoconservatism. Its dive into the murky waters was also assisted by other developments, sentiments and philosophies, but those I shall discuss in later chapters.

2

Perhaps it is worth spending some more time to explore the parallels between the two mythological creeds: American exceptionalism and socialism. After all, they are the dominant ingredients in the quasi-fideistic stew of neoconservatism. Both creeds borrow freely from the phraseology and allusions of Christianity, while rejecting its inner substance and any cultural, social or political manifestations thereof.

Socialism derives its content from the French branch of the Enlightenment, while Americanism mostly, though not exclusively, came out of the Anglo-Scottish branch. The two greatly overlap and they converge fully in their shared conviction that their political systems provide comprehensive answers to every problem of life, even those that ostensibly have nothing to do with politics. They share a propensity for what T.S. Eliot so accurately described as "dreaming of systems so perfect that no one will need to be good". Hence, whatever their protestations, they both despise Christendom with its serene certainty that the real problems of life can have no political solution.

This is not to say that politics and economics should be ignored – only that they fall short of the core around which it

103

DEMOCRACY AS A NEOCON TRICK

is possible to build a civilisation worthy of the name. A society that fails to realise this and forges ahead regardless may become wealthy and powerful, intermittently. What it will remain consistently is primitive of culture, infantile of emotion and capricious of temperament.

The quasi-religions of both Americanism and socialism also mimic Christianity structurally by bifurcating into two streams: hermetic and crusading. Democratic socialism seeks to draw others into its orbit by dangling before them a political and economic system that will act as an irresistible magnet by simply being there and setting an example. Similarly, hermetic monks and anchorites, though proselytising whenever an opportunity presented itself, did not actively seek such opportunities. They stayed in their cells and cloisters, toiling around the clock to save their souls and by their example to light up for others a straight path to salvation.

Aggressive socialism, on the other hand, mimics the crusading spirit of the Middle Ages. It too wishes to shine a beacon onto a darkened world, but this type of socialism is also prepared to force the outlanders to toe the line should they prove incomprehensibly reluctant to do so.

The American creed also shows signs of the same type of mimicry. It too is split into two streams, both based on the underlying mythological premise of American exceptionalism. The hermetic stream (these days called isolationism) prefers to practise its unmatched virtue internally. Others, if they know what is good for them, are welcome to follow, but the hermeticists are more concerned about protecting their own cloister from strangers than about forcing them to join. Hence whatever outsiders may feel about this philosophy, they have no grounds for criticising it: not to cut too fine a point, this is none of their business.

Conversely, the crusaders (usually called interventionists) are ever ready to strike out, converting others not just by setting glittering examples of virtue, but also by setting stubborn infidels on fire. It is this strain of the American self-worshipping religion that acted as an important historical source for today's neoconservatism, and here outsiders are within their right to analyse and criticise. They may, after all, find themselves on the receiving end of proselytising zeal.

Both streams have issued countless statements of intent, but I shall limit myself to quoting only two, made by two US presidents a century and a half apart. Encapsulating the ethos of hermetic American exceptionalism, John Quincy Adams (1825–1829) declared how America felt about faraway lands: "Wherever the standard of freedom and independence has been or shall be unfurled, there will her heart, her benedictions and her prayers be. But she goes not abroad in search of monsters to destroy. She is the well-wisher to the freedom and independence of all. She is the champion and vindicator only of her own."

John Fitzgerald Kennedy (1961–1963) communicated the opposite view, as well as very different character traits, in his inaugural address: "Let every nation know, whether it wishes us well or ill, that we shall pay any price, bear any burden, meet any hardship, support any friend, oppose any foe, in order to assure the survival and the success of liberty." This specimen of demagogic logorrhoea shows that the speaker neither has much intelligence himself nor, more important, expects it in others.

Then again, as with all political demagoguery Kennedy's phrase-making was designed to produce a Pavlovian response in his audience, not to appeal to reason. The listeners were supposed to jump up and scream "let's march!!!", rather than sit back and ask awkward questions. *Any* price, Mr President? *Any* burden? *Any* hardship? Can we put at least *some* limit on those? Does the price stretch to self-extinction? Impoverishment? Social disintegration? And what if our present friends become our foes after we have armed them to the teeth? Are we certain their definition of liberty is the same as ours? And when you say 'we', do you mean yourself, your government or all of us? What if we, 'the people', feel differently from the way your royal 'we' does?

Alas, modernity breeds a populace congenitally incapable of asking such questions forcefully enough, if at all. Whether such unquestioning docility spills out into a tuneless rendition of *Stars and Stripes* or a mighty roar of *Horst Wessel*, and whether the right hand presses flat against the heart or shoots up with its palm outstretched, is only a matter of time, place and response desired by the demagogue.

It is no great surprise that the neocons are in greater sympathy with Kennedy than with Adams. Irving Kristol, the spiritual father of the movement, set out to prove this by stating that "The United States wishes to establish and sustain a world order that... encourages other nations, especially the smaller ones to mould their own social, political and economic institutions along lines that are at least not repugnant... to American values." Screaming Kennedy from every word, this is a far cry from Adams. Establishing and sustaining any world order, however attractive, is not what Adams had in mind, but for Kennedy and the neocons this is an article of faith.

Today's COLLENE, my Collective Neocon, falls in line: "All who live in tyranny and hopelessness can know that the United States will not ignore your oppression or excuse your oppressors. When you stand for liberty, we will stand with you." And further: "America's job is to lead the world." "What's wrong with dominance, in the service of sound principles and high ideas?" "What upholds today's world order is America's benevolent influence – nurtured, to be sure, by American power, but also by emulation and recognition around the world that American ideals are genuinely universal."

Had so many Americans not had the critical faculty bred out of them, in this area at any rate, they would have realised that Kennedy was making a promise of eternally escalating imperialism. Moreover, this was not animated by the crusading spirit of individuals united by their desire to protect and spread their faith. The president was issuing his declaration on behalf of a collective entity: an omnipotent modern state, secure in the certainty that the people will snap to attention whether they wish to or not. The state is primary, the people secondary.

In case the message had not quite got home, Kennedy reinforced it: "Ask not what your country can do for you; ask what you can do for your country!" Allow me to translate from demagogic into English: you are to serve the state, not the other way around. This pronouncement takes us back to ancient Greece, except that neither a Plato nor a Praxiteles nor a Sophocles is anywhere in evidence. Nor, more to the point, is a Pericles.

At the time the first prophets of the American surrogate religion were enunciating their dogma, few Americans – and fewer outlanders – realised what it would eventually come to mean. Whether the prophets themselves realised this is open to discussion. One way or the other, they tended to express themselves more cautiously than Kennedy, along with his, and our, contemporaries. One word they studiously avoided was 'democracy', and it fell upon a Frenchman to explain to the Americans that their everyday political vocabulary just would not be complete without it.

The American religion gets its St Paul

After a new creed has been revealed, it always takes people some time to catch their breath and figure out what it all means. As every religion worthy of the name is multifarious, and typically more than just a religion, people need help to identify the single most important thing. St Paul provided this service for budding Christians by singling out the *sine qua non* of their creed: we are justified by faith in Jesus Christ; all else is derivative. In seeking to come to terms with their secular religion, republican Americans got similar, if delayed-action, help from an aristocratic Frenchman.

Alexis de Tocqueville (1805–1859) travelled through America for a few months in 1831–1832. The resulting book, *Democracy in America*, came out in 1835–1840 and has been since rightly regarded as a classic work of political science. It was Tocqueville who first described democracy as the defining feature of the new republic, and it was he who not only extolled the virtues of democracy but also warned about its dangers.

Characteristically, neither the Founders before Tocqueville nor their followers, such as Lincoln, after him hardly ever even mentioned democracy, and they certainly never singled it out as the salient trait of American politics. This came about later, when the United States began to pursue global aspirations implicit in the American religion.

As do all observers, especially those who claim impartiality, Tocqueville brought much personal baggage to his task. Born in the heyday of Napoleonic expansion, and living in a country almost destroyed by revolutionary mayhem and imperialist wars, Tocqueville looked at American democracy with an eye trained on a different political landscape, that of France. And that terrain was littered with the charred remains of Christendom, of its religion certainly, but also of its political, social and cultural ethos.

The writer's parents had only just managed to survive the Terror by escaping to England, and surely they must have shared their harrowing experiences with baby Alexis. As the atrocities had been perpetrated largely in the name of liberal, republican democracy, it is natural that Tocqueville would devote a great deal of attention to this political idea as practised across the Atlantic, hoping it would do better there than in his native land. It is also natural that, though he mostly looked at America through rosy spectacles, his eye was at times jaundiced.

Unlike so many political scientists who approach their field as if it were structural engineering, with people acting as inanimate struts, Tocqueville realised that a state is a building erected on a spiritual, and therefore metaphysical, foundation. Moreover, his own agnosticism notwithstanding, he knew from the experience of France that no secular alternative to Christianity could give the building the same sturdy stability. However, all claims to the contrary, no observer is ever unbiased and Tocqueville was no exception.

A liberal *par excellence*, he desperately sought signs that in her democratic undertaking America was solving all the problems that had reduced the French revolution to mass slaughter and mad expansionism. Bitten by the rabid dog of revolution, France had run amok, attacking every country she could get her teeth into. Could the same rabid cur become a cuddly puppy in America? Was the disease merely a local French epidemic or a congenital blight of the modern political state? Tocqueville hoped it was the former, pushing aside the gnawing fear that it might be the latter. In particular he yearned to believe that the Americans had reconciled the seemingly irreconcilable: the revealed faith of Christendom and the utilitarian rationalism of the Enlightenment.

Travellers to foreign lands can usually find what they look for, a confirmation of a pre-existing bias. A visiting art historian will marvel at Italy's Renaissance architecture, the Vatican museums

THE AMERICAN RELIGION GETS ITS ST PAUL

and the Uffizi. A gourmet will joyously float from the pesto of Liguria to the meaty delights of Emilia-Romagna. A priest will admire the fervour of the crowds filling St Peter's Square during a papal address. And a leftie activist will not suppress a QED smirk at the sight of the contrast between the prosperity of Milanese neighbourhoods and the squalor of Calabrian slums. It takes years of living in a foreign land to form a broader judgment of it. Yet Tocqueville, though a more observant and intelligent traveller than most, had only a few months.

Since his interests were not so much ethnographic as political, he shared the problem of most political tourists, especially those seeking in a revolutionary country a vindication of their own beliefs. Someone like America's Vice President Henry Wallace, a communist in all but name, could travel to Russia in 1944, see the Kolyma labour camps and hail them as a benign smithy of the new man. He then compared them favourably to "our own TVA".[11]

He had a point, but not in the way he meant it: both Kolyma and 'our own TVA' were towering monuments to rampant statism. However, the salient difference was that in the camps so beloved of Comrade Wallace millions died horrific deaths. In no way comparing an evil dolt like him with an honourable sage like Tocqueville, one still has to remark that the Frenchman suffered from a similar travel sickness, although in a milder form.

Both scarred by the Enlightenment and weaned on it, the writer was delighted to see that Christianity did not seem to have gone out of fashion in America, as it had in his native land. Had Machiavelli not said that "there is no surer sign of decay in a country than to see the rites of religion held in contempt"? Tocqueville knew his classics and he had learned from France's experience that contempt for religion tended to equate contempt for human dignity, liberty and eventually life.

Hence Tocqueville hailed the seeming strength of Christianity in America, but not for any fideistic reasons. Sandwiched

---

11 The Tennessee Valley Authority, a federally owned corporation at the time of the Great Depression.

as he was between Voltaire and Renan, Tocqueville was more religionist than religious: though nominally a Catholic, he believed more in the social utility of Christianity than in its transcendent truth. In this he was similar to many Enlightenment figures and especially Voltaire, with his cynical *croyance utile*. For the author of *Candide*, and incidentally for modern French deconstructionists, religion was a useful tool for keeping the servants in check. Clever people like him obviously knew better. Characteristically neither Voltaire nor other such religionists minded in the least that what they proposed was in effect a society built on what they considered to be a lie.[12]

That was an error of judgement. After all, if Christianity was only an elaborate ploy to feed the people a self-serving falsehood, thereby keeping them from getting ideas above their station, then the resultant society would be built on subsiding metaphysical foundations. Sooner or later it would collapse. If thinkers of the Middle Ages believed society should nurture Christianity because it was true, the Enlightenment brigade believed society should keep Christianity even though it was false. In both instances Christianity was paramount, but the difference is more telling than the similarity.

Though Tocqueville was a much deeper and less ideological thinker than Voltaire, he proceeded from the same premise. That affected the acuity of his vision, making him susceptible to mistaking appearances for reality.

What Tocqueville failed to realise, probably because his metaphysical antennae were not as finely tuned as his sociological ones, was that the wall between religion and everyday life desired by Jefferson had already been erected. Real religion found itself outside the rough-and-tumble of American life – it was the chauvinistic pseudo-religion that ruled in its midst. The country as a whole no longer worshipped God; she worshipped herself. Tocqueville, blinded and deafened by the fireworks of pietistic shrieks going off everywhere he went, confused the two:

---

12 Lamentably, one can observe the same attitude among many of our contemporary thinkers, even seemingly conservative ones, not just the Derridas and Foucaults of this world.

THE AMERICAN RELIGION GETS ITS ST PAUL

"… there is no country in the whole world in which the Christian religion retains a greater influence over the souls of men than in America, and there can be no greater proof of its utility, and of its conformity to human nature, than that its influence is most powerfully felt over the most enlightened and free nation of the earth."

Add the prefix 'pseudo' before 'Christian', get rid of the superlatives, and the statement will become irrefutable. But note that the stress here is on utility, as if Christianity were some sort of management system or a how-to guide on running a business. Anyway, one would like to see the set of criteria by which America could have been regarded as the most enlightened country on earth, unless of course her 'enlightenment' was spelled with the initial capital.

Tocqueville's requirements for awarding this accolade clearly did not include cultural attainment, as one can infer from his other observations in the same book, such as: "The inhabitants have a sort of prejudice against anything really worthy of the name of literature, and there are towns of the third rank in Europe which yearly publish more literary works than all the twenty-four states of the Union put together."

This situation began to change, at least quantitatively, shortly after the publication of *Democracy in America*. However, elsewhere in the book Tocqueville observed that egalitarian democracy is by its very nature not conducive to cultural greatness. That surely is correct, which can be proved empirically by comparing the number of masterpieces, literary, musical, pictorial or philosophical, produced under aristocratic and democratic regimes. One could also argue that both the paucity of culture and propensity for unchecked democracy are parallel symptoms of general decadence.

Tocqueville then complimented Americans on the nature of their religious convictions that did not "spring from that barren traditional faith which seems to vegetate in the soul…" This was so different from the writer's own country where "the spirit of religion and the spirit of freedom [pursue] courses diametrically opposed to each other…" Obviously, to Tocqueville traditional faith could only be barren and vegetating, not vibrant and living. Nor, possibly because the distinction does not exist in his mother tongue, did he grasp the difference between freedom and liberty.[13] Yet the difference is there, and it points to the fundamental, unbridgeable cleft between Christendom and the Enlightenment.

Liberty is physical. The word describes the desired upshot of eliminating arbitrary restraints on human behaviour. Just like Luther proclaiming that "every man is his own priest", the secular Enlightenment creed leaves the decision of which restraints are arbitrary and which are not to personal choice. This naturally creates too wide a divergence of opinion to serve any practical purpose – and opens the door for the state to barge in and dictate its own limits of liberty. Inevitably many are bound to regard such limits as tyrannical, rightly or wrongly. Such malcontents have to be quieted down for the state's business to proceed unimpeded. What transpires, either instantly or over time, is self-refutation: real, tangible liberties have to be suppressed for mythical Liberty to be affirmed.

Freedom, on the other hand, is spiritual and therefore truly inalienable, in the sense in which 'rights' are not. It describes a personal, non-coerced choice between good and evil, vice and virtue or, if one would rather, God and Satan. In fact, the doctrine of free will is perhaps the most important dogma of Christianity, this side of the Trinity. As a distant echo of a world long since past, even in modern English usage 'freedom' is mostly used to describe not physical but spiritual realities. Hence we talk of freedom, not liberty, of conscience or speech.

Had Tocqueville been as interested in metaphysics as in politics, he would have realised that the situation in France and elsewhere in Europe used to be praiseworthy for being natural: religion and politics must operate in different realms and on different levels, with the former taking precedence in case of an overlap, such as for instance when defence of the faith becomes

---

13 This may be the translator's fault, though one can understand his predicament. Does one translate *liberté* as 'freedom' or 'liberty'? The distinction is valid, yet even Frenchmen fluent in English can seldom grasp it.

an issue.[14] They must indeed 'reign in common over the same country', but not in the meaning that Tocqueville assigned to this concept. When they begin to tread on each other's toes, both will suffer – religion immediately, politics soon thereafter. Religion can only contribute to politics by improving both politicians and their flock as human beings, not by affecting the political process directly.

When politicians step out of moral line, it is the church's duty to step in and admonish them for being bad – not as politicians but as men. It is not the remit of a Christian prelate to pontificate, as our Archbishops like to do, on the advisability of banking regulations or taxation reforms, a situation that inevitably arises when the embrace between church and state becomes too intimate. Partly because he did not realise this, Tocqueville failed to grasp the seminal difference between true equality, that before God, and its pernicious simulacrum, social equality of all before the state and its functionaries.

Thanks to their supposed ability to fuse Christian impulses with utility, Tocqueville thought Americans were able to rise above individualism (a quality he deplored on general principle, perhaps confusing it with selfishness) and direct their personal pursuits of happiness towards common good. He identified democracy – more than, say, free markets or the rule of law – as the vehicle able to carry the nation to that idyllic oasis by pooling private interests through universally and evenly distributed votes.

The belief that millions of private interests can be merged to produce public virtue was in the air at the time, thanks to the works by John Locke, Adam Smith, David Hume and other liberal empiricists. Their mistake was in thinking that 'the invisible hand' could work social miracles by itself, unassisted by the metaphysical soul and the institutions dedicated to saving it. It cannot: unless they are united in faith and a morality that can

---

14 Prince Charles sees his role as our future monarch as being not the customary 'defender of the faith' but as the 'defender of faith', meaning all faiths. This means he simply does not understand the makeup of the realm. There is only one faith he is constitutionally obliged to defend, that on which Britain's established religion is founded.

only come from faith, people may create an economy, but they will destroy society. And sooner or later even their economy will begin to resemble a snake biting its own tail. The same goes for democracy or any other political system: where they arrive depends on whence they start.

Tocqueville provides yet another example of a brilliant thinker led astray by a false metaphysical premise. He did not sense that untethered democracy runs contrary to the spirit, and indeed the entire history, of the West. Moreover, he arbitrarily co-opted Christianity into acting as an adjunct to democracy: "Most of English America was peopled by men who, having shaken off the pope's authority, acknowledged no other religious supremacy; they therefore brought into the New World a Christianity which I can only describe as democratic and republican... From the start politics and religion agreed, and they have not since ceased to do so."

Christianity can be neither democratic nor republican nor political in general: it operates in a realm infinitely higher than one in which political doctrines reside. As we have seen, politics and religion did agree in America but, in order to function in this happy union, religion had to turn itself into sanctimonious jingoism with Freedom Bells on.

As to the pope's authority having been shaken off, what about the million-odd Catholics who had settled in America by the time, about ten percent of the free population? They, according to Tocqueville, formed "the most republican and democratic of all classes in the United States." How did that come about?

The writer's explanation is revealing: "For Catholics religious society is composed of two elements: priest and people. The priest is raised above the faithful; all below him are equal." Therefore, "among the various Christian doctrines Catholicism seems one of those most favourable to equality of conditions." More so than, say, Calvinism, where the priest is a mere prayer leader rather than a conduit between a man and his God, God's liturgical stand-in? Really. But then religion was never Tocqueville's main interest.

Let us leave aside for the time being the empirical observation that 'equality of conditions' is not, nor was at the time, any more present in any democracy than in any monarchy. Neither is this the right medium to belabour the point that the intricate multi-tiered hierarchy of Roman Catholicism is unlikely, by itself, to foster the spirit of social (as distinct from spiritual) egalitarianism in its adherents.

What is truly important is that Tocqueville unwittingly put his finger on the inherent all-encompassing statism of any democracy. The logical inference from his statement is that in a democracy it is the state that soars so high that, viewed from its dizzying height, all people seem equal in size. The state, in other words, becomes the simulacrum of God.

If that is what Tocqueville meant, I would be in sympathy with his observation, if not his conclusions. But he did not, so I am not. Let us just repeat that the kind of idealised social equality Tocqueville extolled did not exist then and does not exist now in America, nor can exist in any other country. The only place where it can possibly thrive is in prison, with the inmates all equal before the God-surrogate figure of the warder. A perfectly Catholic arrangement, that, if Tocqueville is to be believed.

Christianity to Tocqueville was thus a kind of licence to socialism when the word was just being coined (this momentous linguistic event is believed to have occurred in 1834). In other words, he simply did not understand Christianity any better than did the flower children of the 1960s, with their silly insistence on Christianity being a form of social and economic egalitarianism, with the iconic murderer Che Guevara as the modern answer to Jesus. Thence came the rosy tint on Tocqueville's spectacles through which he observed America. Thence also came his seminal contribution to the surrogate religion of American exceptionalism.

Such intellectual muddle was widespread in France at the time, and hardly less so now, what with her manic worship of *laïcité* steadily growing in scale and intensity since 1905. Alas, there is always a price to pay for smug secularism: it starts at intellectual confusion and moral ambiguity, and ends at political feeblemindedness and cultural barbarism.

2

For all that, Tocqueville was an important thinker. It is just that he came into his own only upon leaving the shaky grounds of metaphysical exegesis to find himself on the *terra firma* of observation and prophecy.

In contradiction to his ill-advised philosophising on democratic republicanism being the political expression of Christianity and therefore ideal, Tocqueville pointed out the structural defects of democracy. In particular, he talked about democracy fostering "a depraved taste for equality, which impels the weak to bring the strong down to their level." Though a champion of political egalitarianism, Tocqueville was in a way repeating Aristotle's thought that democracy arises when people think that if they are equal in one respect, they are equal in all.

It goes without saying that Tocqueville saw nothing wrong in a healthy, as opposed to 'depraved', taste for equality. However he did anticipate the danger of one becoming the other. He observed correctly that aristocratic regimes, though seeking to control the bodies of men, allowed the soul to soar, whereas democracy "leaves the body alone and goes straight for the soul". What may result if we are not careful is a new type of despotism, "the tyranny of the majority," which will ineluctably lead to rampant statism.

"It [democracy] does not tyrannise," wrote Tocqueville, "but it compresses, enervates, extinguishes, and stupefies a people, till each nation is reduced to nothing better than a flock of timid and industrious animals, of which the government is the shepherd."

As with most political definitions, Burke said it better: "The tyranny of a multitude is a multiplied tyranny." Another aphorist, Lord Acton (d. 1902), admittedly armed with the benefit of Burke's and Tocqueville's earlier insights, put his finger on the problem: the main conflict during the French Revolution, he wrote, was "a great struggle between democracy and liberty," thus suggesting that the two terms so often uttered in the same breath just might be mutually exclusive.

Similar thoughts have been expressed both before and after Acton by statesmen not commonly perceived as haters of democracy. For example, Thomas Jefferson once echoed Plato by observing that, "A democracy is nothing more than mob rule, where fifty-one percent of the people may take away the rights of the other forty-nine." The Founders issued many such statements, and it was with horror that they watched their cherished republic gradually turning into a democracy. Their clearly enunciated aim was to create not a democracy, but what they called republican popular government. They obviously did not believe that the two terms were synonymous – even though the neocons with their well-practised sleight of hand claim the Founders believed just that, the unfortunate choice of words notwithstanding. The neocons simply ascribe to the likes of Jefferson the same lexical laxity from which they themselves suffer.

Rather than talking about democracy, Jefferson and other Founders singled out consent of the governed as the defining feature of the state they saw in their mind's eye. These days we are so used to the term that neither its validity nor its virtue is ever subjected to scrutiny. As do so many liberal notions, 'consent of the governed' derives from Hobbes and mostly Locke, the inspiration behind both American and French revolutions, and therefore the modern world.

An idealised picture Locke must have had in mind was that of 'the people' coming together at some instant in the past to decide on accepting or rejecting the post-Christian idea of secular government unaccountable to any absolute moral authority. Upon mature deliberation they chose to give their consent to the liberal, secular state. No doubt a show of hands must have been involved, all perfectly equitable and democratic.

This idea is doubtless attractive and it would become even more so if any evidence could be found to suggest that this meeting of minds ever took place. Alas, no such evidence exists. In fact, no modern attempt to replace a traditional monarchy with a 'liberal' republic, be that the English revolutions of the seventeenth century, the American and French ones of the eighteenth, or the Russian ones of the twentieth,

DEMOCRACY AS A NEOCON TRICK

involved campaigning for the 'people's' consent or asking them what they wanted.

What they all did involve was unbridled violence unleashed in 'the people's' name by a small cadre of subversives and their variously named revolutionary committees. In most instances, including the American Revolution, 'the people' not only did not give their explicit consent but in fact withheld even their tacit approval. When such reticence was detected, the revolutionaries, acting in the name of 'the people', would inevitably resort to violence, its extent restricted only by expediency, not any moral considerations. They could kill hundreds (Americans), thousands (Englishmen), hundreds of thousands (Frenchmen) or millions (Russians). Whatever was needed.

In the process, such old terms as 'treason' acquired a new and broader meaning. During the period demarcated by the Declaration at one end and the Constitution at the other, American revolutionaries routinely treated as traitors those who resisted exorbitant taxation, albeit with representation. The death penalty was only threatened, but any punishment short of that was widely used: imprisonment, draconian fines, confiscation of property. Also treated as traitors, and here the death penalty was often not just threatened, were the Tories, those who refused to forget that only a few short years earlier they had been loyal and sworn subjects of King George III.

By contrast, compare the treatment of 'the Great Condé' by his cousin Louis XIV, that most absolute of monarchs. Not only was Condé one of the principal instigators and military leaders of the strife known as *La Fronde*, but he also twice led Spanish armies against French royalist troops. On all three occasions he was soundly thrashed by the Vicomte de Turenne, who nonetheless never rated the 'Great' soubriquet in French historiography.

In any modern state, including the USA, Condé would have been put up against the wall and shot – with or without the benefit of trial. Why, William Joyce, 'Lord Haw-Haw', was strung up in 1946 merely for having aired Nazi propaganda during the war. Thus by the standards of liberal democracy the Great one was a traitor who did not deserve to live. Yet by the

THE AMERICAN RELIGION GETS ITS ST PAUL

standards of an organic state of Christendom that France was at the time he was a naughty child who ought to be grounded, or in this instance exiled to his castle in Chantilly. All in all, it is hard not to feel that consent to be governed is dangerously near consent to be tyrannised.

Since neither Locke nor his French followers could pinpoint the granting of 'consent' to any specific historical event, they had to talk about some nebulous metaphysical 'compact' or 'social contract', to use the phrase first used by Democritus and later popularised by Hobbes and especially Rousseau. As Joseph de Maistre showed so convincingly, this idea is invalid even at an elementary logical level.

According to the legal principle going back to the Old Testament, for any contract to be valid it has to be adjudicated by an authority holding sway over both parties, one whose judgment they accept as binding. In any reasonable sense such an authority has to be institutionally superior to the two parties. That is why, for example, when the seller and buyer of a house sign a contract transferring ownership, they have to have the document notarised by a legal official empowered to act in that capacity by the state.

The only authority that can be deemed superior to both the state and the individual is God. Hence frequent, if insincere, appeals to the deity in various founding documents of the early liberal states. Yet one would look in vain for any reference in the Judaeo-Christian Scriptures either to 'government by consent' or to 'social contract'. Nowhere does it say that a third of the electorate, a proportion considered adequate in most modern democracies including Britain, can cast their vote in a way that will give them absolute sovereignty over the remaining two-thirds. (Jefferson's reference to 'fifty-one percent' has a distinctly archaic ring to it.) What both Testaments do repeat time after time is that "all power is from God" – not from some mythical agreement.

An important aspect of 'consent', as understood by Lockeans everywhere, is that it is irrevocable: once given, or presumed to have been given, it cannot be reclaimed by any peaceful means. Yet in no conceivable way could it be true that a third or even a fourth of the population voting in a government has given consent on behalf of the rest of the people as well. This is patently ludicrous, as is the whole idea of consent, which in reality is neither sought by politicians nor given by voters.

Any real agreement includes terms under which it may be terminated. In the absence of a higher adjudicating authority, no 'social contract' can have such a clause. Therefore violence is the only recourse either party has, meaning that in a modern state a revolution is not so much an aberration as a logical extension of the 'social contract', the only way for the people to withdraw their 'consent'. This implicit principle was made explicit both in the Declaration of Independence and a similar document later issued by the Confederacy – with both the insurgents and the rebels having the power of their convictions.

In any logical interpretation of Locke, a society can remain peaceful not because of the people's meaningful consent but only because of their docile acquiescence. In other words, the people can give 'consent' only passively, not actively – by refraining from overthrowing either the government or the whole political system by force. Thus Hobbes and Locke, along with their American, English, French and Russian followers, had no option but to sanctify the people's right to revolution. But the people at large never perpetrate revolutions – this function is usurped by a small group of activists and ideologues ('professional revolutionaries' in Lenin's parlance) who combine radicalism with deviousness.

These chaps are seldom, and never merely, driven by noble motives. Hatred is always present as a significant animus. In the case of modern revolutions, this hatred is invariably levelled not at any particular abuses singled out as pretexts but at the traditional order as such. Depending on the pet issue of the day, this target may be packaged in a box labelled as 'monarchy', 'absolutism', 'popery' (a bee in the bonnet for both Hobbes and Locke), religion in general, 'taxation without representation' – the tag does not really matter.

Hence, not to cut too fine a point, Hobbes and Locke were issuing a *carte blanche* to arbitrary violence as the only option for withdrawing 'consent' never given in the first place. The people, or rather those acting in their name, would henceforth feel justified to rebel against any legally instituted authority for any reason exciting them at the moment. If it is 'popery', that will do famously. If it is 'taxation without representation', that will work just as well. If it is 'bloodthirsty tsarism', even better. In most instances, the existing government would be predictably replaced by one palpably more abusive.

Jefferson could not, or possibly would not, think about such matters deeply enough. But his statement on the coercive potential of democracy is unequivocal: whether imposed by a minority or a majority, tyranny is tyranny – it will always remain the opposite of liberty. This was a hint at the truth: as Lord Acton remarked, even though liberty is portrayed as the *raison d'être* of democracy, the two just may be at odds. Earlier the same dichotomy was spotted by John Stuart Mill who idolised Tocqueville. Under the Frenchman's influence Mill too began to talk about 'the tyranny of the majority', which he saw as potentially perilous to his cherished liberty.

The philosopher in Tocqueville neither dared nor was able to develop this thought to its logical conclusion, but the observer in him was unerring. America's first historian, George Bancroft, writing at roughly the same time as Tocqueville, had similar misgivings about the central premise of democracy. He was scathing about the Founders' belief that "the common judgment in taste, politics and religion is the highest authority on earth, and the nearest possible approach to an infallible decision."

A true political philosopher would have realised that an attenuating liberty is not a potential side effect of unchecked democracy but rather its inevitable consequence. But Tocqueville did not think this was a problem Americans or, following their example, eventually Europeans could not solve. They just had to be aware of the potential pitfalls and stay at their most vigilant to avoid them. Echoing Montesquieu, Tocqueville believed that the best way to combat the problem was to divide central government into three branches, always making sure that the legislative branch did not amass too much power. That would prevent selfishness, corruption and excessive materialism from coming to the fore. Add to this freedom of the press and association, and the damaging potential of democracy would not come to a head.

Tocqueville signposted several potential pitfalls democracy may have in store, including, prophetically, that of institutionalised corruption perpetrated by the state. His fear was that at some point those seeking political office or trying to stay in it would rely on bribery, not just persuasion. "The American Republic will endure," he wrote, "until the day Congress discovers that it can bribe the public with the public's money." That day is upon us and has been for several decades not just in America but in all Western democracies. Yet another one of Tocqueville's prophecies has come true, and both the economic and social consequences are here for all to see.

But to Tocqueville the deepest pitfall was cultural: America's geographic, historical, religious and moral uniqueness made the country a sterling exception from other nations, but the same factors "have singularly concurred to fix the mind of the American upon purely practical objects". That, hoped Tocqueville, was not necessarily as much of a problem for them as it would be for Europeans, but do let us cease to view all democratic notions through the prism of America. America was exceptional, which is to say inimitable, and destined to stay that way. Yet in a different context he remarked, "I know of no country in which there is so little independence of mind and real freedom of discussion as in America." Tocqueville did not connect this pandemic uniformity with fixation on 'purely practical objects', but the link is unmistakeable.

Americans tirelessly extol their own individualism, without grasping the paradox of this fine quality, as it is applied in their country, undeniably begetting uniformity.[15] John Stuart Mill yet again referred to Tocqueville to point out this congenital defect of democracy: "M. de Tocqueville... remarks how much more the Frenchmen of today resemble one another than did

---

15 'With notable exceptions' is a disclaimer I always imply, if not always enunciate, when generalising about national characteristics. This, however, does not mean that no national characteristics exist.

THE AMERICAN RELIGION GETS ITS ST PAUL

those of the last generation. The same remark might be made of Englishmen in a far greater degree." And of Americans in a greater degree still.

Bred into them is the individual pursuit of happiness, which is to say of "purely practical objects". Consumerism consumes them so thoroughly that any intellectual, spiritual or cultural enquiry, if it is undertaken at all, is lowered to the level of a quaint hobby and thereby trivialised. The main business of life is business, and one can detect a certain tightening of jaw and disappearance of levity whenever a conversation with Americans veers towards the serious things in life – this even among those who until then have been chattering about things like the delay of the dominant-tonic resolution in Wagner.

However, business operates with few variables and these, technical details apart, differ little from one area to the next. Inordinate devotion to commerce is bound to produce an understated interest in things of the spirit, those in which free discussion can latch on to infinite intellectual possibilities. In as much as a nation is united mostly on the basis of its material desiderata, "genuine freedom of discussion" has but a small place – there is not that much to discuss.

Tocqueville also observed, and warned against, another danger of egalitarian democracy, its reliance on "the idea of the indefinite perfectibility of man". "Aristocratic nations," he wrote, "are by their nature too much inclined to restrict the scope of human perfectibility; democratic nations sometimes stretch it beyond reason." A throwback to Christendom would observe that the scope of human perfectibility is restricted by original sin, not by aristocratic nations, but this is not an argument Tocqueville could have made. However, his comment on democracy is as accurate as ever.

Actually, democracy mongers have no option but to profess their belief in the inherent goodness of man: if they shared Western civilisation's founding dogma of man being not only fallible but indeed fallen, they would find it hard to peddle the contrary faith in the redemptive goodness of majority opinion. This belief is only peddled, rather than sincerely held: any averagely intelligent person would know that talent for statesmanship cannot be spread more widely than, say, talent for musical or literary composition. And yet, by being asked not only to elect their representatives but to do so on the basis of a sober assessment of their policies, all citizens are presumed to be equally able to go through the mental rigours involved.

That presumption is not just counterintuitive but simply false. Hence, if we juxtapose two statements, 'the majority is always right' and 'the majority is always wrong', it is the second that is nearer to the truth. Surely Churchill was right when suggesting that "the best argument against democracy is a five-minute conversation with the average voter" – yet another example of a putative admirer of democracy either having second thoughts or not being such a fervent admirer in the first place.

Aristocratic regimes were organic specifically because they developed gradually out of the Christian premise for our civilisation – including original sin and its secular reflection, the natural inequality of men in every practical, and especially political, way. Being an ideological contrivance, democracy has to abandon this premise and instead rely on its reverse: Rousseau's idea of man being perfect to begin with (until he was corrupted by civilisation in general and Christendom in particular) and yet tautologically perfectible.

Tocqueville, being in many ways a child of the Enlightenment, thought he was describing a preventable malaise of democracy, rather than its congenital defect. Yet no democracy can exist without deifying man, specifically the common man, to some extent, trying to force the square peg of humanity into the round hole left by religion. Because God is perfect, man can be almost perfect. Because God is self-sufficient cosmically, man can be self-sufficient politically.

Unlike animals, people can improve themselves, declared Tocqueville irrefutably. St Paul said the same thing and he showed exactly how such an improvement could be achieved. Yet to Tocqueville it is democracy that gives people almost endless opportunities to become better.

The implication is that an aristocratic regime of Christendom would deny them this opportunity, forcing people to remain in their bestial state. However, the example of any country that has consecutively experienced both regimes shows this is simply not so: it was under monarchies that Austria created a great music, France a great literature, Holland a great art, and Germany a great just about everything – and what have they created under perfect democracy? Contrary to Tocqueville's belief, one gets the impression that the more realistic, and therefore pessimistic, is the nation's underlying assessment of the people's potential for improvement, the more fully will this potential be realised.

To repeat, Tocqueville's problem was that he started from a wrong philosophical premise. He was fully aware of the potential dangers of egalitarian democracy, as he knew that Rousseau's theory was wishful thinking. But the liberal in him craved the hope he could not find within the Enlightenment dungeon in which he had locked himself. In the name of that hope he shackled his prophetic powers and reached for something that does not exist: a regime eventually becoming perfect and, once the birth pains have been alleviated, churning out perfect people.

In the process he unwittingly gave Americans what their home-grown talent could not quite deliver: a slogan for intellectual self-justification. If democracy was the new religion, Tocqueville was its St Paul: he explained to the Americans what their new religion was really all about.

Yet for the time being the Americans neither heeded his warnings nor needed his explanations, much as they admired them. The Founders and their immediate descendants were sage enough not to focus on democracy as the distinguishing feature of their republic. Although actual democracy would continue to expand throughout the nineteenth century with, for example, property and tax restrictions on franchise gradually falling by the wayside, American statesmen did not inscribe the word on their banners.

Even Lincoln's Gettysburg Address, though talking about "government of the people, by the people, for the people" does not feature 'democracy' among its 278 words. Why did he not just say 'democratic government' instead? That would have reduced the Address to an even 270 words, and surely brevity is important.

Hence for Lincoln "government of the people, by the people, for the people" was not tantamount to democracy, not wholly at any rate – just as democracy did not equate 'popular government' or 'consent of the governed' for the Founders. Put another way, Lincoln expressed his ideal for the substance of government without being entirely sure that democracy was its only possible or desirable form. If so, Lincoln was nothing short of prescient. These days we do see many examples of the democratic form containing an out-and-out spivocracy for which the people are an irritating irrelevance, or else merely a source of revenue.

It took Americans and the West in general another half a century to lose their erstwhile ability to distinguish between form and content. As the West moved further and further away from its metaphysical essence, the substance of government crumbled away and only the form remained. People have forgotten, have been brainwashed to forget, that what matters is not method of government but the kind of society it produces.

The smug, mechanistic adoration of the democratic form has overshadowed everything else. Democracy became deified, and, in common with other deities, acquired the presumption of infallibility. Asking probing questions about democracy became an exercise in futility; doubting it a sign of madness. God is not to be questioned; he is only to be worshipped. Americans in particular, when looking at another country, tend to ask one question only, or at least first: "Is it democratic?" That is all they need to know to form a positive or negative view of the place. It seldom occurs to them to ask fundamental questions about democracy itself, nor to consider why it became the focus of their nationhood relatively late.

Democracy as a battle cry

1

Throughout the nineteenth century, America's expansionism and attendant proselytising were mostly contained within her own continent and, later, within Central America and the Pacific. The key signposts on the road to the American imperial realm as it exists today were:

- The Louisiana Purchase of 1803, whereby Napoleon foolishly sold to the USA a territory of 828,000 square miles for roughly three cents an acre – thus doubling the country's territory and consequently expanding slavery twofold
- The 1812 war with Britain in which America claimed a 'moral victory' but suffered a strategic defeat in her failure to conquer Canada
- The Monroe Doctrine issued in 1823, stipulating that the USA would regard as an act of war any European attempt to colonise territories in North or South America or indeed to play any active political role in the region
- Annexation of the Republic of Texas in 1845
- The Mexican War of 1848 with the ensuing annexation of the Southwestern territories, including California
- Expulsion of the French from Mexico in 1866 during the reign of Napoleon III, whose foray into that part of the world represented the only serious challenge to the Monroe Doctrine until the Cuban crisis of 1962
- The Alaska Purchase of 1867, adding another 586,412 square miles to the American territory for the derisory price of two cents per acre – even a better deal than the Louisiana Purchase

- The Spanish war of 1898 as a result of which Spain turned over Puerto Rico, Guam and the Philippines to the United States
- Turning Hawaii into a US territory in 1900

The Monroe Doctrine was a statement of geopolitical intent, a quasi-legal justification of US domination over the Western Hemisphere. It was only *quasi*-legal for being unilateral: other countries both within the Monroe Doctrine sphere and outside it recognised America's power but not necessarily her legal or moral right to wield it.

Thus, for example, when in 1895 the United States insisted on her right to mediate a border dispute between Venezuela and British Guiana, she was rebuked by Britain. Countering the assertion by US Secretary of State Richard Olney that his country was 'practically sovereign' in the Western Hemisphere, Britain responded that the Monroe Doctrine fell far short of being international law. A parallel with other documents issued by America, especially her Constitution, begs to be drawn: Americans find it difficult to acknowledge the existence of countries with a different way of looking at the world that for them does not necessarily centre around the United States as the sole possible reference point.

At the same time, expansionism, inherent to any revolutionary republic, trumped all constitutional considerations. Indeed, territorial expansion, especially by violent means and at the expense of other nations, was not mentioned in the Constitution. 'Consent' on the other hand was its ironclad presupposition. Yet the Louisiana Purchase brought under federal control a vast population whose consent to be governed by the United States had been neither given nor even sought.

Just like the colonisation and subsequent annexation of Texas, the Purchase also spread slavery over a vast territory where it had been previously outlawed. By the same token, naked aggression against Mexico, depriving her of more than half of her territory, had no constitutional justification, nor any grounding in international law. It sprang not from such worthy motives but from simple gonadic aggression coded into the DNA of any revolutionary state.

The American geopolitical developments of the nineteenth century were unadulterated expansionism mostly pursued by military means, with the partial exception of the two Purchases, where force was implicitly yet credibly threatened but not actually used. When each new step was debated in US Congress, well-meaning phrases were uttered, as they always are by any aggressive modern power, but those were kept strictly in the background of the rhetoric based on cold-blooded national interest, not ideology.

Though America did not become a fully fledged empire in the nineteenth century, it laid out the necessary groundwork. In fact, perhaps the most significant geopolitical development of that century was that as a result of her expansion America emerged as a potentially significant imperial power. As such, she was to find herself in competition with other empires representing the last vestiges of the organic states of Christendom: Austro-Hungary, Germany, Russia – and especially Britain, or the British Empire as it was then known.

Many historians like to reduce America's brewing confrontation with the traditional empires to her seeking economic dominance, easier access to world markets and other physical gains. These no doubt played a significant role, but of equal importance were more intangible stimuli. Primary among them was a typical neophyte's resentment against the traditional establishment, observable not only among individuals but also among nations.

Also at play were even deeper psychological and philosophical issues. America correctly perceived herself as the flag bearer of modernity, with its inherently aggressive animosity towards every physical and metaphysical manifestation of Christendom. Though never actually enunciated, an understanding clearly existed that America's march towards fulfilling her manifest destiny was in danger of being slowed down or even stopped by the organic states of Europe battling for their survival.

The physical and the metaphysical converged at a point where America sought the status of a world empire, heir to the

Romans and, more immediately, to the British, with its concept of 'liberal interventionism'. Yet those two world empires did not gain dominion over much of the known world exclusively by force. The threat of military chastisement was always offset with the promise of cultural, political and economic rewards. The Romans and the British did not just wish to claim the bodies of others; they also craved their souls. They did not just want to conquer; they also wanted to civilise. 'White man's burden', under various names, was part and parcel of all successful imperial expansion, even where no chromatic variances existed between the empire builders and their human material.

Americans too must have realised that the New World could only conquer by extinguishing the old way of life and replacing it with something, anything new. Exactly what that could be was a secondary consideration; destruction was the real imperative. First things first. Obviously, the USA could not realistically hope to expand the Monroe Doctrine all the way to Europe, using the document as the mock-legal justification for crushing the traditional empires by force. Yet the bubbling proselytising spirit of the American religion could not be securely contained within the Western Hemisphere.

The Old World, aka Christendom, congenital hostility to which was part of America's genetic makeup, had to be conquered, but that could only be achieved by subtler means than cannon boats. Since the USA could not fight a shooting war against the world, her offer had to have enough seductive appeal to attract Europeans, particularly if they had good cause to be disaffected with the traditional order.

All such considerations stayed in the metaphysical background to some necessary physical steps. But before any such steps could be taken, the American offer had to be expressed and then sold to the world as a concise, unequivocal slogan that could then do duty both internally and externally. America had to proselytise the world by relying on both her body, which is to say economic dynamism fuelled to a large degree by geopolitical expansion, and on her soul, which is to say... what exactly? Presumably the two founding documents of the American republic provided an answer to that question,

DEMOCRACY AS A BATTLE CRY

but one could hardly inscribe their full text on the banners of expansionism.

Taking stock of all available options Americans had to enlist a word that appeared in neither document. Tocqueville had to be taken off the mothballs and turned against his own continent to proclaim that the soul of America was her democracy. As America was divine, this soul was a particle of God's essence and therefore universal. Hence it was America's holy mission to address democratic deficits anywhere in the world.

Only then did democracy gain currency to a point where it took pride of place among all other possible desiderata. Democracy became useful shorthand for a neatly summarised novelty and, in order to act as an all-conquering slogan, the word had to expand its meaning beyond a mere method of putting a government together. The new meaning had to be transcendent: democracy had to stop being just a word and instead become the Word, or else the holy spirit proceeding from its deified father, the United States, overlooking the world from the crest of a shining hill.

America now had a metaphysical banner under which she could ride into physical battle against the Old World. But first there had to be a battle she could join, and she had to wait for it to come, for initiating one was beyond America's capabilities. She did not have to wait long. Traditional states of Christendom duly obliged by uniting in a suicide pact known as the First World War.

2

That war was historically unprecedented in every respect, either physical or metaphysical. The former requires no additional commentary: thousands of scholarly and popular books have exhausted the issue of geopolitical power play and military strategies based on the mass use of new weapons, such as machineguns, tanks, gas and aeroplanes. The latter, however, has not been commented upon enough.

For the United States was not the only country that was driven by the spirit of hostility towards Christendom. In a display of self-hatred seldom seen in history, European empires had come to share the same destructive animosity. They too had acquired the urge to expand not just in the national interest, and certainly no longer to carry their civilisation to those who could benefit from it, but simply for the sake of expansion itself. Yet thanks to the technological advances of which modernity was and remains so justly proud, each of those empires now represented both an irresistible force and an immovable object. Mutual annihilation was the only possible result.

The role played by America in the First World War is both instructive and germane to the theme of this essay. At first glance this was not America's fight: her geopolitical or economic interests would not have been unduly threatened by any possible outcome. At the same time Wilson's sloganeering along the lines of 'making the world safe for democracy' would have sounded frankly ludicrous to any other than a pre-brain-washed audience. Such an aim presupposed that the Great War was waged against democracy, and only General Pershing in shining armour was there to save it.

That simply was not the case if we divest the word 'democracy' of its subliminal implications, still at that time intelligible to Americans only. All major combatants were already either democracies or constitutional monarchies – or else were fast moving in that direction. Even Germany had a strong parliament that had to vote on war credits for the generals to take over.[16] Had the vote gone against such credits, there would have been no war. Russia's Duma, while less robust than Germany's Reichstag, was getting stronger by the day, and few doubted that the country would soon become a fully constitutional monarchy.

So the big slogan would seem to be a big lie, but only if we insist on using words in their real meaning. As by then modern simulacra had taken over much of political vocabulary, the word 'democracy' did not really mean political pluralism, certainly not just that. It meant modernity's rule, as spearheaded by America.

---

16 The vote in favour was nearly unanimous, with only the German Leninist Karl Liebknecht voting against.

By the time the United States entered the war, Russia had already been paralysed by the pacifist propaganda waged by the Bolsheviks and mostly paid for by the Germans and Americans. She had been almost knocked out of the conflict and, with her armies deserting *en masse*, was months away from falling into the grip of the worst tyranny the world had ever known. At the same time on the Western front supposedly civilised people were no longer fighting a war; they were engaged in mass murder for its own sake. Under such circumstances, it did not take a crystal ball to predict that any possible conclusion to the massacre would come at a cost to traditional institutions. As the flower of Christendom was being mowed down, so was the habitat in which it could stagger back to life.

3

The neocons' idol Woodrow Wilson did not need fortune-telling appliances to predict such an outcome. Happily for him, this was precisely the outcome he craved, one that had come to him as a clarion call from the American grassroots. Unlike, say, the Clemenceaus of this world, he had heard this call of America-led modernity not as a distant echo but in every tonal detail, and responded by employing every modern technique at his disposal.

Two years before America's entry into the war, Wilson had set up the greatest advertising agency ever seen. Called the Committee on Public Information, it included a team of America's leading propagandists headed by George Creel whose own political sympathies lay far on the Left. Their task was clearly defined: America had a mission to convert the world to her way of life and everything it signified. And in one word? Why, democracy of course.

The president had come to the conclusion that this mission could be fulfilled only by entering the war. Ergo, the American people who in their ignorance opposed such a move had to be made to see the light. Anyway, the American people hardly mattered: Wilson had in mind not just parochial interests but a programme for all mankind, and if the programme could be put into action only at a cost to American lives, then so be it. American lives were to be sacrificed at the altar of American exceptionalism, and this was the first time the seeds of this poisonous tree were planted. The tree has since grown to luxuriant maturity and we can admire the glorious shadow it casts over the Middle East, with the neocons, heirs to Wilson's legacy, acting in the capacity of gardeners.

Having won the 1916 re-election on the mendacious slogan "He kept us out of the war", Wilson went on to demonstrate that every means was suitable for dragging America into the slaughter. Technically neutral until April 1917, she had begun to violate the provisions of neutrality from the start. The House of Morgan, for example, floated war loans for Britain and France in 1915, and at the same time war supplies were flowing from America across the Atlantic in an uninterrupted stream. The Germans were thus provoked into unrestricted U-boat warfare (not that they needed much provoking), which in turn helped Wilson to build a slender pro-war margin in Congress.

Nor was Wilson bashful in putting his agenda across, when, for example, demagogically describing the bloodbath as: "... this great war in which there is being fought out once for all the irrepressible conflict between free self-government and the dictation of force... a struggle whose object is liberation, freedom, the rights of men and nations to live their own lives and determine their own fortunes, the rights of the weak as well as of the strong, and the maintenance of justice by the irresistible force of free nations leagued together in the defence of mankind."

Wilson knew exactly what he was after: the destruction of the traditional world and its replacement with a world of modernity led by America. That is why the propaganda spewed out by the Creel Committee went beyond amateurish attacks on the bloodthirsty Hun. Every piece of promotional literature put out by Creel, every speech by Wilson was an incitement to revolution, both political and social, across Europe.

Thus America had no quarrel with the industrious people of Germany; it was the oppressive Junker class that was the enemy.

No sacrifice was too great to liberate the Germans from their own domestic tyrants. No peace, no armistice was possible until the existing social order and political arrangement were destroyed – in other words, until a revolution took place. Likewise Wilson had no quarrel with the quirky people inhabiting the British Empire; it was the Empire itself that he abhorred. Even though for tactical reasons that particular message could not yet be enunciated in so many words, dismantling the offending institution was clearly one of Wilson's key objectives. A fanatic of a single world government, Wilson was at the same time a great champion of national self-determination. Anticipating a possible confusion on the part of the reader, there was no contradiction there, at least not to a modern mind. The first was the end; the second, the means.

It is instructive to see what the founders of neoconservatism thought of Wilson's transparent imperial ambitions. Thus, for example, Irving Kristol, the father or at least godfather of this movement: "…the whole point of the Wilsonian 'crusade' was to rid the world of imperial politics." Later on I shall devote a whole chapter to Kristol's thought, as it still continues to inform neoconservatism on both sides of the Atlantic. A more accomplished man than any of his followers, Kristol still evinced the same muddled thinking – indeed institutionalised it. His description of Wilson's desiderata would be unassailable had he added the adjective 'traditional' before 'imperial'. As it was, Kristol simply paid a characteristic neocon tribute to Wilsonian neo-imperialism.

For the traditional world contained within the European empires to perish, these empires had to be broken up into constituent elements. The marginal peoples of the empires, all those Czechs, Poles, Finns and Serbs could not make good any promise of self-determination without a prior destruction of all organic states. QED. It was no concern of Wilson that the dismantling, say, of a jumbled but still workable Austro-Hungarian empire would lead to the creation of artificial and ultimately untenable states. For example, fashioning a federation out of the culturally and religiously hostile peoples of Yugoslavia was tantamount to pushing the countdown button on a time bomb. But such concerns were never a factor in his calculations.

Nor did it matter to Wilson on which side a traditional government fought. He was as hostile to the British and Russian empires, with which America was allied, as to the Central European ones, against which she fought. So it stood to reason that he would welcome the demise of those empires, even at the cost of reversal in the fortunes of war. Thus, when Russia's tsarist regime collapsed, Wilson was ecstatic. Here was another democracy hatched out of the dark recesses of absolutism. It mattered little that the new 'democracy' was so weak that it could neither keep her troops at the front nor indeed survive beyond a few months. For America this was not about winning a world war but about winning a war for the world.

That is why Wilson, Lloyd George and their followers in the ranks of likeminded intelligentsia in both countries constantly downplayed the risk of Bolshevik takeover, and failed to respond to it properly once it had taken place. Wilson, in fact, contributed to the Bolshevik revolt by personally facilitating Trotsky's return from New York to Petrograd.

The role of Germany in providing a similar service for Lenin is well known and, after 70 years of lying Soviet denials, universally accepted. Out of fairness we should similarly acknowledge the tireless efforts of President Wilson who had to countermand his own State Department to make sure the future leader of the Bolshevik uprising, armed with a crisp US passport, found himself aboard a transatlantic liner. The affair caused some awkwardness: as American newspapers had just published documented evidence of Trotsky's dependence on German funding, in effect Wilson was helping an enemy agent. But such incidentals were not allowed to interfere with his global vision.

4

Bolsheviks were mortal enemies of Christendom, which is why the likes of Wilson found them less objectionable than any traditional empires. A modern state may have democracy written on its banners, but instinctively it will always feel closer to modern totalitarianism than to traditional autocracy or even parliamentarianism. Deep-seated cultural affinity overrides intellectual posturing whenever the going gets tough. This explains the otherwise inexplicable benevolence of many 'democratic' statesmen towards either the Bolsheviks or the Nazis or, as in the case of Lloyd George, both.

In his memoirs Lloyd George, the British answer to Wilson, implies as much: "Personally, I would have dealt with the Soviets as the de facto Government of Russia. So would President Wilson. But we both agreed that we could not carry to that extent our colleagues at the Congress, nor the public opinion of our own countries which was frightened by Bolshevik violence and feared its spread."

Implicitly neither Wilson nor Lloyd George shared that fear. They were, however, mortified by the thought of any possible restoration of traditional government in Russia, which at that time could only have been a constitutional, not absolute, monarchy. That is why their support for the White movement in the Russian Civil War was lukewarm at best. To both Wilson and Lloyd George the Whites were out to restore the tsarist empire that would present a greater danger to their interests than the Bolsheviks ever could. Still, they had to mollify the public in their own countries, and the public was not yet prepared to accept the on-going massacre of millions in Russia as the march of progress – especially since not all eyewitness accounts of it could be suppressed.

For example, early in 1918 Sidney Reilly, later to enter popular lore as the 'Ace of Spies', pleaded from Moscow that his superiors in London shift the emphasis of their policy from the war to the Bolshevik revolution: "This hideous cancer [is] striking at the very root of civilisation," wrote this well-known sceptic who then went on to prove that his mind was not fashionably open at all: "Gracious heavens, will the people in England never understand? The Germans are human beings; we can afford to be even beaten by them. Here in Moscow there is growing to maturity the arch enemy of the human race... At any price this foul obscenity which has been born in

DEMOCRACY AS A NEOCON TRICK

Russia must be crushed out of existence... Mankind must unite in a holy alliance against this midnight terror."

But Reilly was a foreigner, an ex-Russian with an obvious axe to grind and, to mix the metaphors, an Old World chip on his shoulder. He was also a Jew, born Rosenblum, of which Bruce Lockhart, at the time the senior British official in Russia, never stops reminding us in his memoirs. In other words, Reilly could never be trusted.

Instead it fell upon Lloyd George to express the dominant emotion he shared with Wilson: "Our attitude [towards the Bolsheviks] was that of the Fox Whigs towards the French Revolution." "A Bolshevik Russia is by no means such a danger as the old Russian Empire." "Bolsheviks would not wish to maintain an army, as their creed is fundamentally anti-militarist." "There must be no attempt to conquer Bolshevik Russia by force of arms." "The anti-Bolshevik armies must not be used to restore the old Tsarist regime and re-impose on the peasants the old feudal conditions under which they held their land."

Admittedly, there was the minor matter of Lenin having betrayed the Alliance and signed a separate peace with Germany, while 'the anti-Bolshevik armies' were committed to honouring Russia's obligations. Hence HMG had to be seen as providing some token support to the Whites. But there were strings attached.

Note the strands out of which these strings were woven, for these tie into a convenient knot the notion of democracy in its modern meaning, or rather modern absence of meaning. In every pronouncement of their leaders, in their every publication and, more important, by their every action the Bolsheviks were attacking the very essence of political pluralism. Lenin in particular, echoing a similar thought once expressed by Jefferson, always stressed that power was to be the exclusive property of a tiny conspiratorial cadre or even a single dictator, "who could achieve so much more by himself".

This was a long way removed from even the limited democratic element in the tsarist political mix, and surely Wilson and his friends knew this. But the knowledge they had in their heads was trumped by one residing in their viscera – the

Bolsheviks were today's enemies of the Americans' historical enemies. Therefore they were the Americans' friends or at least colleagues. They were the lesser evil.

Hence the Allies were only willing to supply surplus munitions if the Whites were to agree to "renounce class privileges", "refrain from restoring the former land system" and "make no attempt to reintroduce the régime which the revolution destroyed" [that is, the short-lived parliamentary democracy]. These demands were strikingly similar to Lenin's desiderata, and wholly consistent with the revolutionary propaganda spewed out by Creel, with Wilson whispering in his ear. The Allies also insisted that the Whites, if victorious, should agree to dismember the Russian Empire, granting independence to every ethnic group that desired it.

The Whites were as perplexed as they were indignant, especially since a few months earlier their officers had been fighting side by side with their American and English comrades-in-arms. White generals, such as Denikin, Wrangel and Yudenich, did not possess elastic dialectical minds, an asset Wilson and Lloyd George shared with Lenin and Trotsky. Their reply came straight from the heart: "We do not trade in Russia." As a result they were denied any other than token support, which spelled their demise. The last chapter of the great war was written.

5

The First World War is often described as Europe's suicide, and in some ways it was just that. Above all, however, it was the murder of Christendom within Europe's borders, the ultimate triumph of modernity. The inner impulse that injected murderous energy into Europe largely came from the desire to destroy the habitat in which Christendom could return to life. Since de facto power had already swung to America, the only combatant to emerge from the war not just unscathed but better off, she was in a position to act as puppet master.

The easiest way to demonstrate this is to apply the ancient *cui bono* principle. Indeed, the First World War knocked out the political cornerstones of traditional Europe: the British, German, Austro-Hungarian and Russian Empires. In the process, whatever trust had existed between Europeans and their governments was gassed out of existence in Flanders and shot up to pieces in East Prussia. Trust was replaced by cynicism at best, hatred at worst. As a result, all the underlying ideas of the traditional world were compromised and Europe was left at the mercy of the larcenous rule by simulacra.

Democracy was one such: it was not any meaningful democracy for which the world was made safe, but its simulacrum. Real democracy, which is to say an elected legislative element of government, counterbalanced by other elements, was part and parcel of traditional statehood in the West. Such democracy could not therefore be relied on to act as an aggressive weapon against tradition, nor as the battle cry of American supremacism.

For democracy to act in that capacity, it had to become absolute, uncontested and unchecked. In other words, meaningful, limited, down-to-earth democracy had to step aside and be replaced by its deified simulacrum, which in due course would indeed become a neocon trick. In the United States, this *faux* democracy became synonymous with America, freedom, prosperity, rule of law, justice, fairness – in short, every good thing in life. Democracy became an equivalent of Good, which is to say God. The borders between democratic and other states no longer separated one country from another. They separated good from evil.

Democracy therefore had to acquire the attributes normally associated with God: it had to be portrayed as omnipotent, omnipresent and omniscient. This enabled it to dovetail neatly with the pre-existing notion of America carefully cultivated since the birth of the new republic. The syllogism was as simple as it was spurious: America is divine; America is democratic; ergo, American democracy is divine.

Yet modern democracy falls far short of such a lofty perch in everything that counts. This should become instantly clear to anyone attempting a dispassionate analysis based both on correct premises and empirical evidence. It was mainly to preclude such analysis that democracy had to be deified: one does not decorticate God for fear of being smitten by his divine hand. However, since democracy is not God it ought to be open to an exegesis going wherever historical evidence will take it. This is what I propose to attempt in the next chapter, by the simple expedient of comparing what modern democracy purports to be to what it actually is.

'A deviant constitution'

1

This is how Aristotle described democracy, and the Greek understood politics better than any other thinker of his, or possibly all, time. (Incidentally, most great thinkers among his Athenian predecessors and contemporaries, including Socrates and Plato, shared Aristotle's contempt for democracy.) Since in the West of the twenty-first century the Aristotelian assessment of democracy has not survived as anything other than a matter of antiquarian interest, perhaps we should wonder why. And in doing so raise some basic questions that democracy has not had to answer for quite some time.

According to Freedom House, the Washington-based think tank with neocon leanings, in 2007 the world could boast 123 electoral democracies – up from 40 in 1972 and from zero [*sic*] in 1900. In other words, just over a century ago even America, never mind what Freedom House doubtless sees as a vestigially tyrannical Europe, did not qualify for the ultimate accolade of politics. Democracy then is strictly a modern phenomenon that is barely 100 years old.

I have not studied the set of criteria for a real democracy on which the West had been failing so miserably until Woodrow Wilson gave it a leg up. One suspects women and pre-pubescent youngsters not voting had something to do with that rating, and also possibly the less than dictatorial powers then wielded by the lower houses of the West's parliaments.[17] On

---

17 US Congress is not bicameral in any real sense. The Senate and the House of Representatives divide between them the functions that in Britain

the other hand, one may be so bloody-minded as to question the validity of countries like today's Venezuela and Columbia meriting admittance to Freedom House's wide church while, say, Edwardian Britain being denied this honour.

Or else one may be perceptive enough to realise that this is yet another example of a simulacrum trumping reality, or else of form negating content. As long as the mandated proportion of the population are entitled to vote, even if most choose not to do so and others are tricked by boldfaced deception, Freedom House and other democracy mongers are happy.

Never mind that in some places the votes are meaningless, bought, falsified or even coerced at gunpoint. Never mind that it often takes much ingenuity for some 'democratic' governments to keep the vote count in their favour below a hundred percent. Never mind that at least two-thirds of today's 'democracies' are the kind of hellholes that make the populace nostalgic for the old-fashioned tyrants of yesteryear (Russia is a prime example of this, along with most other ex-Soviet republics).

As long as those pieces of worthless paper drop, rustling reassuringly, into the ballot boxes, Freedom House is satisfied. Form is everything, substance nothing. Therefore words can no longer mean what they do mean – they must mean whatever is expedient at the moment. Prime among such elastically desemanticised terms is 'democracy', which now means something different not only from its etymology but also from what it used to signify when our grandfathers were young.

Halfway along the Freedom House timeline, Winston Churchill quipped in his 1947 Commons speech that, "Democracy is the worst form of government, except for all those other forms that have been tried from time to time." This one-liner from the master of the genre is widely quoted not so much for its wit as for its intrinsic truth. Alas, wit can often obscure truth.

---

are discharged by the Commons. The division is purely procedural and does not reflect representation of divergent interests. That is why both the senators and the congressmen are drawn from the same pool of human material, with 60 percent of the former and almost 40 percent of the latter being lawyers by education (roughly the same proportion as among the Framers).

'A DEVIANT CONSTITUTION'

Snappy phrases are hard to resist, nor should they be resisted under right circumstances. Show me a man with a talent for a *mot juste*, and I shall show you a man with a sharp mind, if not always a deep one. The reverse, however, cannot be assumed: deep minds do not always coexist with a talent for coming up with epigrams off the cuff. By way of illustration, Oscar Wilde and Groucho Marx had this talent, while Thomas Aquinas and Immanuel Kant did not. Unfortunately these days epigrammatic witticisms of the past are used to mask the absence of serious thinking at present, and all-encompassing democracy is largely responsible for this development. This is not to suggest that one should expect systematic analysis from a political soliloquy (God forbid) – only that we ought to strain our mental faculties to distinguish one from the other.

One suspects that Churchill's idea of democracy, formed as it was at a time when, according to Freedom House, democracy was nonexistent, differed from Freedom House's. Though both a staunch monarchist and a committed parliamentarian, Churchill clearly did not believe he was living a double life. To him there was no contradiction in a strong monarchy being balanced by an elected lower house, with the hereditary upper chamber making sure the balance did not tip too much to either side. That was the essence of England's ancient constitution, one that so many American visitors claim does not exist because it has not been written down. In fact, a written constitution is a bit like a prenuptial agreement specifying the frequency of sex: if you have to write it down, you might as well not bother.

In previous chapters I argued that the practice of true democracy involves a populace immersed in public affairs. How else could people govern themselves if not by being keen students of the minutiae of politics and ardent participants in them? As we start parsing the concept this way, we suddenly realise to our horror that true democracy, whether we regard it as good, bad or indifferent, is impossible in a Christian or even formerly Christian world. All that is possible is the Freedom House version of it, a formal shell devoid of meaningful substance.

Quite apart from Christianity having redirected people's

aspirations inwards, and therefore away from any all-consuming interest in public affairs, people cannot govern themselves for purely technical reasons. Government involves making decisions, and modern government demands making perhaps millions of them every year. Just calculate the number of solutions a single section within one ministry must find or at least pretend to have found every day, multiply this by the number of sections, then by the number of ministries, and you will realise that a single voter cannot possibly practise a hands-on approach to running or even following public affairs.

The best he can hope to do is transfer his political power to a representative who will then make decisions on his behalf. Making such decisions would not involve solving the technical problems required to run various departments of the state. Those will fall into the domain of appointed, which is to say unelected, bureaucrats. Elected representatives would simply pass laws, establishing rules by which the bureaucrats must play the game. In doing so, wrote Burke, the parliamentarians ought to act as the people's representatives, not as their delegates. They should be guided by the people's interests, not necessarily their wishes. This is the essence of Burkean democracy, and he thought it through when the word still had a real meaning, if one already not wholly consonant with its etymology.

Burke could not even fathom the complete reshuffling of the social pack that happened a century after his death. He rightly assumed that his political ideas brought sense to the status quo, charting a route towards gradual, prudent development. This was by no means tantamount to stagnation, desperate clinging to the past at the expense of constructive change. "A state *without the means* of some change is *without the means of its* conservation," wrote Burke. But before a call to change is heeded it must be leavened with prudence, and for once someone else had earlier expressed the same thought more epigrammatically. Addressing the Commons in 1641, Lucius Cary, 2nd Viscount Falkland, encapsulated the nature of political prudence: "If it is not necessary to change, it is necessary not to change."

Little did Burke realise that the event he so warmly welcomed, the American Revolution, bolstered by the one he so expertly tore to shreds, the French equivalent, would inaugurate a decisive and probably irreversible shift throughout the Western world. William Pitt the Younger read the signs with greater clarity when he referred to the American Revolution as "most accursed, wicked, barbarous, cruel, unnatural, unjust and diabolical" – yet another example of a Tory assessing a revolution more accurately than a Whig, even one in possession of a sublime mind.

In the modern world emerging out of the ruins of tradition, parliamentarians solve the conflict between being representatives or delegates by being neither. Their loyalty is vouchsafed only to themselves and the empowered class to which they all belong. This class is not social but political; it is defined not so much by birth, wealth or education as by proximity to power. In this it is but a simulacrum of the ruling classes of yesteryear, and the difference between the two is salient. Old rulers were drawn from a pool admittance to which could be gained either by birth or by merit or ideally a combination of the two. Such people typically concentrated on controlling the public affairs of the state without devoting much attention to controlling the private affairs of their subjects.

As Tocqueville correctly showed, the new ruling class has to lay claims, false as they may be, to be the embodiment of 'the people', another term gaining wider usage in modern times.[18] In effect this means that the elite has to control its flock in ways that would have been unthinkable to the *ancien régime*'s monarchs and aristocrats. Since most career politicians lack essential qualifications for their job, they have to trick 'the people' into believing otherwise. The process is long and unrelenting: it is not so much about educating the voters' minds as about training their reflexes. The relationship between the elite and 'the people' begins to resemble that between a circus trainer and a monkey, and paradoxically the distance between them grows much greater than it ever was in the organic states of Christendom

---

18   As it comes across nowadays, 'the people' is an exclusive club. The likelihood of belonging to it is inversely proportionate to one's income, education and social status. Thus a doctor or a successful businessman is not part of 'the people', but a drug addict subsisting on government handouts is.

laying no claim to the people governing themselves.

The supposedly nonexistent English constitution suspended the sticks and carrots of social influence in fine balance: all estates were represented in the division of power. The people had their interests, if not necessarily their wishes, adequately represented in the Commons by parliamentarians who, in Burke's apt description, were their constituencies' representatives but not delegates. The people thus had a legal defence mechanism they could activate at the slightest threat of tyranny from above. Unfortunately, the liberal principles that lay at the foundation of this constitutional arrangement also had an offensive potential.

The new people, the flotsam washed ashore by the demise of Christendom, acquired social and political power, and they were not about defence: an important part of their reason for being was assault on the traditional order. Now they had made their debut on the historical stage, they were ready to use parliamentary representation as an aggressive weapon. All they had to do was to make sure that their greater numbers would tell and, in order to achieve that, franchise had to be pushed towards universality.

Nowadays those who jealously guard modern democracy against invective miss an important point, which is that they are in fact defending not real democracy but its simulacrum. Britain, along with other countries of the West, has had two democracies, not one. The first belonged to the traditional world, the second belongs to the modern one. The first was genuine and organic; the second, the one still with us today, bogus and contrived.

2

The democratic aspect of the English constitution reflected the traditional sense of justice and social balance. Both sprang from the creative nature of Christendom which, for all the blunders it may have committed, was out to shape a world that would agree with its understanding of God. Since achieving this understanding required a great deal of creative imagination,

'A DEVIANT CONSTITUTION'

this faculty grew so strong that there was enough left over for secular matters as well.

America-led modernity, on the other hand, is by its very nature a cultural vandal. It was brought into this world at least partly to do away with Christendom, a mission of which it is aware either consciously or viscerally. To that end it hijacked the concept of democracy and turned it against itself. Expanding the franchise *ad nauseam* was the surest way to undo a constitution based on the assumption that voting was not an automatic right but a privilege to be earned. That assumption inexorably leads to the concept of limited democracy, for privileges cannot be earned by everyone, and certainly not equally.

But even a limited democracy can never work in the absence of a strong, well-informed electorate. After all, only responsible voters can elect a responsible government. Edmund Burke estimated the number of those fit to vote in his contemporaneous eighteenth-century England at 400,000, which then constituted about eight percent of the country's population. The same proportion today would produce an electorate of approximately five million. Since the actual number is almost 10 times as high, one may be forgiven for getting the impression that the requirement for responsible voting has been dropped somewhere along the way. In any case, are there in Britain today even five million people who would satisfy Burkean, as opposed to purely formal, demands for responsible voting? Somehow, after half a century of comprehensive schooling, one doubts that.

Limiting the franchise would be the only way of reverting to a democratic arrangement that would have a sporting chance of elevating to government only those fit to govern. This thought would sound less blasphemous if we took the historical perspective, without even going too far back.

For franchise was severely limited throughout much of the West's history. The most notable limitation was the disfranchisement of women in all the established democracies. In the USA women got the vote as late as in 1920, in the UK in 1921, in France in 1944 – and in Switzerland the fair sex had to wait until 1971 to start dropping forms into ballot boxes. Restricted suffrage does not therefore contradict the founding tenets of Western polity; the size of the franchise is a matter of transient consensus, not transcendent principle. This may not tally with Freedom House's notion of democracy, but we shall have to live with that.

It cannot be repeated too often that 'one man-one vote' is not so much a constitutional concept as an aggressive strategy designed to bring about the dictatorship of the new political class and the inevitable demise of Christendom. The success of this strategy is largely owed to those good Western people who, unaware that they have fallen victim to an awful trick, cannot find it in their hearts to say anything bad about democracy. They have accepted, if only by default, the originally American insistence on seeing democracy as an omnipotent God-surrogate, not merely a form of government to be judged dispassionately on its merits. Many may be aware of severe problems in their societies but few realise that these are directly linked to democracy, or rather its formal simulacrum.

Let us extricate ourselves from this thrall of democratic form for a moment and ask a subversive question: so what kind of society do we wish to emerge at the other end of political process? After some debate, most people will probably settle on four essential attributes: justice, liberty, security and stability. At the same time, intellectual honesty compels one to admit that, if queried, most of the same hypothetical people, regardless of their political affiliation, are likely to express the conviction that democracy of universal suffrage is the best, some will say the only realistic, route to these ends.

So before we do anything else, it is important to strip unlimited democracy of its non-partisan mask. Unlike the limited democracies of Hellenic antiquity and Western polity, universal suffrage is a radical idea that first came to the fore during the halcyon days of the Enlightenment, which inspired both the American and French Revolutions. Original sin was no longer recognised as anything other than a quaint fairytale that holds no significance for public or private affairs. Man was pronounced to be good to begin with and, what is more, infinitely improvable. It followed logically that good and further

'A DEVIANT CONSTITUTION'

improvable people, all of them, were equally qualified to choose their leaders and govern themselves. It also followed that any other form of government was unthinkable. Once Americans elevated universal suffrage to secular sainthood and spread this fideistic notion high and wide, active opposition to it became impossible in the West. Expressing even timid reservations about this kind of democracy has become increasingly more difficult and intellectually suspect.

The benefits of unchecked democracy are held to be self-evident, which is just as well for they are impossible to prove. Yet in traditional Western thought even God was regarded not so much as self-evident as a proposition awaiting philosophical and evidential proof, if not strictly of a forensic variety. Democracy these days may be on its way to being deified but, as it is has not yet achieved that divine status, one feels justified in holding it to scrutiny.

The eighteenth century, with its demolition of religion, deprived governments of an eschatological aspect. Yet for a political system to persevere in eternity, it has to be presumed to have started there. Traditional monarchy satisfied that requirement; newfangled republicanism did not. Hence other redemptive creeds were bound to appear to fill the vacuum. In the nineteenth century democracy elevated man to a God-like status and gave him a DIY technique for expiating secular sin. In the previous century the *philosophes*, abetted by British empiricists, had even managed to weave scientific threads into the democratic promise, presenting democracy as a social answer to the scientific revolution of the sixteenth and seventeenth centuries, a trick that was to stand both socialists and communists in good stead.

Socialism and communism, modernity's other redemptive creeds, are unlimited democracy's first cousins once removed; they activate the same response mechanisms marching in parallel with democracy and just a step behind. Like universal suffrage, both are weapons in the modern armoury aimed at eradicating the last vestiges of Christendom. Socialism is democracy with logic; communism is socialism with nerve. All such beliefs

153

spring from a characteristic liberal contempt for human nature – a condition disguised by cloying encomiums on the goodness of man. In fact, if man is presumed to be virtuous, he is likely to turn out bad. It is only when his fallen state is accepted as axiomatic that a path to virtue becomes clear.

Democracy of universal suffrage is almost as pregnant with mendacity as communism is, which is suggested by the very etymology of the word. 'Democracy' implies the promise of self-government and the premise that such an organisational arrangement will *ipso facto* preclude tyranny. This is simply not the case, as the democratically elected Messrs Hitler, Perón, Mugabe, Putin, Lukashenko, Ahmadinejad, Yanukovych and Macías Nguema (who gratefully murdered a third of the population of Equatorial Guinea that had voted him in) demonstrate so vividly.

It also implies that sovereign power rests with the people. Yet modern democracies, along with their ultimate supranational extensions, such as the European Union, never tire of demonstrating how far this is from the truth. Witness the travesty involving the democratically held referenda in EU member countries. At various times, Denmark, Austria, Ireland and France returned results that the ruling supranational elite found unsatisfactory. Without a moment's hesitation, and with no regard for democratic principles to which it professes undying devotion, the European Union put its foot down and the boot in. People's choice is all fine and well, provided it is the choice the bureaucrats favour at the moment. Otherwise, people will have to choose again – and keep choosing until they get it right.

Neither is unlimited democracy a particularly time-honoured creed. The word 'democracy' in both Greece and Rome had no one-man-one-vote implications, and Plato used it in the meaning of mob rule. Another disciple of Socrates, Alcibiades, called it 'unequivocal folly', while Aristotle described it in the words I used in the title to this chapter. As we have seen, the American Founders hardly ever used it at all. Under the influence of America, which increased *pari passu* with her imperial power, towards the end of the nineteenth century the word spread, as the more intelligent modern men found it a useful smokescreen, while the more gullible among them

'A DEVIANT CONSTITUTION'

actually believed the implicit promise.

Yet in reality the promise of democracy is larcenous when democracy is unchecked by the power of other estates. By atomising the vote into millions of particles, democracy renders each individual vote meaningless. What has any weight at all is an aggregate of votes, a faceless, impersonal bloc. Consequently, political success in democracies depends not on any concern for the good of the people, but on the ability to put such blocs together.

This has little to do with statesmanship. Coming to the fore instead are such qualities as disloyalty, cynicism, a knack for demagoguery, photogenic appearance, absence of constraining principles, ability to tell lies with convincing ease, cold disregard for *bono publico*, selfishness and an unquenchable quest for power at any cost – all typically, though not exclusively, post-Christian traits.

Tocqueville – and remember that he was a champion of democracy – warned against this with his usual prescience: "I do not know if the people of the United States would vote for superior men if they ran for office, but there can be no doubt that such men do not run." It ought to be remembered that Tocqueville formed his ideas of American statesmen on the basis of John Adams, Thomas Jefferson and James Madison, to name but a few. One wonders what the Frenchman would say today, observing modern politicians in action. The reliable guess is he would feel that what has come true was not his prophesies but his nightmares. The former, after all, were always leavened with optimism.

When they succeed, our newly elected leaders fear they will be found out. Hence they strive to put some serious acreage between themselves and the people who have elected them. They seek to remove every remaining bit of power from the traditional local bodies, which stay close to the voters, and to shift it to the centralised Leviathan, claiming all the time that the people are governing themselves. The subsequent transfer of power to international bodies, which is to say as far away from the national electorate as geography will allow, is a natural extension of the same process. This explains the otherwise inexplicable rise of the European Union, for one has yet to hear any rational argument in its favour.

Thus expanded franchise inevitably leads to greater centralisation, and for that reason it is wrong to complain, as today's conservatives so often do, that growing centralisation undermines democracy. This is like saying that pregnancy undermines sex.

The burgeoning political centralisation of modernity also reflects a deeper trend, that of reversing two thousand years of Christendom and reverting to idolatry and paganism. People have been hollowed out, their metaphysical certitudes removed or inverted, the resulting vacuum filled with idols whose selection is left to individual choice independent of any group affiliation or loyalty. Falling by the political wayside is the familial localism inherent to Christendom. It has been replaced by hysterical adulation of central government, leading *in extremis* to totalitarianism. In an important way, however, all modern states are totalitarian, in that they seek control over areas hitherto seen as being off-limits for governmental meddling. In that sense the differences between, say, the USA and the USSR are those of degree and tactics, not principle.

While perpetrating centralisation run riot, the ostensibly democratic, but in fact neo-tyrannical, state acquires more power over the individual than any monarch ruling by divine right ever saw in his dreams. French subjects, for example, were shielded from Louis XIV by several layers of local government, and the Sun King wielded more power over his loftiest courtiers than over the lowliest peasants. The King was aware of this, and his famous pronouncement on the nature of the state fell more into the realm of wishful thinking than reportage.

By contrast, a freely voting French citizen or British subject of today has every aspect of his life controlled, or at least monitored, by a central government in whose actions he has little say.[19] He meekly hands over half of his income, knowing

---

19 Britain boasts a CCTV camera for every 14 of Her Majesty's subjects, making surveillance one of the few areas in which we lead the world. Communist China, for example, has fewer cameras even in absolute terms, never mind per capita.

that the only result of this transfer will be an increase in the state's power to extort even more. Clutching the few remaining notes, he hopes that Leviathan, no longer athirst, will let him keep them for his family. He opens his papers to find yet again that the 'democratic' state has dealt him a blow, be that destroying his children's education, raising his taxes, devastating the army that protects him, closing his local hospital, letting murderers go free or undermining his country's sovereignty. In short, if one defines liberty as a condition that best enables the individual to exercise his freedom of political choice, then democracy of universal suffrage is remiss on that score.

Nor is understated (and diminishing) liberty the price we pay for security. Unlimited democracy, whose penchant for aggressive statism is predetermined both historically and psychologically, has demonstrated time and again its chronic inability to avoid murderous wars – or at least to win them quickly once they become unavoidable.

This was proved in the twentieth century, the first in which modernity ruled supreme from beginning to end. Traditional polity, already reeling in the run-up to that fateful century, died as it unfolded. With its congenital mendacity, modern democracy tried to pass defeat for victory, even as Robespierre and Danton had tried to convince the French that martial law was liberty. Modern opinion-formers seem to forget that the 'victory' in the first big war of the century empowered two satanic creeds, while the second delivered half the world to one of them.

Midway through the twentieth century the publisher Henry Luce described it as 'the American century'. If so, then its score is hugely negative, and our advances in murderous gadgetry are only a minor factor in this. This observation trumps the claim the neocon founding mother Jeane Kirkpatrick originated (and today's neocons love to repeat), that democracies do not fight one another. Her proud boast is not quite correct even factually, with various authors citing up to 50 examples of both warring sides being democratic (in the Freedom House sense of the word). It is also dubious logically, implying as it does the false assumption that for a democracy to commit wanton aggression against a non-democratic state is somehow more moral than to attack one that holds elections. And at a more fundamental level the claim is downright bogus, for democracies have amply demonstrated their ability to set up a world order that makes wars more frequent and sanguinary than they ever were in the past.

Since the time unlimited democracy achieved the PR status of the only possible alternative to tyranny, hundreds of millions have died violent deaths. Universal suffrage implies universal military service, a fact that is at least as responsible as technological advances for the amount of blood spilled in modern wars. If medieval princes had to beg their vassals to spare a few men for the army at wartime, today's democracies can simply conscript the entire population if they so wish, and prosecute anyone who refuses to join up.

Still, conscription would be just if defence of the realm were at stake. But modern democracy is not about defence of the realm, which after all is one of the few legitimate functions of government. It is about manipulating votes here and now. Few modern politicians are capable of thinking beyond the next election they realistically expect to win; few voters are capable of thinking beyond the quiet comfort of today. Witness the current reductions in the West's military budgets, rendering us impotent to counter any real, as opposed to imaginary, threats. Money spent on defence is money that politicians will not be able to use to bribe voters with corrupt, and corrupting, handouts. Such bribes are primary to them, while defence spending is strictly subordinate.

Giving people the vote was easy; teaching them to cast it in an enlightened and responsible fashion has proved impossible in conditions of universal suffrage. As a result, most people have got to a point where they see nothing as worth dying for. This means that the next time the West is under lethal threat they will be unlikely to find the backbone to fight – unless they felt that fighting would be the only way to preserve their comfort. Any other concession, including independence, would be proffered with alacrity, unless of course they could find someone to do their fighting for them. Rome had this kind of arrangement with the Vandals and the Goths, and we all know what happened in the end. So much for security.

Neither does unlimited democracy provide stability. Quite the opposite, one can argue that the democratic body politic carries the rogue gene of instability, even as it is forever plagued by the demons of *ad infinitum* centralisation. Here too, this most factional of political systems suffers from the heredity of its liberal mother and radical father. That is why democracy infinitely gravitates towards social democracy (a euphemism for socialism which is itself a euphemism for the unchallenged dictatorship of the modern state), leaving little room for conservatism, which is a popular if imprecise word for traditional Western politics.

Looking at the three major European democracies of today, Britain, France and Germany, it would be hard to argue that democracy is a factor of political stability. In a mere century, Britain has gone from being an empire governed by constitutional monarchy to being a crypto-republican province of the European Union; France, from being an international power to being first a part of Germany and then her junior partner; and Germany – well, we all know about her. Having started the twentieth century by keeping some vestiges of traditional polity, the glorious trio ended it as a set of snuff movies starring Christendom as the principal attraction.

The USA is unique in that it was conceived as a modern state and created as such in a wasteland shorn of traditional influences. With little indigenous heritage to dispose of, pursuit of happiness proceeded apace, creating the 'happiest' society the West has ever known and consequently the least Western. But the downside of pursuing happiness and not, say, virtue, justice, honour, dignity, truth or salvation goes beyond the yawning ennui America tends to induce in throwbacks to Christendom.

For in spite of all the lip service Americans pay to God in their Pledge of Allegiance, the USA is a modern, which is to say relativist, state. Without the underlying supremacy of absolute moral strictures, society loses its moral fibre, which has many unpleasant ramifications not only internationally but domestically as well. Law enforcement, for example, is difficult in the absence of an absolute criterion with which to distinguish between *malum prohibitum* and *malum in se*. Without this distinction law becomes amoral and runs the risk of becoming arbitrary.

More important, when God's law is no longer recognised as an authority superior to man's regulations (positive law), the law loses its link with human nature, becoming instead an instrument of coercion. Law is replaced with legalism. As a result, people treat it with fear but without respect, and fear alone is not a sufficient deterrent. That is why a high crime rate is an automatic levy unlimited democracy imposes, and the more modern the society, the higher the crime rate.

Business activity, central to the pursuit of happiness, also has to become amoral in a modern democracy. Not doing anything wrong disappears as an in-built starting point and is replaced by not getting caught. By itself that would be almost bearable if so many clever people did not spend their time, and waste ours, by thinking up cloying encomiums of what they call 'free enterprise'.

However, freedom is a child of responsibility. When 'responsible' walks out, 'free' becomes an orphan. If certain of impunity, a modern businessman would market potassium cyanide instead of potassium chloride, this to the chorus of 'conservative' economists singing hosannas to both the merchant and his victims for striking important blows for free enterprise. In fact the crisis tearing the world apart at this writing bears palpable testimony to the immoral, indeed amoral, nature of today's business activity. One should never forget, even when extolling modern achievements, that the same company that gave us synthesised aspirin also gave us Zyklon B. In fact during the war this notorious compound constituted about 75 percent of I.G. Farben's turnover, and never mind aspirin.

In America and other secular societies the inherent amorality of modern business is dressed up by elevating commercial activity to a moral high ground it never used to occupy in Christendom. Someone like Milton Friedman or George Gilder will drive us to distraction explaining that the cycle of free enterprise has more to do with charity than with acquisitiveness. In that sense they resemble their supposed antipode Marx who also had a knack for creating in his head a picture of economic life that had little to do with reality.

One wishes Messrs Friedman, Gilder and their friends studied the American economy as it is, rather than the idealised picture of it they see in their mind's eye. They would then realise that the New Deal corporatism that dominates the pursuit of happiness in America today has little to do with free enterprise. Rather than glorifying indiscriminately the founding institutions of America, they would perhaps see that this freedom-stifling corporatism is directly traceable back to the pursuit of secular happiness canonised in the Declaration of Independence.

3

The nature of human society is such that nothing exists in isolation. The popular ditty about the human body ("The toe bone connected to the heel bone, the heel bone connected to the foot bone, the foot bone connected to the leg bone" and so on) is fully applicable to the body social and political.

By controlling some sinews, muscles and blood vessels, unlimited democracy, or rather the political class that acts in its name, in effect exercises influence over the whole body. This is best demonstrated on the example of the economic crisis that started in 2008 – note how the degeneration of some realms brings about the demise of all others: a broken toe effectively renders both legs useless.

Toe bone: Christianity stopped being a determinant of human behaviour in the West. This formed a vacuum, which nature abhors and people try to fill. As is the human tendency, the void left by something real is best filled with its simulacra rather than its obvious opposites. It is always easier to build a new philosophy of life on the foundations of the old one, rather than starting from scratch. Thus the canonised pursuit of happiness provided the body of the new creed, while democracy tried to become its soul. Fused together, the two were bound to produce a consumers' society so despised by Plato, among others. What was the Greek's bogeyman became America's ideal.

Heel bone: The notion of original sin and its redemption

defined the morality of Christendom, while Christ's absolute goodness set an example of how man could try to improve himself and overcome his own wickedness. However, modern people accentuate the meliorating possibilities while ignoring the reason for which the melioration is necessary. The central idea of the Enlightenment was to replace the notion of original sin with that of original virtue.

Rather than starting out compromised and then improving by the grace of God and a lifelong quest, all men were declared to be equally good to begin with. As many manifestly did not end up good, the fault had to lie with their social, political and economic environment. Since improving that environment now had to be seen as the panacea, the philosophical edifice of modernity was erected on termite-infested foundations.

Foot bone: Equality of virtue logically presupposed equality of condition, especially of economic condition. Democracy of universal suffrage lends itself more easily than any other political arrangement to being portrayed as a system ideally suited to egalitarianism. Of course even modestly educated people could not help noticing that no society in history had ever come close to winning this glittering prize. Therefore they had to be brainwashed into believing that democracy of universal suffrage possessed the divine ability to render the hitherto impossible possible. Those who would not be brainwashed had to be marginalised.

Leg bone: Society, especially its political aspect, thus became stratified into the brainwashers and the brainwashed. The laundering effort had to be constant and escalating, for otherwise it could lose the centrifugal force required to keep up its momentum. Gradually, at the expense of qualities traditionally associated with statesmanship, the political class had to acquire a raft of skills involved in operating the brainwashing *perpetuum mobile*. The brainwashed masses, on the other hand, had to be trained to equate happiness with material wealth.

Knee bone: Striving for material wealth had to be reconciled with the original egalitarian premise of modernity. The two were at odds: as in any other human endeavour, some people are better than others at making money. Just like a sporting contest, economic activity presupposes the emergence of not only winners but also losers.

"Democracy," wrote Aristotle, "arose from men's thinking that if they are equal in any respect, they are equal absolutely." This presumptive absolute equality had to be extended to the economy. Even the least successful layers of the population had to have their expectations built up, lest they might unplug themselves from the democratic process, thereby weakening the political class's hold on power.

To do so, the promise of wealth, or at least comfort, had to be substantially divorced from the ability to earn it. Since in reality the two go hand in hand, the political class came to be judged and rewarded on its ability to subvert reality, creating an illusion of a narrowing gap between ability and expectation. As failure to do so could spell its own demise, success in this illusion-building endeavour first became the main determining factor of political success, and eventually the only one.

R.G. Collingwood's analysis of the collapse of the Hellenic economy presages the collapse of ours: "The critical moment was reached when Rome created an urban proletariat whose only function was to eat free bread and watch free shows. This meant the segregation of an entire class which had no work to do whatever; no positive function in society, whether economic or military or administrative or intellectual or religious; only the business of being supported and being amused. When that had been done, it was only a question of time until Plato's nightmare of a consumers' society came true; the drones set up their own king and the story of the hive came to an end."

Thigh bone: Enlightenment economists established a parallel between universal suffrage and private enterprise in people's minds. Both were supposed to be based on individual responsibility for one's future, either political or economic. This was a parody of Christian individualism, distorting it first by shifting it into a politicised material arena, and second by trying to legitimise a dubious political idea by letting it bask in the borrowed warmth of a sound economic one. As a result, unchecked democracy and free enterprise became so inextricably linked

DEMOCRACY AS A NEOCON TRICK

that the failure of one was widely presumed soon to lead to the failure of the other.

Since unlimited democracy was founded on the fallacious premise of egalitarianism, its practitioners now had to falsify the process of free enterprise as well, making sure its products could be more evenly distributed between the consumers and producers. Failure to do so would jeopardise the status of those currently in power and undermine the future of the whole political class. Putting it crudely, votes – and the power they confer – had to be not only requested but also bought.

Back bone: This had to be done with some delicacy: the success of wealth redistribution depended on the existence of wealth to be redistributed. Therein lay the problem, for the only way to avoid a potential conflict was to undermine the organic distribution of wealth in a free economy where many earned increasingly higher wages and few made increasingly greater profits. This arrangement had to be replaced by its pernicious simulacrum: an enlargement in the size of groups making a living without earning it, and the consequent plunder of wealth actually earned.

The entitlement group was bound to continue to grow, for human nature is such that the availability of unearned income and the number of those desiring it exist in a symbiotic relationship. The process of redistribution, rather than being organic, had to become coercive: wealth producers were to be forced to part with greater and greater proportions of their wealth to support the expectations of greater and greater numbers of those who felt entitled to consume without earning.

Neck bone: Acting as a middle man with megalomania, the state had to appropriate vast and growing chunks of the nation's wealth. As a result the state grew in direct proportion to the amount of money it could extort from wealth producers. Such inordinate growth conveniently tallied with the principal motivation of the political class: acquiring, expanding and retaining its own power.

Consequently any residual reality that had persisted in post-Enlightenment democracy was painted over until it could no longer be seen. This vindicated the prognosis of Thomas

'A DEVIANT CONSTITUTION'

Jefferson, one of the principal agents of the new order: "The Democracy will cease to exist when you take away from those who are willing to work and give to those who would not." The only thing required to turn this exercise in clairvoyance into philosophy would have been the admission that 'the Democracy', which is to say its modern simulacrum, is bound by its very nature to produce such a lamentable situation sooner or later. As the state depends on the support of the indolent Paul, it has to buy it by robbing the industrious Peter.

Head bone: Wealth producers had to be squeezed with taxes, but they could not be squeezed dry because otherwise they would have stopped producing wealth. Tax revenues alone therefore could not satisfy the growing expectations of the nonworking classes. Yet those expectations had to be satisfied if the political class was to rely on their continued support. The only other mechanism available to the state was increasing the supply of money, which is to say either borrowing or printing it.

Hence the historically staggering inflation rate that has grown in exact parallel with the growth of the entitlement underclass. For example, in Britain the last 50 years of the 'American' twentieth century saw a cumulative inflation of 2,000 percent, compared to a mere 10 percent between 1850 and 1900. Hence also the suicidal public debt accumulated by most Western governments and the burgeoning size of their public sector. America's public debt currently stands at $16.7 trillion and Britain's at over £1 trillion, with both growing fast. No economy can support such a burden without its knees buckling at some point – just the cost of servicing Britain's debt is already greater than her shrinking defence budget.

This, schematically, is the principal origin of today's crisis. It is also sufficient grounds for pessimistic predictions: the cancerous economy of the West may show a temporary remission, but ultimately it will get worse rather than better until it can reverse the toe-to-head journey and begin a gradual movement in the opposite direction. This would necessitate such a cosmic shift in our understanding of democracy, justice, fairness and happiness that one cannot confidently offer optimistic predictions. Those of a complete collapse spring to mind more naturally. Whether the West will then be able to do a Phoenix and rise from its ashes can only be a matter of futile conjecture.

The economy is but one area of life where democracy reveals the destructive rogue gene it carries. Exactly the same degeneration is observable in our anaemic culture, disjointed social life, urban decline, increase in random violence and unrest. As a minimum, this observation ought to give rise to a dispassionate weighing of democracy's pros against its cons. Instead COLLENE reassures the public that we are doing famously and "decline is a self-fulfilling prophecy". (Just as Stalin declared that "life has become better, life has become merrier" when millions were dying in concentration camps or of starvation.) Most democratic states are embarked on this unceasing brainwashing effort, otherwise known as their educational policy, and it has created populations where the numbers of those capable of weighing democracy's pros and cons are steadily declining.

At the same time the numbers of those who are ready to pay obsequious knee-jerk tributes to democracy are growing despite its demonstrable failures. This paradox testifies to the success of democracy's agitprop effort. One day the same paradox may yet spell democracy's demise.

4

The post-Enlightenment fusion of politics and economics has been with us for over two centuries, a long enough time for the two to blend into one in the minds of most people. This is understandable for these days they are both based on the same philosophy, best exemplified by two Scottish friends, Smith and Hume, along with many other Enlightenment empiricists.

The blend seems so natural that it is easy to forget at times that, in historical terms, it has been around for only an instant. Until then people had been accepting, indeed worshipping, a different order for millennia, and their notion of happiness had never been defined in strictly material terms. Happiness was to be found in the realm of the spirit, which precluded anything resembling our modern egalitarianism.

In that realm it was no humiliation for the common man to accept the authority of those whose accomplishments were greater than his own. A communicant seeking happiness in salvation was prepared to let his priest teach him what happiness was and how it could be attained. A student seeking happiness in wisdom found it easy to rely on his teacher to instruct him in true sagacity. Neither democracy nor free enterprise was essential to the pursuit of such happiness, and one could easily see how under some circumstances they were more likely to be detrimental.

For most people, the principal economic desideratum of their lives was survival, not Smith's cherished "bettering one's condition", which he saw as "that great purpose of human life". Note the implicit rejection of any spiritual purpose, later echoed by Max Weber: "Man is dominated by the making of money, by acquisition as the ultimate purpose of his life." As far as happiness was concerned, people used to be compelled by the dominant ethos to seek it not in a progressively improving standard of living but in a steadily refining spiritual and moral fibre. That built a big, though not inexhaustible, moral capital on which the neonatal bourgeois order could draw so successfully.

Max Weber was justified in linking capitalism with specifically Protestant work ethic. For it was John Calvin who managed to attach a moral and even transcendent value to acquisitiveness, thus providing a key link between the old and new orders. Calvin treated wealth as God's reward for such virtues as honesty, thrift, sobriety, hard work. One had to be good in order to become rich, which made wealth a telltale sign of goodness.

Hume and Smith, who both were, not to cut too fine a point, atheists, recognised the vital importance of the faith they themselves did not possess. They realised that turning Christianity into a merely private affair would deprive it of its crucial public significance. In the absence of faith the process of 'bettering one's condition' would bring to the fore vices no longer offset by antithetical virtues. Selfishness, greed, avarice, ruthlessness, all useful qualities to have in a fiercely competitive economic environment, would no longer be mitigated.

Neither Smith nor Hume could fathom that within a century or two their own atheism would become the dominant superstition of Western society. They were certain that individual stores of Christian virtue, though now nationalised and pooled together, could still apply the necessary brakes to the rolling juggernaut of the new order. The braking action did not even have to be, according to them, particularly strong. Developing this line of thought they came up with a theory that has since animated political and economic discourse to such a great extent that it is now barely questioned. Hume, Smith and their admiring contemporaries repainted the traditional picture of society to portray it as a sort of crucible.

When theologians were turning into philosophers, philosophers into *philosophes* and *philosophes* into intellectuals, Calvinist or similar virtues still received their requisite lip service – people were not yet ready to accept the demotion of virtue to the status of quaint personal choice. But private vices were no longer seen as inhibitors of public virtue. Like in arithmetic, where two minuses multiplied produce a plus, in social life too tossing a mass of private vices into the crucible of the new order was supposed to smelt them into one overriding collective virtue.

It was reluctantly accepted that most citizens freely electing their leaders in politics and freely fending for themselves in the marketplace would always act in their naked self-interest. The fallacy sold to the public by Enlightenment thinkers was that the sum total of naked self-interests could *by itself* produce public good. This was the eighteenth-century politico-economic answer to alchemy: presumably the gold of goodness could be extracted from the pig iron of crude, occasionally wicked pursuits. Democracy in politics would then marry free markets in economics to give birth to widespread happiness.

Such is the orthodoxy vociferously, if at times uneasily, accepted by all political economists of the Right, from Hayek and von Mises to Friedman and Gilder, and then on to those politically active people who are these days described as conservatives. They never even attempt to answer some simple questions begging to be asked. Are you sure people will play

'A DEVIANT CONSTITUTION'

along? What if their free choices in politics and economics prove to be catastrophically wrong? Smith and Hume were confident that, push come to shove, they could fall back on the unused capital of Christian ethics to prevent such an outcome. But their modern followers know that this particular ace has slipped out of its hole and dropped on the floor.

Christianity has been downgraded to one of many equally valid options on the table. You choose Christ, he chooses Buddha, they choose atheism – does it really matter any more than our preference in socks or ties? No one seriously believes this archaic nonsense anyway, and even those few who do often fail to see its connection to the main business of life, the pursuit of economic happiness.

What was bound to transpire is totalitarian economism, the economy acting as the sole *raison d'être* and redeemer of the new, post-Enlightenment order. The Calvinist model has been turned on its head: it is no longer the pursuit of virtue that is rewarded with wealth. It is now the frenzied pursuit of wealth that is somehow supposed to produce virtue. Interestingly, totalitarian economism is where *soi disant* conservatives and confirmed socialists converge. Both groups see economic happiness as the be-all and end-all of life; they disagree only on the means required first to achieve and then to distribute wealth. Like Orwell's animals, they reduce everything to a single issue. They just cannot agree on the number of legs.

They all ignore the catastrophic consequences of destroying the foundations on which the West was built. This they do not out of ignorance but because for them to admit such a far-reaching oversight would be tantamount to committing intellectual suicide. So they prefer the ostrich way out and persist in their folly. Their heads buried in the sand, they credibly feign deafness when confronted with the simplest of questions: What if the people's free political choice is to prefer slavery to liberty? What if a free market produces a situation where the people opt to push free markets out of existence?

It is naïve to suppose that common men can have the uncommonly good sense to distinguish between equality of opportunity and equality of outcome. Nor is it realistic to expect that the worse-off would be so thankful for what in historical terms is absolute wealth (never being short of what Dr Johnson called 'the necessaries') as to overlook that, relative to them, the better-off live in the lap of luxury. Only someone imbued with Judaeo-Christian ethics could accept such iniquity with equanimity, but this particular gift has stopped giving.

The transition from Christian infinity to infinite economic expectations was guaranteed to breed mass resentment. Already in the 1830s Tocqueville felt justified in remarking that Americans "are forever brooding over advantages they do not possess." Such resentment can never be adequately contained within the restraints of liberal democracy not fortified by a unifying religion. In the end the market will become less and less free, while democracy will become less and less democratic. Both will eventually be reduced, if they are not already, to formal shells emptied of whatever content they used to have. At that point both free enterprise and democracy will devour themselves.

Only religion can contain the congenital megalomania of both democracy and free enterprise by limiting the lust for political power in the former and for economic power in the latter. Left unchecked, such lamentable cravings will destroy not only democracy and free enterprise but indeed the whole society. A free Western society is only possible when it mainly rests on small government in its politics and small businesses in its economy. A trade guild uniting people of all classes is unlikely to foster class resentment to the same extent as a modern labour union or for that matter a giant multinational corporation. A small, mostly local government can maintain people's vital interest in politics much more effectively than any all-encompassing national (and especially supranational) democracy.

While the transition from Hellenic to Christian civilisations involved a steady progression from big to small, the transition from Christendom to modernity was vectored in the opposite direction. Modernity thus denied not just the faith of Christendom but also the political and economic principles that lay at its foundation. This could not have gone unpunished and it did not. The inordinate and unstoppable growth of the state and specifically its welfare extension is the punishment exacted, and its cataclysmic consequences are there for all to see. At the same time history shows that an uncontrolled quest for more and more capitalism will sooner or later produce fewer and fewer capitalists, not more. As a result, society will become alienated from both politics and production, which ostensibly are designed to be all-inclusive.

It fell upon a theologian, rather than an economist or political scientist, to express this principle most succinctly. In his 1931 encyclical Pope Pius XI did not equivocate: "Just as it is gravely wrong to take from individuals what they can accomplish by their own initiative and industry and give it to the community, so also it is an injustice and at the same time a grave evil and disturbance of right order to assign to a greater and higher association what lesser and subordinate organisations can do." The pontiff thus issued an unmistakable warning: moving away from the founding tenets of our civilisation will have dire consequences, and not only for the tenets.

In fact we can safely move from the future tense to the present – this situation is upon us. Reflecting the moral convergence of Right and Left politics, the erstwhile command economies are meeting the formerly free economies on the middle ground of socialist corporatism, just as democracies are meeting totalitarian regimes halfway. Neither side really wants to be in this no man's land. They both realise that they have effectively lost their historical claim to legitimacy.

Deep down they resent the rule by simulacrum. They want the real thing as they see it, but both sides know there is precious little they can do about it. They acknowledge they have lost; it is now a matter of negotiating the most favourable terms of surrender.

The last nail in the coffin of Christendom

1

The previous chapter should not be construed as merely an attempt to disparage the modern, America-led notion of democracy, particularly as it is practised within America herself. In fact it is conceivable that this form of government suits the country best. After all, from the time *The Mayflower* deposited the first settlers on a Massachusetts beach, and certainly after 1776, the country has effectively severed her links with Europe's organic polity. Europe, with everything it represented, survived in the collective American psyche, if at all, only as a source of residual resentment.

Hence the inherent conflict between deified democracy and Western tradition did not, nor does not, get most Americans excited. In fact, they are more likely to see it as an argument *pro*, not *contra*. Wherever the Old World is different from America, it is inferior – in politics or anything else. Europe is moribund and irrelevant, a relic of the past and hardly anything else. Americans tend to feel that their own democracy is so robust as to be immortal, forgetting that secular immortality does not exist. That European democracy has long since morphed into social democracy, socialism by another name, does not bother Americans unduly. They themselves have been touched by the divine hand, and Old World problems cannot possibly extend across the Atlantic. American virtues are impervious to European vices.

In the same vein, few Americans stop to think why almost everything man-made in their country is ugly, and even when such a thought crosses their minds they do not gasp with horror. The great Greeks, however, had a ready explanation for ugliness. They considered what Aristotle called 'transcendentals' and what Plato specifically identified as Truth, Beauty and Goodness to be the inseparable ontological properties of being. Leaving theologians to decide whether or how this prefigured the Holy Trinity, one can still infer that a deficit in any element of the inseparable triad would automatically produce a failure in the other two.

A constitutionally secular state from her inception, America turned her back on Truth – hence her awful cities.[20] In fact, most of them are not only aesthetic abominations but also planning disasters. They do not even have much to recommend themselves functionally. Inhabitants of the sprawling, faceless bungalow areas at the outskirts have to fight miles of bumper-to-bumper traffic to get to the wedding-cake downtowns where most jobs are. Compare, for example, Houston, Texas, which is about 80 miles across, to London, whose diameter is only about 10–15 miles and whose population is roughly four times greater; or to Paris, four by six miles, providing home to approximately the same population as Houston. Londoners and Parisians still live in reasonable comfort and sufficient space, but most of them do not court coronaries travelling to and from work.

Many Americans are not devoid of aesthetic sense, and when they get to see Paris, Rome or London, typically in their student days or as part of their retirement tour, they no doubt can spot that those places are rather more beautiful than Detroit, Dallas or Denver. But they tend to see the Old World as a contiguous Disneyland: a nice playground for children, which is to say Europeans, but an irrelevance for grownups, which is to say Americans.

A professor of something or other in the Midwest once wrote to me, "You Europeans are welcome to your symphonies and paintings. We in America have something much more

---

20 Once European countries went secular they stopped producing beauty as well. Most European cities still look good, but only because there is enough architecture left there that goes back to Christendom.

important." He did not specify what that might be and I did not press for an elucidation. But had I done so, 'democracy' would probably have been the answer. The visceral rancour was unmistakable, the underlying historical animosity just as evident – this regardless of the fact that Western European countries are nowadays scarcely less 'democratic' than the good old U S of A.

Americans see democracy as their exclusive property and also as a potential platform from which to launch an aggressive proselytising campaign against the traditional West, whatever is left of it. By itself, this perception is innocent enough, provided its offensive potential remains unfulfilled. EU members apart, sovereign countries have every right to arrange their affairs as they see fit. In fact, if American democracy were strictly designed for internal consumption, we would have no moral right to criticise it too vociferously. Alas, this is not the case: the proselytising aspect of the American secular religion has never been dormant, and at present less so than ever. It received a tremendous boost from two of history's most murderous wars, both breaking out during the 'American century'.

The First World War, America's first great success at imposing her version of democracy on the hitherto organic states of Christendom, effectively put Western tradition in a coffin. The Second World War nailed the lid shut.

2

Earlier I commented on the kinship between modern unchecked democracies and their totalitarian cousins. What brings them close together is not just their clean break from the traditional polity of Christendom but also their shared, and often pooled, efforts to eradicate every survival of the organic Western state. This may not always be based on a conscious decision springing from mature deliberation and an intellectually rigorous weighing of the pros and cons. Often it is an expression of an innermost intuitive conviction that resides in an area lying deeper than the one producing sequential thought.

In the case of modern Western leaders it is probably both,

and Franklin D. Roosevelt was the quintessential Western leader. Just like Woodrow Wilson, who saw in the First World War an opening for indulging their animosity towards traditional polity, Roosevelt had grasped the subtext of the Second World War even before the text was written. His immediate goal was to get America out of the Great Depression, something his statist New Deal had failed to do. But that was only part of the story.

If history has proved anything, it is that people and governments tend to feel about wars differently. Most people do not like them, but most governments, especially democratic ones, do. This is easy to understand for, as I have argued earlier, unchecked democracy inexorably degenerates into ever-growing centralisation and statism, and statism thrives on social and economic turmoil. The same goes, ten-fold, for war. War is the ultimate expression of the innate statism of modern states, the sustenance on which they build up their muscle mass. The state has emerged stronger, and the individual weaker, out of every modern war.

Like babies, all modern states were born covered in blood. No modern state, whenever it came to life, was delivered without the midwifery of a formative war. In England, it was the Civil War. In the USA, ditto – more so even than the Revolutionary War. In Russia, ditto. In Spain, ditto. In France, the post-revolutionary Napoleonic wars. In Germany, the Franco-Prussian War. In Italy, the war of liberation from Austria. And collectively, modern statism vanquished finally and irreversibly as a result of what was perhaps Western man's greatest, and definitely stupidest, crime: the First World War. In all instances, people had to die in large numbers so that the modern state might be born and then weaned on the congealing red liquor.

Swords may sometimes be beaten into ploughshares, but this only occurs when the modern state feels it can increase, or at least maintain, its strength without having to fight a war. When it feels differently, the ploughshares will be quickly beaten back into swords. And once they have vanquished, the weapons can then be recast into the strongest chains binding the individual hand and foot.

There exist only two reasons for modern states to refrain

The Last Nail in the Coffin of Christendom

from fighting wars. One, they feel they do not need a war to increase their power at the time. Two, they fear they may not remain in power as a result. Neither of those conditions pertained in late–1930s America, and Roosevelt worked hard to drag the country into the war against the express wishes of the very *demos* in whose name he supposedly governed. In that FDR followed the example of Woodrow Wilson, who 20-odd years earlier had performed a similar trick for, one suspects, similar reasons.

With that precedent to learn from, Roosevelt knew exactly how to milk a military conflict for all it was worth. If Congress and the people were likely to prefer peace to war, they had to be left with no choice. To that end Roosevelt desperately hoped that either Germany or Japan would launch a pre-emptive strike, the sooner the better. Germany would not come out and play. Japan, being starved of essential raw materials by the American blockade, would. She really had no choice: when in the summer of 1941 the US government suddenly froze all Japanese assets in American banks, simultaneously imposing an embargo on the export of oil, Japan's foreign trade instantly shrank by 75 percent and her oil imports by 90 percent.

Did Roosevelt merely hope for something like Pearl Harbour, or did he deliberately provoke it? This is no place to come down on either side of the debates that have raged ever since on FDR's exact role in those tragic events. Suffice it to say that, no matter how much we despise conspiracy theories, it would be hard to deny that quite a few perfectly non-theoretical conspiracies have been hatched in modern history. Russian Bolshevism, for example, was one. So was German Nazism.

While Roosevelt was obviously a more benign politician than Messrs Lenin or Hitler, nothing in his track record suggests he was incapable of deviousness. While his methods were different from those used by his more extreme colleagues in other countries, he pursued the same ends all modern politicians do: great, preferably unlimited, power. Whether they worship at the altar of unlimited tyranny or unchecked democracy is immaterial in this respect.

Roosevelt remembered that it was usually wartime leaders

who went down in history as great statesmen. And his place in history was important for FDR, as it is for any egotistic politician. So I would be inclined to think that in this instance the conspiracy theorists just may have a point, especially since they have a corpus of circumstantial evidence going for them, not to mention the old *cui bono* principle.

One such bit of evidence is the memorandum that Arthur H. McCollum, a senior officer in naval intelligence, sent to Captain Knox, Roosevelt's top military advisor, on 7 October, 1940. Having outlined the possible ways of provoking Japan into war, McCollum concludes, "If by these means Japan could be led to commit an overt act of war, so much the better." Intelligence officers seldom submit reports, or especially reach conclusions, they do not think their superiors want to see.

What I find amusing is that earlier in the memo McCollum describes Russia as neutral. In fact the USSR was at the time Hitler's closest ally. It was the misnamed Non-Aggression Pact that had kicked off the Second World War a fortnight after it was signed. It was the two predators who had divided Europe between them. It was their two-pronged attack that had defeated Poland in 1939. Even as McCollum put pen to paper, it was Nazi planes flying on Soviet fuel that were raining Soviet-made bombs on London. And it was endless trainloads of Russian strategic materials that were flowing into the veins of the Nazi military monster. But then Western intelligence services always have been inept when dealing with Russia.

By then Nazi Germany had shown the way to virtual riches by stimulating her own economy with massive infusions of capital into rearmament and public works. Following suit, Britain steadily reduced her unemployment and, once the war started, eliminated it altogether. In the USA the war also got rid of unemployment and doubled the country's GDP, burying the depression under an avalanche of tanks, planes and lorries.

The debit side of the ledger was the 300,000 Americans killed, most of them out of touch with the deep subtexts of the conflict. They had a job to do and they did it bravely and nobly. However, the long-term geopolitical result of their sacrifice was far from noble. By assisting in the defeat of brown and brown fascism they were instrumental in handing half the world over to the red variety. Though the chromatic distinction is clear enough, one struggles to see any difference between the two in principle.

3

Neither Roosevelt nor any other prominent American ever admitted that his fervent faith in American, which is to say unchecked, democracy was largely motivated by hostility to Christendom, along with its cultural, social and political tradition. They did not have to: their animus can be inferred not from their words but from their actions, always the more reliable telltale sign with men of action.

Similarly motivated American businessmen, all fanatical champions of democracy, systematically built up the war machines of both Soviet Russia and Nazi Germany. The US administration did not bat an eyelid. Why? The argument that in a free country the government has no way of telling businessmen where and how to invest does not cut much ice. Any government in the world can stop the flow of strategic materials to a potential enemy, and US laws, like those of any Western country, contained sufficient provisions for such action. In fact, we have already seen that Allied governments had no qualms about stopping supplies of arms to the Whites during the Russian Civil War.

Yet the US administration did nothing to stop a flow of armaments and other strategic supplies to Stalin's Russia even when she was allied with Nazi Germany between 23 August, 1939, and 22 June, 1941. Moreover, no political or economic conditions for aid were imposed on the Soviet Union – unlike in the case of both the Whites and, later, the British Empire. The US administration was so obliging that the Soviets did not even have to steal military technology during the period when no diplomatic relations existed between them and the USA. One example is typical.

Experts agree that Soviet tanks were the best throughout the Second World War and in the immediate run-up to it. The most prominent machines were the light BT series led by the BT-7M, the medium T-34, probably the best all-purpose tank of the war, and the heavy KV-1 and KV-2, later augmented by the IS series. None of those would have existed in their actual superb form without the negligence, or perhaps even acquiescence, on the part of the US government.

For, while the Russians eventually produced the best tanks, Americans could boast the best tank designer. Though J. Walter Christie, a prophet without honour in his own land, failed to catch the imagination of the US defence establishment, he was enthusiastically appreciated by the Soviets. It was thanks to his contributions that the Soviet BT tanks were dominant against their Italian and German rivals in the Spanish Civil war and also against the Japanese in the 1939 battle of Khalkhin Gol, while the T–34 became legendary over the next decade.

Both tanks featured the unique suspension and sloping armour developed by Christie and first used in his prototype M1928 and M1931 tanks. In 1930 the Soviets bought two M1931s complete with plans, specifications, spare parts and production rights, put them in boxes marked as farm tractors and shipped them home – this at a time when the Soviet Union was not only barred from obtaining war materials in the United States but was not even diplomatically recognised by America. It is clear that, had he been allowed to, any customs inspector could have told the difference between a tractor and a tank, even with its turret removed. Equally clear is that the US government, while playing hard to get in the diplomatic arena, acted on its inbred anti-traditional imperative in areas that counted.

4

While Henry Ford was not the only major businessman who helped either Hitler or Stalin or both, his is a more interesting case than most. In his public persona Ford was and still is regarded by American conservatives as one of them. This political tag pre-supposes the championing of traditional values and individual liberty in the face of collectivist oppression. And sure enough, in his public pronouncements Henry Ford did

THE LAST NAIL IN THE COFFIN OF CHRISTENDOM

come across as holier than James Madison – if one overlooked the rabid anti-Semitism immortalised in his robust pamphlet *The International Jew*.

Even so, one still should not be too hasty in letting Ford or, say, J.P. Morgan get away with a claim to conservatism. A slight delay should be caused not by what they said but by what they did.

Ford had been financing Hitler's movement since before the Putsch, which was first reported by the *New York Times* in December, 1922. In recognition of this support, Hitler had a wall of his private office decorated with a portrait of Ford. In 1928 Ford merged his German holdings with I.G. Farben, a chemical cartel that also financed Hitler from the start and whose impressive product range later included the Zyklon B gas custom-made for the needs of Germany's growth industry.

Ford's holdings in Europe prospered during the war, thanks in part to extensive use of free labour generously supplied by Auschwitz. In 1938 Henry Ford was awarded the Grand Cross of the German Eagle, the highest Nazi decoration for foreigners (which incidentally had been turned down by Francisco Franco).

But Ford's greatest reward was the opportunity to profit from the war on both sides of the conflict. His plants in Germany and France assisted the Nazi war effort as much as his Detroit facilities helped the Allies. The war was to Ford an opportunity, not a threat. There is even evidence that the US Air Force spared American holdings in Europe, including Ford's factories. Either the RAF Bomber Command was not party to that arrangement, or else Sir Arthur Harris got carried away, but in March, 1942, the RAF hit the Ford plant at Poissy. Justice was done, however, when the Vichy government paid Ford 38 million francs in compensation, with profuse apologies for having been lax in their anti-aircraft defences.

Lest one may accuse Ford of playing favourites, in 1929 he signed an assistance agreement with another champion of democracy, Stalin's Russia. This agreement culminated in 1933 when Ford's plant was completed in Gorky. While known to every Russian as the maker of GAZ lorries, it is also known for its true military output to those who are aware of the real function of such factories in Soviet Russia.

Also in 1929 the Americans built the Stalingrad 'tractor' factory, then Europe's largest tank manufacturer. The entire facility was built as modules in the United States, transported across the Atlantic and re-assembled in Stalingrad by American and German technicians. Later, again with American help, the Stalingrad plant was cloned in Cheliabinsk and Kharkov. It was in those plants that Christie's designs were adopted and turned into the greatest tank force the world had ever known.

It is generally believed that businessmen like Ford or Morgan, who greatly contributed to the military potential of both the Bolsheviks and the Nazis, were atypical. In fact the opposite is true.

Modern business may be amoral but, underneath the surface, it is not apolitical. The likes of Ford and Morgan were driven not only by a desire for profits but also by the proselytising spirit of the American religion. Since its communicants tend to see traditional Western governments as infidels, simple logic would suggest that regimes that are hostile to Christendom would then be regarded as long-term, if not immediate, allies.

5

One would think that, having been thrust into an alliance with Stalin's Russia, America would regard it as strictly an *ad hoc* marriage of convenience. Elementary honesty should have prevented American leaders from portraying their combined war effort as a crusade for democracy. After all, Stalin's regime was every bit as hideous as Hitler's and, unlike the latter, could not even boast the distinction of having been democratically elected. How then could Roosevelt claim that the struggle against Nazism represented a fight for democracy?

Such a claim would indeed have been impossible had the word 'democracy' still been used in its real meaning. That, however, was no longer the case and to Roosevelt the word meant something entirely different: a slogan to be inscribed on the banners of the new world order. Democracy was thus fully synonymous with virtue. Anything that promoted the new order, such as Stalin's nightmarish regime, was *ipso facto* democratic, if at one remove, and anything that did not, such as Britain with her ancient parliament, was not.

Churchill's views on both democracy and Bolshevism were different and much closer to the truth. In that spirit, throughout the war he kept bombarding Roosevelt with warnings about the real nature of Bolshevism. Specifically, Churchill was pushing for a strategy aimed not only at defeating Nazi Germany but also at containing the likely post-war Soviet expansionism.

In this undertaking the prime minister enlisted the help of William Bullitt, the first US ambassador to the Soviet Union, whose own dealings with the Soviets were rather ambivalent. Nevertheless he knew the Soviets well and had few illusions about their nature or indeed intentions. When in 1943 Bullitt conveyed to Roosevelt Churchill's misgivings about Stalin, FDR replied in a way that vindicates my arguments: "I just have a hunch that Stalin is not that kind of a man... and I think that if I give him everything I possibly can and ask for nothing from him in return, *noblesse oblige*, he won't annex anything and will work with me for a world of democracy and peace."

If FDR had really meant that drivel, that surely would have been clinical proof of a rapidly progressing senility. However, as not only 'democracy' but also 'peace' had become the shorthand for the new order, Roosevelt was perfectly sound. Stalin was to him a true ally in that his desiderata were largely consonant with Roosevelt's. Churchill, on the other hand, was committed to the preservation of what was left of the British Empire. That made him an American ally only technically. In every meaningful way Roosevelt felt that Churchill's aspirations clashed with America's, while Stalin's overlapped with them.

That is why the flow of American supplies to Stalin never abated even during the two years when he was officially allied with Hitler. When Hitler's pre-emptive strike forced Stalin into an alliance with Western powers, the floodgates, already ajar, were flung wide open and American supplies turned into a mighty stream flowing in one direction only.[21] Moreover, America's assistance was indeed offered as generously as Roosevelt indicated in his reply to Bullitt. Both at the time and in the subsequent decades America neither received nor even requested any payment for her wartime supplies to the Soviet Union. What's a few billion among friends?

America's arrangements with the moribund British Empire, whose commitment to the democratic values touted by the USA was manifestly firmer than Russia's, were entirely different. Britain had to pay for everything in cash, IOUs being accepted only grudgingly and with the understanding that no defaults would be allowed. Specifically in 1940, when Britain's survival hung by a thread, all transactions had to be done strictly on a cash-and-carry basis.

Alas, both cash and precious metals were rapidly running out, and Britain had to dump all her overseas investments at derisory prices to settle her accounts with the transatlantic champions of democracy. The entire gold reserves of the British Empire had to be used up to pay for vital American supplies, especially food and medicines. The practical value of American military supplies proper was less critical – after all it was the homemade Spitfires and Hurricanes that won the Battle of Britain, and it was the homemade ships of the Royal Navy that rendered an invasion of Britain impossible.

That victory was won at the expense not only of British lives but also of Britain's post-war economic prospects. Churchill knew this was coming. On 7 December, 1940, he wrote to Roosevelt, pleading that the brutally unsentimental terms on which American aid was being proffered would consign Britain to a position in which "after the victory was won with our blood and sweat, and civilisation saved, and the time gained for the United States to be fully armed against all eventualities, we should stand stripped to the bone. Such a course would not be in the moral or economic interests of either of our countries."

---

21 Those interested in the details of these transactions could do worse than look up Prof. Anthony C. Sutton's book *National Suicide: Military Aid to the Soviet Union* or, better still, his seminal three-volume study *Western Technology and Soviet Economic Development.*

THE LAST NAIL IN THE COFFIN OF CHRISTENDOM

Roosevelt acknowledged receipt and promptly collected Britain's last £50 million in gold.

Churchill pretended not to understand that 'such a course' was precisely in America's 'moral and economic interests'. Morally, the demise of the traditional British Empire, the last major stronghold of Christendom's political order, played into the hands of the American ambitions of leading the post-Christian world. And economically, British cash helped America to overcome the Great Depression and indeed emerge from the war better off than she had been before it.

6

By delivering half the word to the Soviets, the post-war order set the scene for both strengthening the PR appeal of democracy and, as a natural consequence, erasing the last vestiges of Christendom from Western politics. While an alliance with Stalin had made appeals to democratic virtue ring hollow, a confrontation with the Soviets helped such appeals to come across with crystal clarity. Democracy could now be positioned as the only possible alternative to communism. The world faced a choice between the voting booth and the torture cellar. Presumably no other options existed.

Western, especially American, leaders could now feign innocence as the Soviets perpetrated on Eastern Europe all the same horrors they had rehearsed on Soviet citizens – exactly the outrages that the treaties of Yalta, Teheran and Potsdam championed by Roosevelt had freed them up to unleash. That was of little consequence. What mattered was that the Americans' thirst for democracy had been slaked: Stalin had undertaken to hold elections in Eastern Europe. Yet predictably elections within the Soviets' sphere of influence turned out to be a cynical sham, with puppet regimes installed and propped up by Soviet bayonets.

Western governments could now take stock of the situation. To their horror they realised, or rather finally permitted themselves to realise, that the Soviets had ambitions reaching beyond the low-rent part of Europe. Stalin could now put his foot down and match up American power strategically all over the world. In this the Soviets were ably assisted by a worldwide network of agents,[22] some of them ensconced in the upper echelons of all Western governments, with many others claiming a huge share of voice in the press.

The United States and her allies had to face up to the imminent danger of losing their strategic dominance, and it fell upon Winston Churchill, now divested of high office, to enunciate their concerns. Having lost the first post-war election, he no longer felt bound by loyalty to the treaties in which he had played such a prominent, if subservient, part. On his visit to Fulton, Missouri, Churchill again demonstrated his way with words: "From Stettin in the Baltic to Trieste in the Adriatic, an iron curtain has descended across the Continent."

(The words Churchill demonstrated his way with were not necessarily his own. He probably borrowed the phrase from the book *The Apocalypse of Our Times* written by the Russian essayist Vasily Rozanov in 1919, shortly before he starved to death. The book was translated into English in 1920 and Churchill must have been taken with its brilliant prose: "With clanging, creaking and squeaking an iron curtain is lowering over Russian History. 'The performance is over.' The audience got up. 'Time to put on your fur coats and go home.' We looked around. Neither the fur coats nor homes were any longer there.")

Churchill was right in general principle, as the Soviets demonstrated by blockading Berlin in 1949. But he was too modest in detail, for their designs were more ambitious than just gaining control over half of Europe. In 1945 they occupied North Korea and established a communist state north of the 38th parallel. In 1949 they succeeded in installing Mao in China, and at the time it looked as if the communist bloc was becoming an immovable monolith. Already in 1947 the American journalist Walter Lippmann published the book *The Cold War*, which term, a translation of the French *la guerre froide*, he coined to describe the Soviet-American confrontation.

A cold war is unlike the normal kind in that the use of

---

22 At least 500 government officials, including two of FDR's closest advisors at Yalta, were Soviet spies, and one of them, Alger Hiss, was later imprisoned.

military force is merely threatened, while the actual hostilities are waged with words. A cold war is just like the normal kind in that it too needs spiffy slogans inscribed on its banners. The word 'democracy', though used widely from the beginning of the century, could now do credible service as the distinguishing feature of the West in its clash with demonstrably non-democratic communism.

The new syllogism behind it was beautiful in its simplicity, if not quite unassailable in its logic: Unlike the Soviet Union, America is democratic. Unlike the Soviet Union, America is good. Ergo, democracy is good. Thus it was under the banners of democracy that Western countries closed ranks in the Cold War against Soviet beastliness. No other slogan, and certainly not a crusading call to arms against godlessness, would have worked as well: by then the West was almost as godless as the Soviet Union.

The lines were clearly drawn and it was the Cold War that drew them. The intellectual domain of Western politics was no longer divided into conservatism (aspiring to cling on to the fragments of Christendom) and modernism (hostility to any such aspiration). The line of demarcation now ran between anticommunists, those probably in the majority, and communist sympathisers, those in a vociferous minority.

A war, even a cold one, forges all sorts of unlikely alliances. For example, in the 1930s the loudest anti-Stalin voice belonged to Leon Trotsky, an equally if not more hideous monster, but a man who had lost out to Stalin and thereby became his enemy. Suddenly anticommunist Western politicians, some of whom had detested Trotsky when he had been in power, found themselves in partial sympathy with his message.

Similarly the post-war confrontation, especially after the Soviets acquired the atom bomb in 1949 and the hydrogen one in 1953, drew under the banners of anticommunism many vaguely rightwing or conservative groups and even significant portions of leftwing ones. Real or feigned affection for democracy was in many instances the sole unifying element among them.

Conservatism, in the real sense of the word, took a step

back and exited pursued by the Russian bear. It certainly became impossible to be critical of unchecked democracy, a political system that runs against the grain of Christendom and therefore conservatism. Any such critic would have been instantly branded as either a communist (if he was broadly on the Left) or as a fascist (if on the Right). Such demonisation is still with us, and even in our PC times one routinely overhears conservatives, or those perceived as such, being described as fascists.

For reasons on which I shall expand in the next chapter, conservatism had a particularly rough ride in the United States, and eventually its road became bumpy in Europe as well. But the time has come, now that I have referred several times to *real* conservatism, to define the term properly.

Conservatism and the Babel of politics

1

In the Bible, erecting "a tower, whose top may reach unto heaven" with the subsequent disintegration of language was severe punishment: "Go to, let us go down, and there confound their language, that they may not understand one another's speech."

However suspicious one may be of Biblical literalism, it is hard not to notice the lexical chaos reigning in our political taxonomy. Particularly relevant to the subject of this essay are the varied interpretations of conservatism – so varied that anyone can nowadays use the word to convey not only the entire gamut of political convictions but also one's attitude to them.

For example, when Tony Blair boasted of the progress his government had made in combating 'the forces of conservatism' he felt no need to add a pejorative modifier. The word 'conservatism' was derogatory enough by itself. Of course Mr Blair, possessed as he is of rather understated intellectual rigour, would probably define conservatives simply as those reluctant to vote Labour. Unlike many other definitions, this one has the advantage of clearly demarcated if excessively broad limits, which stands it in good stead in the rough-and-tumble of political demagoguery. Once outside that environment, however, it loses substance altogether.

Predictably Blair's opposition to his bogeyman has earned him numerous plaudits from the neocons, such as this one from COLLENE, my composite source: "…Tony Blair is… almost perfectly neoconservative on foreign policy…" Blair was equally perfect on domestic policy as well, specifically by allowing his rampant statism to create an economic crisis from which Britain still has not recovered fully. But the neocons do not emphasise such accomplishments too much.

In Britain the word 'conservative' tends to take on a capital initial even in spoken English, thereby identifying a member or supporter of the Tory party, for which true conservatism is at best a nostalgic echo from a distant past. In America the word tends to denote a free-market libertarian, what used to be called a liberal until the word was shifted leftwards. Specifically in America's southern states, 'conservatism' usually includes an aspect of populism, terms that traditional conservatives would regard as mutually exclusive. In Russia 'conservative' means Stalinist; in Australia conservatives call themselves liberals. In France, the first Western country to have introduced universal male suffrage, *conservateur* is usually used as a term of abuse.

Granted, it is not just different times but also different countries that bring forth different mores, emphasising therefore different things they wish to conserve. Nevertheless when a word can mean so many things it ends up meaning nothing at all, which leaves a lexical black hole. Hence any group, the neocons and the libertarians being obvious examples, can squeeze itself into that hole and claim conservative provenance, usually for nefarious purposes. So much more important it then becomes to define the word precisely.

2

According to Lord Hailsham, former chairman of the British Conservative Party, "Conservatism is not so much a philosophy as an attitude, a constant force, performing a timeless function in the development of a free society, and corresponding to a deep and permanent requirement of human nature itself."

Fair enough, conservatism is not so much an ideological bias as a matter of intuitive, visceral predisposition. But a temperamental proclivity is a liquid that needs to flow into a particular vessel, for otherwise it will end up as an amorphous puddle on the floor. A vague longing has to be put into words for it to become definable. And an ability to choose the right words

CONSERVATISM AND THE BABEL OF POLITICS

cannot be acquired without a considerable training of mind and senses, which is not something everyone can do even in a society committed to egalitarian uniformity.

Just as there is more to a religion than just faith, there is more to conservatism than just 'an attitude'. Both faith and attitude require the forklift of doctrine and philosophy to rise above a personal idiosyncrasy to the height of a social phenomenon, a dynamic creative force. What Lord Hailsham referred to is not conservatism but a predisposition for it, a base on which a structure can be erected.

A useful parallel would be the difference between musicality and musicianship. A child with an innate musical sense, a good ear and what is loftily called psychomotor coordination may still never become a musician unless he is taught how to play an instrument. And even if he has learned the requisite mechanical skills, he will never become a *serious* musician unless he grasps the spirit animating Western music and has the mind to understand how this spirit is revealed through tones and harmonies.

By the same token, before he can become a fully fledged conservative, a visceral conservative defined in Lord Hailsham's terms still needs some intellectual and spiritual training to relate his intuition to specific ideas. Hence what Lord Hailsham talked about is an essential but not a sufficient condition. But essential it is, and I shall return to his definition in the context of neoconservatism.

Logic would demand that conservatism be defined first positively, in terms of things its proponents wish to conserve, and then negatively, in terms of things they wish to oppose. Thus the only definition with a chance of achieving universality in the West would have to revolve around the deep meaning of the Western world, its natal inspiration and the force that has sustained it through centuries. You will notice that the accent here is not on specific countries but on the West at large, which approach must of necessity focus on things all Western nations hold in common.

Hence before we define conservatism we must first define the Western world. Since throughout these pages I use the term interchangeably with Christendom, no equivocation on my part is possible. The Western world came out of Christianity the way Eve came out of Adam's rib, or rather almost the same way. For the West had plenty of other formative influences as well, Greek philosophy and Roman legality being prime among them. These added finishing touches to the life-giving force, making it irresistible. But the force did come from the obscure event that took place in Galilee during the reign of Tiberius.

The resulting entity took a long time to develop fully and it grew up to be highly complex, including as it did so much more than just a religion. As a matter of fact, no religion can ever stew in its own juice for long – if it does, it ceases to exist before long. In order to survive as a true religion and not just a sect, it has to excrete and wrap around itself a particular cocoon of ethics, morals, social and political organisation, culture, overall way of life. In time this cocoon may take on an importance all its own, with people ignoring or even forgetting its original source. But even in the absence of such a development the way of life produced by a religion is often as important to society as the religion itself.

Calvinism provides a prime example. While reforming the Reformation, Jean Calvin produced a large body of theology, thousands of pages densely packed with small print. Practically none survives to this day as anything other than a matter of academic interest to those passionate about intellectual archae-ology. But the way of life produced by Calvinism is as robust as ever, and it is one of the phenomena responsible for the prevalence of atheism in today's West. Encouraged to use their own judgment to doubt everything and dispense with the most fundamental doctrines of Christianity, people felt empowered to get rid of all the others as well, in due course including first the God in Christ and then the God in God. This was not what Calvin had in mind, but the law of unintended consequences has never been repealed.

Modern democracy and economic activity also owe much to Calvinism. Religious self-reliance was bound to produce a quest for economic and political self-reliance: if people felt free to choose any God or none, so much more justified they felt in taking charge of their economic and political lives. In other words, though Calvinist theology is dead, Calvinism lives on. This shows that the way of life spun out by a religion can at times outlive its founding tenets.

It is the Christian, specifically apostolic Christian, way of life that defined and shaped the West. It is this way of life that in modern times has been under sustained attack from all sorts of quarters, for reasons I commented on earlier. From this the definition of conservatism flows as naturally as wine out of the bottle, for it becomes instantly clear what it is that conservatives wish to conserve: Christendom, whatever is left of it. Similarly, once we have established what conservatives are for, we shall instantly know what they are against: any further attempts to destroy the multifarious heritage of Christendom.

This definition of conservatism is unacceptable to the neocons. Thus Midge Decter, one of their shining lights: "It's this notion of a Christian civilisation. You have to be part of it or you're not really fit to conserve anything. That's an old line and it's very ignorant." Old this line may be, but its ignorance could only be demonstrated by coming up with an educated alternative. Neither Miss Decter nor any other neocons have so far provided any, certainly not one that can withstand even cursory examination, never mind scrutiny. Her outburst does raise the question of which civilisation she would rather claim as her own, but this is not a question to be answered here.

Because Christendom has so many facets, conservatism must reflect them all – never forgetting that they are indeed facets of the same whole, rather than unconnected phenomena. These days it is fashionable to talk about social or cultural conservatism, as distinct from the political kind. Such a separation is philosophically unsound, rhetorically artificial and psychologically unlikely.

If someone does insist on it, one has to doubt his sincerity or else his mind: he either only pretends to be a conservative or simply does not understand what the word means. For example, it is hard to imagine a true political conservative preaching the social delights of a classless society, as John Major once did when he was still prime minister. Nor should a man get a free ride when claiming to be a social liberal but a fiscal conservative, which presumably means he loves the welfare state but hates to pay for it.

On the other hand it is usually easy to guess a man's political views without ever bringing up politics during, say, a dinner-table chat. For instance, it is highly unlikely that a political conservative would express enthusiasm for pop music, 'conceptual' sculpture, garden cities, vegetarianism, same-sex marriage, facial metal, yoga or body art. And it is impossible that in writing he would ever choose BCE and CE over BC and AD. Neither is it probable that someone on the left of the political spectrum would dismiss out of hand any music amplified by electric or electronic appliances. Nor can one easily imagine a political conservative sporting a tattoo, say 'ACAB' on his knuckles.[23] Such telltale signs may of course mislead, but not often.

The conservative tree has sprouted many branches, but they are all attached to the same trunk, and apple blossoms are not going to appear on an elm. The metaphorical trunk is the civilisation of Christendom brought to life by the faith that created it, and a conservative is a person who strives to cultivate the tree or at least to keep it from dying.

In view of this definition of conservatism, a natural question arises: is it possible for a true Western conservative not to be a Christian? For someone who subjugates all his thoughts and most of his feelings to relentless logic, probably not. But people are not always logical and never merely so. Most of us find it hard to tie a multitude of intellectual strands and emotional nerve cells into a single ganglion, which is why most of us frequently hold contradictory beliefs. This certainly applies to the issue of compatibility between conservatism and atheism.

Faith, after all, is neither an intellectual attitude nor a 'lifestyle choice'; it is a gift in the literal sense of the word, something presented by an outside donor. We can seek it, but whether we gain it is not entirely up to us. However, the way we view the world is a product of individual quest, and so are our resulting actions. Therefore even if someone has no faith he may still be

---

23   For the benefit of non-British readers, or those British ones who have led a sheltered life, 'ACAB' stands for 'All Cops Are Bastards'.

able to grasp its historical significance to our civilisation with its every manifestation.

Anyone well-disposed towards Western civilisation, regardless of his religion or absence thereof, has to feel at least residual affection for Christianity, the faith that gave birth to this civilisation. Consequently conservatism is incompatible with aggressive atheism, hatred of Christianity à la Richard Dawkins or A.C. Grayling. It may however occasionally coexist with agnosticism, a mournful admission that one is denied faith even though one acknowledges its paramount, irreplaceable importance.

These days we are witnessing the birth of a new intellectual type: the clerical atheist, which is the exact opposite of the erstwhile anticlerical believer. The new type illustrates the previous paragraph: clerical atheists have no faith but, all else having failed, they see no viable alternative to the church as a social and cultural adhesive. Deep down their thinking is unsound because the church can contribute to the lasting health of society only if its tenets are widely believed to stand for the truth. Clerical atheists seem to believe that the church is useful even though it stands for a lie. Ultimately they are in for a letdown, but political conservatism is not beyond their reach.

Be that as it may, empirical observation suggests that any large gathering of political conservatives will feature a greater proportion of believers than any other political group. Conversely, a predominantly atheist group of any kind, be it cultural, political or social, is unlikely to include many conservatives. Group association has a certain inner logic to it, and it cannot be defied *en masse*.

This consideration by itself would be sufficient to doubt the conservative credentials of the neocons, few of whom, especially the younger generation, have any religious beliefs at all. Interestingly, when even practising Christians become thoroughly imbued with neocon views, they often abandon their faith – and one could cite quite a few examples, both American and British. Such apostates sense that the nature of their political creed makes it incompatible with Christianity.

By detaching our civilisation from its origin, modernity was hoping to unleash its creative potential. All it showed in effect was its ability to destroy: pollarding tree branches has a beneficial effect on the tree's growth; severing its roots does not. T.S. Eliot diagnosed the condition accurately: "If Christianity goes, the whole of our culture goes. Then you must start painfully again, and you cannot put on a new culture ready-made... You must pass through many centuries of barbarism."

We are currently living through such centuries of barbarism, which explains why conservatism, defined as a quest to preserve what is left of Christendom, has such a hard time in the West. This is true of any aspect of conservatism and certainly its politics. It would be no exaggeration to suggest that no truly conservative party is currently holding, or vying for, power anywhere in the West. Even individual politicians who have conservative convictions can remain in politics only by either concealing such views or diluting them beyond recognition.

3

In the immediate post-war years American, and to a large extent any other, conservatism became so tightly fused with anticommunism that for all intents and purposes they became one and the same. It was not so much Jesus Christ as Joseph Stalin who brought focus to the American Right. In a way, if communism had not existed American conservatives would have had to invent it in the hope of giving themselves a political *raison d'être*. For, while an American may develop conservative tastes in, say, music or architecture, political conservatism is somewhat more problematic, for neither an obvious source nor a reliable outlet for it exists.

Thus American political conservatism got to be described in largely negative terms based on what it was not or stood against. Implicitly such apophatic politics was tantamount to accepting communism as the frame of reference. This was inadvertently emphasised by a southern senator, Strom Thurmond if memory serves, in a conversation about Dwight Eisenhower. In an offhand remark the senator said that Eisenhower was a communist. "Not at all," objected his interlocutor. "Ike is

CONSERVATISM AND THE BABEL OF POLITICS

an anticommunist." "I don't care," retorted the indomitable politician, "what *kind* of communist he is." He probably did not mean that the way it sounded but, as a starting point of political thought, anticommunism is indeed nothing but communism with an opposite sign.

It is hard for an American to pass the litmus test of political conservatism encapsulated in the question "So what is it about our political system that we wish to conserve?". The French have the same problem and for the same reason: both countries, America more or less from birth and France in its present form, came to life as revolutionary republics denying the very essence of conservatism. Both chose democracy as the encapsulation of their political selves, though only Americans ended up perching it on top of a totem pole. Hence both are at odds with the real desideratum of conservative politics: preservation of the traditional order of Christendom, as it applies to our time.

An American conservative would probably answer the lapidary question about conserving something by the magic shibboleth 'the Constitution of the United States'. But as I argued in a previous chapter, commendable though that document doubtless is, conservative it is not – even though of necessity the Constitution has had to act as the tight boot into which conservatively inclined Americans have had to shoehorn their political convictions.

Yet in the immediate post-bellum period and for several decades thereafter such primal doubts and uncomfortable questions could be shunted aside, more or less. No semantic and philosophical subtleties were needed to unite the Right and Centre of US politics in a common cause: resisting world communism in general and the Soviet Union in particular.

Two landmark cases shook Americans out of their complacency in 1950: Alger Hiss, a high official in the State Department and foreign-policy advisor to FDR, who earlier had been charged with being a Soviet spy, was sent to prison for perjury when he denied it. Prosecuting the case for the House Committee on Un-American Activities (HUAC), the young congressman Richard Nixon nailed Hiss to the wall. Since then the 'liberal' papers, such as the *New York Times* and *The Washington Post*, never relented in their concerted efforts to destroy Nixon by digging up any dirt they could find. He kindly obliged by giving them, at Watergate, more than they could hope for. In no way wishing to exculpate Nixon, one could still wonder how principled a stand those papers would have taken had a similar offence been committed by, say, one of the Kennedy brothers.

Then the communists Julius and Ethel Rosenberg starred in an atomic-espionage trial, also involving David Greenglass, Harry Gold, Klaus Fuchs and Morton Sobell. The Rosenbergs were electrocuted in Sing Sing and many others were implicated if not necessarily indicted. Specifically, numerous scientists involved in the Manhattan Project were strongly suspected of passing atomic secrets to the Soviets.

The Italian communist Bruno Pontecorvo turned a suspicion into certainty by fleeing to the Soviet Union in 1950. Others, such as Enrico Fermi and Leo Szilard were almost certainly involved, though this was never proven. Robert Oppenheimer, the director of the Manhattan Project, eventually lost his security clearance and consequently his career.

Interestingly, Sergo Beria, son of the Soviet secret-police chief, claims in his memoir that Oppenheimer once visited their house in Moscow before the war. Sergo's veracity is not of sterling quality on many issues, but this does not automatically mean that he lies on all of them. Though Oppenheimer was never indicted for espionage, he himself admitted in 1942 that he had been "a member of just about every Communist front organisation on the West Coast." It says a lot about the competence of US counterintelligence that such an admission did not prevent Oppenheimer from being put in charge of the ultra-sensitive Manhattan Project. It was only much later that he was identified as a security risk.

Though in existence since 1938, it was only in the run-up to the 1950 trials that HUAC (in which another young politician, Robert Kennedy, also distinguished himself) came to the forefront of American politics by accusing a number of entertainment-industry and literary figures of using their media for the purposes of communist propaganda. As a result, stars like Charlie Chaplin, Orson Welles, Paul Robeson, Lillian Hellman,

CONSERVATISM AND THE BABEL OF POLITICS

Dashiell Hammett, Dalton Trumbo and many others were blacklisted, some of them emigrated and only a handful were eventually able to rebuild their careers.

The most vociferous accuser, however, was not any HUAC congressman but a senator from Wisconsin Joseph McCarthy, whose Senate Committee of Investigations is often confused with HUAC. It is with 'Tailgunner Joe' McCarthy that claims of communist penetration of such institutions as the entertainment industry and the State Department are usually associated. The senator himself is still routinely portrayed in the leftwing press and literature as a hideous alcoholic, a deranged fanatic whose anticommunist delusions were caused by an onset of delirium tremens.

'McCarthyism' has become the nemesis of the American Left, while those he accused are still incongruously portrayed as innocent victims. However, the specific take on their innocence has changed: if at the time it was claimed they were not communists but good people, these days they are supposed to be good people specifically because they were communists. At a secure distance, communist sympathies are now seen as innocent idealism, rather than as the clear and present danger they were rightly considered to be in the 1950s.

It has to be said that, true enough, McCarthy was such a shrill and uncouth demagogue that even many of those who sympathised with his cause "deplored his championship of it", in Evelyn Waugh's phrase. All this is well and good, except for one minor matter: McCarthy was right. In fact, when some Soviet archives and the so-called VENONA transcripts were made public, not only was McCarthy vindicated in practically all of his accusations, but indeed they were shown not to be far-reaching enough.

When in 1949 Mao took over China, McCarthy accused The Institute of Pacific Relations and specifically its key figure Owen Lattimore (another advisor to FDR) of acting as Soviet agents of influence, subverting the public opinion to Mao's cause and rendering impossible any muscular action to prevent the communists' victory. In his later career Lattimore was closely associated with Castro's regime and, while it lasted,

Allende's. Though vindicating McCarthy was far from his mind, his actions achieved precisely that purpose.

Given that sort of backdrop, it is understandable that the scene was set for confrontations defined by *pro* and *contra* attitudes to communist influences. Few American *soi disant* conservatives asked themselves how they would express their innermost convictions should communism no longer be an issue. They had no time for philosophical subtleties: the battle lines were too sharply drawn.

Defining and refining conservatism

1

You will have noticed that I devote a great deal of time to discussing American conservatism rather than, say, British. This slant is unavoidable in the context of this essay, and for more than one reason.

First, in view of my understanding of conservatism, the British variety presents few intellectual challenges of definition – it practically defines itself. If the overall quest is to conserve the heritage of Christendom, including its political manifestations, then traditional (as distinct from today's) Toryism is coextensive with my definition of conservatism. The triad of 'God, king and country' may be as primitive as all slogans tend to be, but it is more precise than most, encapsulating neatly the essence of British conservatism, both its transcendent inspiration and political expression.

It is worth pondering the triad to see how it agrees with the definition of conservatism proposed in this essay. The starting point of deliberation for any Western conservative thinker is that all key institutions of Christendom, which is to say of the West, must somehow reflect the teaching of Christ and, on a deeper level, his person. The essence of Christ, as accepted by all apostolic denominations, is that he is both fully divine and fully human, uniting within himself the transcendent and the transient, the timeless and the temporal, the physical and the metaphysical.

In politics the same unity is communicated by the triad of 'God, king and country'. However, the parallel could be made to work even harder if we relate it not to the umbrella slogan but to a specific political system. I would suggest that constitutional monarchy (as unsuccessfully tried in France but first achieved and then debauched in England) underpinned by qualified franchise is the only method of government that truly reflects the essence of Christendom and its founding religion.

A monarch ruling by divine right or some similar claim to legitimacy represents the transcendent aspect of such a system, a factor of constancy linking generations past, present and future on a timeline demarcated by Creation at one end and the Second Coming at the other. At the same time, an elected parliament is a temporal institution translating the people's interests into political action and preventing the monarch from becoming a despot. To achieve a workable balance, Parliament's power must be real but limited, the monarch's power limited but real, and they should both feel accountable to the institution that is itself accountable to God only.

If we accept this as the theoretical starting point, then all that is required to turn it into a practical recommendation is empirical evidence of efficacy. This is in ample supply. When the triad was properly balanced in Britain, all the prime ministers, with one or two exceptions, were greater statesmen than all the subsequent ones, again with one or two exceptions. When the monarchs still held some residual power in the nineteenth century, Britain was an immeasurably more successful country relative to others than she was to become in the twentieth. Clearly, a functioning constitutional monarchy begets better government than the dictatorship of the Commons, otherwise known as modern British democracy, can deliver. This stands to reason, for just as commercial competition improves the quality of goods on offer, so does competition from other estates improve both the parliamentary and the royal breed.

Of course a perfect symbiosis between the physical and metaphysical aspects of political power is hard if not impossible to achieve, which is true of all worldly ideals. All we can expect is a reasonable approximation to the ideal, and I would suggest that England's constitutional monarchy, when it was still in business for real, came as close to it as any other political system ever has.

DEFINING AND REFINING CONSERVATISM

Hence the triad of 'god, king and country', in which the first element reflects transcendent continuity, the third temporal interests represented in Parliament and the second the link between the two. Regarded in this light, the slogan stops being just that, becoming instead the philosophical premise of British conservatism.

It is important to remember that the triad lists its elements in a descending order of importance. Thus eliminating the first element, as has effectively been done in Britain, largely invalidates the second one and runs the risk of destroying the third. Conservatism then becomes problematic, as demonstrated by today's Conservative party, which has become neoconservative at best and downright socialist at worst. But at least British conservatives have a past model they can hope to revive.

Americans, on the other hand, excised the second part of the triad, king, and effectively fused the other two, God and country, together. Falling victim to this surgical procedure was the philosophy of political conservatism, indeed its clear definition. The American religion of exceptionalism stepped in to fill the vacuum thus formed, but this creed can draw its believers from all sorts of political groups, not just conservative ones. This explains how the neocons, a manifestly non-conservative lot, could eventually usurp the claim to conservatism.

Second, the USA emerged in the immediate post-war years as the only power capable of containing, if not necessarily rolling back, Soviet expansion. It therefore assumed, deservedly if perhaps unfortunately, a position of leadership in the Western world. This position was further strengthened by the role America played in the reconstruction of European economies devastated by the war.[24]

The Marshall Plan, put into effect in 1948, was instrumental to European economic recovery, though it cannot claim the whole credit for, say, the German economic resurgence (*Wirtschaftswunder* for short). Britain, for example, received

---

24 America's popular mythology tends to exaggerate her role in winning the war in Europe. Undoubtedly important, it was not sufficient to justify the claim 'we won your war for you'. For example, US troops landing in Normandy on D-Day were outnumbered by those from the Commonwealth.

greater assistance under the Marshall plan than Germany did and yet took several decades, as opposed to a few years, to recover. The success and speed of recovery were mostly owed to the policies adopted by individual countries and the vigour with which they carried the policies out. But the Marshall Plan did help.

It helped the United States as well by advancing the crusading, evangelical ambitions inherent to the American secular religion. Similarly to Prussia using the economic levers of *Zollverein* to drag all of Germany under her aegis in the nineteenth century, or the EU using economic tethers to tie the less successful countries into the Union, America too used its economic muscle not just to assist Western Europe but potentially also to dominate it in the long run. Assuming such a leadership role tallied with the demands of the American religion of exceptionalism – the City on a Hill began to shine its light upon the world not just metaphorically but in a blindingly obvious way.

Third, America's influence began to extend to philosophical matters as well, at least as far as politics was concerned. One-man-one-vote was the American political cult in a nutshell, and no Western European country could be brazen enough to take a sledgehammer to it, not yet anyway. In particular, the American religion proved influential in converting Anglophone infidels, be that in the metropolis or in the fragments of the erstwhile British Empire. Hence the confusion perennially reigning within the ranks of American conservatism gradually turned into a contagion spreading all over the Western world. This included Britain whose conservatives lost their erstwhile clarity of self-identification and have not since recovered it, at least not as a cohesive group.

Fourth, though neoconservatism is now gaining international clout, especially in the Anglophone sphere, its genesis cannot be properly understood outside the American context. The movement appeared largely as a reaction against conservative traditionalism as expounded at the time by the American journal *National Review*, about which later.

Americanism began to affect European thought and mores seriously in the 1950s. Yet for all its burgeoning international influence the American religion was in a bit of a mess internally. Conservatism in particular was adrift even more than it had been originally, when the United States first declared her separation from perhaps the most organic, and at the time the most successful, state of Christendom. So it was in the 1950s that American conservatives attempted to find a firm, unifying intellectual base. The need for it could no longer be put off.

2

In 1953 Russell Kirk (1918–1994) published the book *The Conservative Mind: From Burke to Santayana* (in a later edition ... *to Eliot*) attempting to trace back the genealogy of American conservatism and give it enough shape to correct its amorphous state. Specifically, he derived its origin from Edmund Burke, thereby canonising the great Anglo-Irish Whig as the John the Baptist of American conservatism. Interestingly Burke, though unquestionably regarded as a sublime political philosopher, never attained the same prominence in his own country, where Tory or proto-Tory thinkers in the vein of Hooker, Dr Johnson, Coleridge, Carlyle, Newman, Eliot and Collingwood have arguably had a greater impact on conservative thought.

Kirk recognised not only the philosophical and aesthetic value of Burke's *Reflections on the Revolution in France* but also the nature of its inspiration: "The *Reflections*," he wrote, "burns with all the wrath and anguish of a prophet who saw the traditions of Christendom and the fabric of civil society dissolving before his eyes."

Burke indeed was one of the few contemporaneous thinkers who understood the French Revolution for what it was: modernity's assault on Christendom. His demolition of that outrage is perhaps the best evidence of how a deep mind can harness a bubbling intuitive passion and channel it into the right conduit. Burke would probably have first described himself as a Christian, not as a conservative – even if the term in its present sense had existed at the time. He would have seen his philosophy as an attempt to apply his understanding of life, as informed by his faith, to the quotidian problems of the world.

In that, if not in everything else, Burke was one of the greatest and truest conservative thinkers ever.

Like Burke – and any other reasonably defined conservative – Kirk knew that morality was transcendent, and the link between Christian and social virtue unbreakable. Unlike Burke, however, he lived at a time and in a place where the basic certitudes of civilised society were not only doubted but widely mocked. Burke did not therefore feel the need to summarise his beliefs in a schematic, slogan-like form, but Kirk did. To that end he formulated as stab points his ten underlying principles of conservatism. This was his own Decalogue that, Kirk hoped, would resolve the confusion reigning in America's intellectual and political life:

"First, the conservative believes that there exists an enduring moral order.

"Second, the conservative adheres to custom, convention and continuity.

"Third, conservatives believe in what may be called the principle of prescription.

"Fourth, conservatives are guided by their principles of prudence.

"Fifth, conservatives pay attention to the principle of variety [of class, wealth and status].

"Sixth, conservatives are chastened by their principle of imperfectability.

"Seventh, conservatives are persuaded that freedom and property are closely linked.

"Eighth, conservatives uphold voluntary community and oppose involuntary collectivism.

"Ninth, the conservative perceives the need for prudent restraints upon power and human passions.

"Tenth, he understands permanence and change must be recognised and reconciled in a vigorous society."

Any conservative would accept Kirk's commandments as his own dicta, if possibly not without some modifications. A British conservative, for example, would find it hard to omit a reassertion of loyalty to his country's monarchy and established church (even if he himself does not belong to it). But while perhaps wishing to augment Kirk's Decalogue in some ways, such a hypothetical conservative certainly would not wish to take anything out. More important, he would recognise a kindred spirit and a like mind.

However, what is especially remarkable is not only what is in Kirk's Decalogue but also what is not. Not a single commandment mentions or even obliquely refers to democracy or any other method of government, with only the seventh touching upon economics – and then only tangentially, in its relation to freedom rather than to any specific wealth-producing practices.

This stands to reason: as a Burkean, Russell Kirk had to stress the primacy of the transcendent over the transient. The former was to him immutable; the latter negotiable. Hence Kirk could never be confused with a neoconservative and neither was he a libertarian in the style of Frederick Hayek or Ayn Rand, of whom the former was a significant thinker and the latter a facile, shrill demagogue. Totalitarian economism, even if realised through free enterprise, would have been as alien to Kirk as totalitarian communism.

Libertarianism in particular is often confused with conservatism, mainly because of their shared commitment to limiting the power of the state over the individual. Both accept that a free market is a *sine qua non* of civilised society even though libertarians assign a greater importance to the economy in the general scheme of things. Actually in British Toryism this acceptance is of rather recent provenance, dating perhaps only as far back as the 1970s. But Toryism, like any other doctrine, must develop in order to survive and, what with the alternative shown to be a sure-fire guarantee of despotism, commitment to free enterprise is a useful embellishment – provided it does not assume an inordinately overriding importance.

However, unlike conservatives, libertarians also seek to curtail the influence of the benign associations, including the church, lying at the foundation of any traditional order. Hence libertarians would reject at least half of Kirk's commandments, especially those reflecting Burkean prescription, prudence and prejudice. That is why, while a part of their creed overlaps with latter-day conservatism, a more important part paradoxically has more in common with aggressive socialism, which in turn has much emotional kinship with neoconservatism.

By concentrating on cultural, religious and aesthetic matters, rather than practical politics and economics, Russell Kirk hinted at the difficulties inherent in reconciling political conservatism with the revolutionary DNA of the United States. Kirk's philosophy, though at one with the traditional religion of the West, was in conflict with the American religion in which democracy had become the principal tenet. It is also at odds with what I call totalitarian economism, an essential link of the American religion with everyday life.

Hence Kirk's conservative traditionalism, though influential on American academic thought, has had little impact on American practical life. By contrast, Ayn Rand's fusion of totalitarian economism, political libertarianism and hysterical atheism claimed many disciples acting not just in university halls but in the economic and political arena. This makes her refracted impact both deep and long-lasting.

Rand was the archangel of crude materialism, the nexus at which all strands of modernity converge. While rather feeble in her intellectual constructs, and for a bestselling novelist astonishingly incompetent a writer, she was a natural fisher of souls, claiming many disciples who instantly fell under her spell. For example, Rand exerted a formative influence on Alan Greenspan, the Virgin to her Gabriel, who in his position of Federal Reserve boss was one of the principal architects of the 2008 crisis. Even today, almost three decades after her death, this objectionable woman still claims apostles, most no doubt attracted by her fanatical championing of free enterprise *über alles*.

Few are repelled by Rand's strident tone or the way in which she fuses the values of cutthroat capitalism with fascistic philosophy and aesthetics. At the centre of all her musings stands the fiscally virile superman, towering over a godless world made in his image. This is couched in the literary equivalent of Nazi and Soviet paintings depicting, respectively, a muscle-bound chap sporting swastika insignia or a muscle-bound chap raising high the hammer and sickle. Replace those attributes with a wrench and a balance sheet, keeping every other detail intact, and Rand's clumsily painted picture will be complete. To reinforce the parallel, whenever Rand delivered herself of views on religion, she matched the hateful rhetoric of her diabolic contemporaries, such as Lenin and Stalin or Mussolini and Hitler. Nor did she defer to them in the hysterical pitch of her effluvia, except that she chose as the object of such outpourings the *übermensch* defined in economic terms, rather than those of race or class. No wonder Rand, having escaped from the Marxist hell of her nightmares, found herself so much at home in the economic paradise of her dreams.

Kirk's haughty disdain for modern democracy, particularly its innate egalitarianism and obsession with the economy, placed him in opposition to most strands of the American Right. It fell upon a magazine to try to weave them all together.

3

In 1955 a young American patrician William F. Buckley founded *National Review*, presented as a journal of conservative thought. That self-description was not quite accurate. For Buckley and his friends sought to fuse together, albeit under the aegis of traditionalism, various factions of the American Right. Specifically they sought to reconcile traditionalists, which is to say conservatives proper, with libertarians and neonatal neoconservatives.

Buckley himself variously described himself as either a conservative or a libertarian, carrying within his own breast the eclecticism plaguing the American Right. An excellent, idiosyncratic essayist, he wrote English with the kind of studied brilliance that to an expert analyst might have suggested this was not his first language. Indeed, as a child Buckley was educated mostly abroad and could speak French and Spanish before he received, at seven, any tuition in English. Later he also did a stint at an English public school, and this international upbringing both added a touch of British to his accent and inoculated him against the more virulent germs of American parochialism.

Buckley first came to national attention in 1951, when he published, with his brother-in-law Brent Bozell, the book *God and Man at Yale*, in which he attacked his *alma mater* for abandoning its founding principles. Since that university produced a great number of American leaders, Buckley's animadversions were rightly perceived as an attack on the American liberal establishment in general. In his student days Buckley (along with his two brothers and later his son) belonged to the inner sanctum of Yale, the secret quasi-Masonic society *Skull and Bones*, boasting among its membership many politicians. For example, three generations of the Bush family were members: the senator Prescott along with his son and grandson, both presidents. Interestingly, the 2004 presidential election was contested by two 'Boners', George W. Bush and John Kerry.

Buckley quickly turned *National Review* into perhaps the most sparkling conservative magazine ever. The simple rota of its editors and contributors speaks for itself: the Americans James Burnham, Frank Meyer, Russell Kirk, John Dos Passos, Jeffery Hart, Max Eastman, Whittaker Chambers, Joseph Sobran, Richard Neuhaus, Milton Friedman, Irving Kristol, Robert Nisbet, Willmoore Kendall, Tom Wolfe; the Brits Robert Conquest, W.H. Auden, Michael Oakeshott, Brian Crozier and John O'Sullivan; the Austrians Ludwig von Mises and Erik von Kuehnelt-Leddihn; the Dutchman Ernest van den Haag; the German Eric Voegelin...

Buckley also tried to recruit Evelyn Waugh, offering $5,000 for 25 articles a year, a higher fee than any of the others were getting (an equivalent of roughly $4,000 per article in today's funny money). Waugh, however, declined the offer in a most elegant letter of rejection: "I appreciate that in the circumstances your offer is a generous one, but until you get much richer (which I hope will be soon), or I get much poorer (which I fear may be sooner), I am unable to accept it."

It is notable that, the odd agnostic apart, most *NR* contributors were practising members of one of the apostolic confessions, Catholic, Episcopalian, High Anglican or Greek Orthodox.

DEFINING AND REFINING CONSERVATISM

Even some of those who started life within Protestant denominations, such as Russell Kirk and the Lutheran pastor Richard Neuhaus, eventually converted to Catholicism.

This is understandable for true conservatives feel at one with history; they place themselves within a much longer historical continuum than do those of different political persuasions. Their spiritual genesis dates back to the first century AD, rather than the sixteenth or especially the eighteenth. Because of this, and also because of its inherently revolutionary nature, they often feel ill-served by unflinching Protestantism. This is what John Henry Newman meant when writing that "To be deep in history is to cease to be a Protestant." Buckley himself was a pious Catholic, an enthusiastic supporter of the Tridentine mass and a bitter opponent of Vatican II. All this reemphasises the link between one's political, religious and cultural convictions.

Contrast Buckley's conservatism with the neoconservative fixation on the present. Lacking a clearly defined spot in the continuum of Western history, the neocons have no option other than believing that the historical dial is zeroed for every generation. Thus, for example, the novelist Saul Bellow, talking admiringly about his late friend Allan Bloom: "He didn't ask, 'Where will you spend eternity?' as religious the-end-is-near picketers did, but rather, 'With what, in this modern democracy, will you meet the demands of your soul?'." Good question. Alas, Bellow did not cite an equally good answer, possibly because none existed.

National Review may not have found the answer either, but at least it looked for one in all the right places. Hence it served for many years as an exhilarating, brilliantly written and influential primer of conservative thought. Many young, virginal minds, including my own, got their first whiff of intellectual conservatism from the magazine in its prime. But nothing in this world lasts for ever, and neither did the halcyon days of *National Review*. For the edifice the editors were trying to erect had structural defects that eventually produced deep cracks in the masonry.

4

Every serious political movement attracts its fair share of riffraff who end up giving it a bad name. That is why serious political thinkers and practitioners try, not always successfully, to dissociate themselves from extremist groups, correctly claiming that they do not belong in the mainstream of their movement. When such movements fail to do so, they invariably lose intellectual, moral and in due course political credibility.

Both Buckley's magazine, the flagship and focus of the conservative movement, and Buckley personally were rather successful in drawing such a line of demarcation. More so than, say, the British Labour Party, whose ranks are still generously peppered with barely reconstructed communists and CND survivals, or our Tory Right that frequently rubs shoulders with BNP types. Our rising political star UKIP would do well to remember the dangers of attracting undesirables. Faults in its vetting may let in BNP sympathisers and other quasi-fascists, which could besmirch not only the party itself but, by association, also the cause of national sovereignty it champions.

Not only was Buckley publicly contemptuous of the John Birch Society, along with similar extremist and nativist groups, but he also dealt ruthlessly even with his closest associates when they came up with racist or anti-Semitic statements. For example in 1993 he sacked Joseph Sobran, his Senior Editor and perhaps the most talented columnist, for publishing remarks in the style of our own dear David Irving.

Yet a close look at the list of *NR*'s major contributors will show an inordinately large number of former communists among them, many of recent provenance: James Burnham, Whittaker Chambers, Max Eastman, Brian Crozier, William Schlamm, John Dos Passos, Frank Meyer, Irving Kristol and quite a few others. Obviously Buckley neither felt ill at ease with such converts nor doubted their sincerity – one even gets the impression he went out of his way to welcome apostates from the hard Left.

In many ways he cannot be faulted for such omnivorism: Buckley and *NR* pursued not only intellectual truth but also political objectives. Their aim was to make conservatism appealing across the board, and for that they felt it was essential to bridge over as many political watersheds as possible. The magazine's original success testifies to the value of political compromise; the subsequent marginalisation of traditional conservatism testifies to the inherent dangers of political catholicity. One way or the other, it cannot be gainsaid that all those recently minted conservatives brought to the movement an awesome combination of intellectual brilliance and literary ability.

James Burnham, the magazine's co-founder and Senior Editor, is a case in point. Born in 1905, he became in the 1930s a famous Trotskyist publicist and propagandist, second in international stature only to his close friend Trotsky himself. In 1933 Burnham was the driving force behind the founding of the American Workers Party which the next year merged with The Communist League of America. In 1937 he left, together with the whole Trotskyist faction, to form The Socialist Workers Party whose guiding light he remained until 1940.

None of this CV points at Burnham's subsequent emergence as America's leading conservative thinker. Yet in the very next year, 1941, he published *The Managerial Revolution*. In this conservative classic Burnham displayed prophetic powers in charting the corporatist course on which global capitalism was embarking. He was also the first thinker of note to point out the numerous similarities among German Nazism, Soviet Communism and Roosevelt's New Deal. They all, according to Burnham, were characterised by the emergence of a new corporatist managerial elite, differing only in the speed and manner of replacing the ousted old classes with the new. In particular, he brought into focus the burgeoning separation of ownership and control in modern capitalism, which could eventually bring about its demise. Observing the state of today's global economy, it is hard to deny the prophetic nature of Burnham's thought.

Another key figure at *NR* was Whittaker Chambers, who went James Burnham one better by having been not only an American communist but also a Soviet spy. Inspired by Lenin's writings and especially impressed by their manly authoritar-

DEMOCRACY AS A NEOCON TRICK

ianism, Chambers, whose own masculinity was somewhat ambivalent, joined the Communist Party in 1925, aged 24. A lucid writer, he became one of the most influential contributors to *The Daily Worker* and other communist publications. In the 1930s Chambers joined a GRU[25] spy ring, also including some key figures of the New Deal government, mostly those employed in the AAA (Agricultural Adjustment Administration). Aware of the gruesome fate awaiting present and former Soviet spies who displayed symptoms of wavering, Chambers began to gather evidence on his fellow spies, hoping to use it as life-saving leverage should the worse come to the worst.

Chambers's Damascene conservative experience was brought on by the Soviet 1936–1938 purges of prominent communists, such as Zinoviev, Kamenev and Bukharin, that effectively wiped out Lenin's original party. Notably, the widely publicised slaughter of millions, which had been such an endearing feature of the Soviet regime from its inception, had had no such eye-opening effect on Chambers. The 1939 Soviet-Nazi Pact was the last straw, and Chambers shared with the FBI his suspicions, though not yet the hard evidence he had secreted away in a hollowed-out pumpkin. At about the same time he joined the staff of *Time Magazine*, where he soon became Senior Editor.

In 1948 Chambers was subpoenaed to testify before HUAC on the charges against Alger Hiss, who had risen to the rank of head of the UN Charter Committee. During that landmark hearing Chambers at first perjured himself by only claiming under oath that Hiss was a communist, while denying he was also a spy. However, after his old friend sued him for libel, Chambers was forced to produce the 'Pumpkin Papers'. Since the five-year statute of limitations for espionage had expired, Hiss was only convicted of perjury, a charge that could have been levelled against Chambers himself, but was not. He was now on the side of the angels.

In 1952 Chambers published his bestselling book *Witness*, which succeeded in converting many New Dealers, including

---

25　*Glavnoye Razvedovatelnoye Upravleniye* (Soviet military intelligence).

DEFINING AND REFINING CONSERVATISM

the jobbing B-actor Ronald Reagan, to the cause of anticommunism. In 1955 the former spy joined the staff of *NR*, to whose pages he went on to contribute many coruscating pieces, including a thorough demolition of Ayn Rand in a review of her awful novel *Atlas Shrugged*.

It was partly under the influence of Burnham, Frank Meyer and Chambers that Buckley turned *NR* into a church wide enough to accommodate many recent converts from communism, along with current exponents of other philosophies more or less adjacent to conservatism and yet distinct from it. This was a sincerely and generously offered embrace, but there was a kiss of death implicit in it – both for the magazine and for American conservatism.

Here I have to admit that my own feelings about political converts who espoused communism as mature adults are less magnanimous than Buckley's were. To explain why, I would like to go back to Lord Hailsham's definition of conservatism as an intuitive attitude, not so much a philosophy, much less an ideology. Earlier I described this as an essential but not a sufficient part of what goes into the makeup of a conservative. However if we accept that such an intuitive predisposition is indeed essential, it is not immediately clear how this can accommodate active membership in a communist party or even passive support of it.

Granted, until his mid-twenties a man's brain is not even wired properly, and even those endowed with innate conservative longings may not yet know how to relate them to specific philosophies or politics. Also, without wishing to overindulge in homespun psychology or physiology, one could still venture a guess that bubbling testosterone and the concomitant propensity for aggression may well lead a youngster to philosophies and movements favouring a violent reworking of government and indeed human nature. Later in life, when such a man, his mind now taking over from his gonads, begins to act true to his conservative nature, only an obtuse doctrinaire will hold his youthful indiscretions against him.

The situation is not quite so clear-cut when the man in question remains a communist well into his maturity. This is

215

DEMOCRACY AS A NEOCON TRICK

especially true if he is as richly blessed with cerebral power as Burnham or Chambers, both of whom saw the conservative light in their mid-thirties. When this is the case, one has to doubt they could indeed have passed the Hailsham test. Consequently one has to doubt the sincerity of their conversion – and look more closely at the net effect of their new activities.

Do let us spell out exactly what the likes of Burnham and Chambers had preached, and what kind of doctrine they had espoused, before the conservative lightning struck them on the road to their Marxist destination. These days one hears all sort of chaps with learning difficulties, some of them working for our major papers, carry on about Marxism being a beautiful theory later lamentably distorted by the Soviets.

That is a pity, for if more people had actually read the *Communist Manifesto* and other such texts one hopes there would be fewer innocents who believe that Marx's ideals were wonderful but regrettably unachievable; or else that Marx's theory was perverted by Soviet practice. In fact, Marx's ideals are unachievable precisely because they are so monstrous that even the Bolsheviks never quite managed to realise them fully, and not for any lack of trying.

For example, the *Manifesto* (along with other writings by both Marx and Engels), prescribes the nationalisation of all private property without exception. Even Stalin's Russia in the thirties fell short of that ideal. In fact, a good chunk, as much as 15 percent, of the Soviet economy was then in private hands (small agricultural holdings, repair shops, construction and other co-ops, some medical care, etc.). And people were allowed to own cottages, flats, the clothes on their backs, radio sets, dovecotes, tools – really, compared with Marx, Stalin begins to look like a humanitarian trying to get in touch with his feminine side.

Marx also insisted that family should be done away with, with women becoming communal property. Again, for all their efforts, Lenin and Stalin never quite managed to achieve this ideal either, much to the regret of those who could see an amorous pay-off in such an arrangement. Then, according to the *Manifesto*, children were to be taken away from their parents, pooled together and raised by the state as its wards (echoes of

DEFINING AND REFINING CONSERVATISM

Plato there). That too remained a dream for the Bolsheviks who tried to make it a reality by forcing both parents to work and leaving no place for their children to go but the state-owned crèches, kindergartens and young pioneers' camps. But that was as far as it went: kindergartens and young pioneers' camps were not compulsory, and those fortunate women who could get by without full-time employment were still free to read Pushkin to their children.

Modern slave labour, such an arresting feature of both Soviet Russia and Nazi Germany, also derives from Marx – and again Lenin, Stalin and Hitler displayed a great deal of weak-kneed liberalism in bringing his ideas to fruition. Marx, after all, wrote about *total* militarisation of labour achieved by organising it into 'labour armies,' presumably led by Marx as Generalissimo and Engels as Chief of the General Staff. Stalin came closer to this than Hitler, but again fell short. No more than 10 percent of Soviets were ever in forced labour at the same time. The rest could still more or less choose their professions, and for some it was even possible to choose their place of employment.

One aspect of Bolshevism and Nazism that came close to fulfilling the Marxist dream was what Engels described as 'specially guarded places' to contain aristocrats, intelligentsia, clergy and other 'noxious insects', in Lenin's heartfelt phrase. Such places have since acquired a different name, but in essence they are exactly what Marx and Engels envisaged. Here Lenin and Stalin did come close to fulfilling the Marxist prescription, but they were again found wanting in spreading concentration camps to a mere half of the world. So where the Bolsheviks and Nazis perverted Marxism, they generally did so in the direction of softening it.

Genocidal or ideological mass murder, another cannibalistic outrage widely practised by both the Nazis and the Soviets, also derives from the teachings of Marx and Engels. Here are a few quotations from their works to give you a taste of this beautiful theory supposedly perverted by the dastardly Bolsheviks:

> "All the other [non-Marxist] large and small nationalities and peoples are destined to perish before long in the revolu-

217

tionary holocaust. For that reason they are now counter-revolutionary... these residual fragments of peoples always become fanatical standard-bearers of counter-revolution and remain so until their complete extirpation or loss of their national character... [A general war will] wipe out all this racial trash."

"In history nothing is achieved without violence and implacable ruthlessness... In short, it turns out these 'crimes' of the Germans and Magyars against the said Slavs are among the best and most praiseworthy deeds which our and the Magyar people can boast in their history."

"...only by the most determined use of terror against these Slav peoples can we, jointly with the Poles and Magyars, safeguard the revolution... there will be a struggle, an 'inexorable life-and-death struggle', against those Slavs who betray the revolution; an annihilating fight and ruthless terror – not in the interests of Germany, but in the interests of the revolution!"

"We have no compassion and we ask no compassion from you. When our turn comes, we shall not make excuses for the terror."

The Marxist perpetrators of the terror in the twentieth century indeed proffered no excuses when their turn came – this was done by their Western acolytes, many of whom operated under discipline imposed by either the Comintern or, as in the case of Chambers, Soviet intelligence services. 'Either... or' is perhaps an inaccurate turn of phrase since in practice the line separating the Comintern from the NKVD (precursor of the KGB) was so blurred as to be nonexistent. Lenin, after all, did explain that "every communist is a Chekist",[26] and that maxim applied internationally as well as domestically.

Hence people like Burnham and Chambers were intuitively

---

26 From CheKa (*Chrezvychainaya Komissiya*), a precursor of the KGB/FSB

DEFINING AND REFINING CONSERVATISM

attracted not to conservatism but to the most cannibalistic theory in history. Moreover, they were doctrinally obliged to regard as praiseworthy the practice of that theory in the Soviet Union, where millions had been murdered and countless other millions enslaved by the time our dynamic duo joined the communist ranks. Nor could they, highly literate and erudite intellectuals, claim ignorance of those crimes: a whole library of books had by then been produced by eyewitnesses, such as the prominent Russian historian Sergei Melgunov.

His book *The Red Terror*, translated into most European languages and published in the West in 1924 when Lenin was still alive, documents thousands of instances of such niceties as skinning people alive, rolling them around in nail-studded barrels, driving nails into people's skulls, quartering, burning alive, crucifying priests, stuffing officers alive into locomotive furnaces, pouring molten pitch or liquefied lead down people's throats. All this went on against the background of mass shootings that in the first five years of Soviet rule, under Lenin's watch, dispatched almost two million in a quasi-judicial way, and millions on top of that without even a travesty of justice. Artificially created famines claiming the lives of millions of Russian and Ukrainian peasants, who were too slow to recognise the glory of collectivised agriculture, were also widely reported throughout the West (by Malcolm Muggeridge among others).

This was the regime that Western communists, such as Burnham, Meyer and Chambers, admired, pledged loyalty to and wished to spread globally. This means they had to believe that murdering and enslaving millions was a fair price to pay for the triumph of their cherished doctrine. Since they persisted in this as mature and highly accomplished adults, it is a safe assumption that they were not innately predisposed to conservatism – especially since, as Marxists, they had to be not just atheists but visceral haters of Christianity or any other religion.

Can a man of that ilk convert to conservatism genuinely and sincerely? The only plausible answer to that question is no – unless, and this is an important proviso, the political conversion was precipitated by the religious kind. If we accept that it is not

219

a man who chooses God but God who chooses the man, then the gift of faith can arrive spontaneously and unexpectedly, as it did to so many scriptural figures, including Saul of Tarsus who until then had been persecuting Christians with unwavering zeal. On some occasions it may take a man years to realise that he has received the gift and to accept it, the slow pace of discovery usually being due to artificial obstacles erected either by his mind or the circumstances of his life.

Whether a man turns to the West's formative faith instantly or slowly, when he does do so the faith becomes an important factor of his life, often the most important one. When this happens to a powerful thinker, he has to reconcile his religion with his thought. If his grasp of history is secure, his logic intact and his honesty unimpeachable, he will have to realise that conservatism is the only political philosophy that can comfortably coexist with Christianity in the same breast.

Actually Chambers did claim that his path to conservatism had been lit by a religious conversion, and one has to take him at his word. A man of his mind and sensitivity could well have experienced a political conversion as a result, and indeed it would have been surprising had he not done so. But Burnham and most other recent communists working for *NR* neither had a similar religious experience nor even claimed to have had one. Burnham, though raised as a Roman Catholic, left the faith as a youngster and never returned to it until the last days of his life (not an uncommon occurrence).

Another former communist apparatchik, the prominent philosopher Frank Meyer who exerted a strong influence on Buckley and *NR*, also waited until his deathbed to convert to Catholicism. Meyer was the author of the philosophy of 'fusionism', an attempt to blend traditional conservatism with other intellectual strands of the Right, especially libertarianism, to present a united front against the dominant 'liberal' ethos.[27] All the ex-communists on the *NR* staff were enthusi-

---

27   I often put 'liberal', especially in an American context, in quotation commas because its chief desideratum, increasing the power of the state at the expense of the individual, is the exact opposite of real liberalism.

astic champions of fusionism and claimed it was a resounding success, as they would.

In fact, by diluting the philosophy of conservatism with foreign and largely alien additives, ex-communist converts made it vulnerable to usurpation by the more dynamic elements within the eclectic mix of the American Right. Such a takeover has happened to so many political movements as to suggest that it is hard to avoid.

For example the Russian socialist movement also sought reconciliation with its most extreme heretical faction, the Bolsheviks, only to be taken over by them in short order. Similarly, in their struggle against the Left, Weimar conservatives initially looked for allies among the Nazis, only to end up in exile if they were lucky or with piano wire around their necks if they were not.[28] In the same vein traditional American conservatives were eventually marginalised by the most aggressive proselytisers of the American religion, the neocons.

Interestingly, both conservative 'fusionists' and the original neocons were led not just by any old ex-communists but mainly by former Trotskyists, adherents of the most internationalist and radical wing of the communist party. In an odd sort of way, Trotsky's cherished doctrine of 'permanent revolution', incessant war against Christendom, struck a chord with the proselytising, evangelical aspect of the American religion and even more so with the interventionist impulses of neoconservatism. That is why the two philosophies have since blended so neatly.

Also it was psychologically easier for a Trotskyist than for a Stalinist to switch allegiance from communism to anticommunism: a Trotskyist was already at odds with Stalin's Soviet Union, the paymaster of the international hard Left. Throughout the late 1920s and 1930s Trotsky was the world's most strident and vociferous critic of both the Soviet Union

---

28   Friedrich Percival Reck-Malleczewen was among the unlucky ones. The conservative author of *Diary of a Man in Despair*, a moving account of life in Germany under the Nazis, he was shot in Dachau a few months before the end of the war.

and Stalin personally. It was Trotsky who set the terms of the anti-Stalinist debate, the one in which the closing argument was in 1940 delivered with an ice axe.

These days, while Leninism is largely regarded as anachronistic, Trotskyism is still alive and kicking. France, for example, has two Trotskyist parties exerting a powerful influence on policy, particularly when the socialists are in power. Only internal bickering prevents them from uniting and contesting elections with a realistic hope of some success.

5

An American correspondent of mine recently replied to my laments by stating, correctly, that neither America nor Britain has had a truly conservative government for at least a century, perhaps longer. As it was only a short letter, she made no connection between that observation and the nature of modern democracy, but it is an obvious one.

The period in question coincided in time with the triumph, indeed appearance, of democracy as defined by Freedom House. This points not just to a temporal, *post hoc ergo propter hoc* overlap but a causal relationship, raising doubts about compatibility between conservatism and unchecked one-man-one-vote democracy. That is of course the only type recognised as legitimate by the neocons and other exponents of the American religion.

Here again Lord Hailsham's definition comes in handy, especially if juxtaposed with Russell Kirk's Decalogue of conservatism. For neither the intuitive predisposition as stressed by Hailsham nor the Burkean prescription, prudence and prejudice as revived by Kirk can possibly inspire the set of qualities required for electoral success under unlimited democracy. This was recognised by even such variously fervent champions of democracy as Tocqueville before Hailsham or his contemporaries Russell Kirk and Irving Kristol, the founder of neoconservatism.

I shall talk about Kristol in detail later, but here he is, decorticating democracy in a way that ought to have nipped his neocon passions in the bud, but oddly did not: "In a democracy all politicians are, to some degree, demagogues: They appeal to people's prejudices and passions, they incite their expectations by making reckless promises, they endeavour to ingratiate themselves with the electorate in every possible way... The status of men and women as consumers of economic goods is taken to be more significant than their status as participants in the creation of political goods."

This quotation shows a number of things, not least that the original neocons were still capable of incisive thinking on politics, even though this ability was as a rule overridden by their ideology. Hence they were also capable of glaring contradictions, leaving the door wide open for the next generation of neocons, made up of those considerably less endowed intellectually and more impassioned ideologically.

What is left in no doubt is that successful democratic politicians, as described so fittingly by Kristol, cannot be drawn from a pool of men who are as intuitively predisposed towards conservatism as Hailsham postulated, or as devoted to fundamental conservative principles as Kirk considered essential. Putting it simply, a true conservative cannot win elections in today's West.

This is not to say that successful politicians cannot add to their bag of rhetorical tricks a few verbal flourishes picked from the conservative repertoire. They can and they do – in fact frequent references to highly commendable things like free enterprise and sound fiscal policies have become *de rigueur* for any candidate for public office, regardless of his personal beliefs, party affiliation or actual plans.

But rhetoric belongs to the political games played in the virtual world ruled by simulacrum; it is action that is real life. And no politician who miraculously manages to keep his conservative instincts under wraps long enough to be elected will be allowed to act on these instincts. The very presence of such a politician on the electoral rolls would indeed be a miracle: modern political parties are good at vetting, and their olfactory sense is of bloodhound acuity.

NR actively pursued political objectives, while at the same time acting as the vanguard of intellectual conservatism in public life. Therein lies an inherent problem for any publication, or for that matter individual, whose function in life is to formulate and communicate a certain political philosophy and then to act on it.

A political philosopher seeks intellectual truth; a democratic politician seeks electoral success. The two desiderata are more nearly opposite than the same – even Plato knew that his dream of a philosopher king was just that, a dream. And Plato only ever spoke of philosopher *kings*, not philosopher MPs or congressmen.

Conversely a political philosopher is not after broad appeal and indeed would be frustrated if he tried to court it: truth is not widely accessible to all men, which is yet another area in which they are demonstrably not created equal. On the other hand, a politician could not remain in politics unless he could command wide support. Hence when a publication (or an individual) attempts to hit the birds of intellectual rectitude and political success with one stone, both will fly away chirping a merry song.

NR eventually discovered the truth of this observation empirically, even though in the short term it defied the odds by doing well in both areas. Acting in the political arena while Buckley was still at the helm, the magazine endorsed five presidential candidates: Eisenhower in 1956, Goldwater in 1964, Nixon in 1968, Ashbrook in 1972 and Reagan in 1976. Of these only Goldwater and Reagan, who both lost, drew the magazine's enthusiastic support rather than just formal endorsement. The others were supported grudgingly because they were correctly perceived to be the lesser evil.

Acting as intellectual inspiration for Barry Goldwater was his speechwriter Harry Jaffa, expert on Lincoln and Buckley's close friend, who had found a publishing haven at *NR* after being ostracised by 'liberal' and neocon publications. As it turned out, Jaffa's talent for spiffy phrasemaking contributed to Goldwater's landslide loss of the presidential election. Delivering his acceptance speech at the Republican National Convention, Goldwater lip-synched Jaffa's masterpiece: "Extremism in the

DEFINING AND REFINING CONSERVATISM

defence of liberty is no vice and moderation in the pursuit of justice is not a virtue."[29]

Since the leftwing press, which is to say the press, was already running cartoons of Goldwater toting nuclear bombs under a big mushroom in the sky, the line of attack became clear: the Republican candidate was a war-mongering extremist. The aphorism has had a long shelf life, and even today's political candidates of the Left occasionally repeat it as proof of their opponents being dangerous madmen.

Yet neither Goldwater nor Jaffa was a true conservative in my (also Hailsham's and Kirk's) understanding of the word. In fact, in his dispute with Irving Kristol, which effectively barred Jaffa's subsequent access to the increasingly influential neocon press, it was the former who came closer to enunciating the conservative position.

The two disagreed on the significance, indeed virtue, of the Declaration of Independence, which Kristol correctly identified as an egalitarian Enlightenment construct. "To perceive the true purposes of the American Revolution," wrote Kristol, "it is wise to ignore some of the more grandiloquent declamations of the moment", by which he specifically meant the Declaration's pronouncement that "all men are created equal".

Jaffa, on the other hand, belied his (and vicariously Goldwater's) conservative credentials by extolling such anticonservative Jacobins among the Founding Fathers as Paine and Jefferson. He defended the very egalitarianism that comes close to being the exact opposite of conservatism: "One must understand that the East Coast Straussians of which he [Kristol] was one viewed the American Founding – or at least its natural rights rhetoric – as flawed. They defend the constitutionalism of the founding, strictly construed, and grounded in a slow-moving tradition, *sans* the natural rights of the Declaration of Independence."

In other words the conservative Jaffa accused the neocon Kristol of defending conservative principles, if only in

---

29 Jaffa was also capable of witty remarks, such as the one in reference to the materialist philosopher Ludwig Feuerbach, "We were baptised in the Jordan, not in the fiery brook."

relation to the Declaration. This sort of confusion is not only widespread but unavoidable in a democratic republic begotten by revolution: its founding tenets leave little leeway for true, clearly defined political conservatism. In such a republic conservatism has no future because it has no past.

Kristol also made a few critical remarks about Thomas Paine, an Englishman who, according to him, never properly understood America. Jaffa retorted by citing the fact that Paine had toted a musket in the battle of Trenton, and what further proof of his understanding America could one possibly need? To see a self-admitted neocon and a self-professed conservative finding themselves on these sides of an argument about Thomas Paine is like seeing a football player come out for the second half of the match wearing the opponents' strip.

For if there ever was a man who denied every conservative principle with every word he uttered and every step he took, it was Paine, one of the most pernicious demagogues the Enlightenment produced, and the list of aspiring candidates is long. Correctly identifying its hostility to Christianity as the driving force of his beloved Enlightenment, Paine published in 1793 the pamphlet *The Age of Reason*, in which he attacked not just Christianity but religion in general. For example Genesis was to Paine "nothing... but an anonymous book of stories, fables, traditionary or invented absurdities, or downright lies." As to Christianity, Paine considered it "a history of wickedness that has served to corrupt and brutalise mankind."

Though an Englishman, Paine took part in both American and French revolutions, and not just as an advocate but also as a hands-on perpetrator.[30] In the former capacity, he defended the American Revolution in his bestselling pamphlet *Common Sense* (1776), while extolling the French version in *Rights of Man* (1791). This much-travelled gentleman indeed treasonously fought on the insurgents' side in the revolutionary war and

---

30 Jefferson too was a hands-on man. Serving as American minister in France, he actively plotted with the revolutionaries, especially Lafayette. Acting in that demonstrably undiplomatic fashion, he influenced the language of the Declaration of the Rights of Man, which as a result bears an uncanny resemblance to the American Declaration of Independence.

subsequently also played an active role in France's revolutionary politics. Though unable to speak French, he was even elected to the National Assembly in 1792.

In his *Rights of Man* Paine attacked Burke's seminal work *Reflections on the Revolution in France* and, for good measure, Burke personally. As a result, he was tried and convicted *in absentia* for seditious libel against the man American conservatives still regard as their spiritual father. That a supposed conservative like Harry Jaffa would admire a man like Thomas Paine is unthinkable, or rather would be to anyone unaware of the intellectual confusion reigning on the American Right.

Yet Jaffa's argument that Paine understood America well was justified, if not the way Jaffa meant it. Unlike Burke, Paine sensed the organic link between the French and American revolutions, and indeed among various strands of the Enlightenment, be it French, German, Scottish or Anglo-American. For all their individual differences, there was an umbilical cord linking, say, Hume and Smith, Kant and Hegel or Diderot and Voltaire with one another and contemporaneous revolutionaries everywhere – their weapons differed, but the target they saw in their sights was the same. They all represented a revolt against every tenet and tradition of Christendom and, their personal accomplishments apart, the only differences lay in the area of tactics and rhetoric. Thus for example Kant, extolling the French Revolution: "…this revolution finds in the heart of all observers the kind of sympathy that borders on enthusiasm." (Obviously Burke's *Reflections* was not on Kant's reading list.)

One can only surmise what policies Goldwater, with Jaffa as his advisor, would have adopted as president. The subjunctive mood is not a productive grammatical category in either politics or history, but reasonably informed guesses can still be ventured. In all likelihood Goldwater's presidency would have combined conservative rhetoric and egalitarian action, the usual mélange one finds among today's 'conservative' politicians of the West. There would have been no room for traditional conservatism there, and in fact Jaffa frequently debated against the true conservatives in the ranks of *NR*, such as Russell Kirk, Richard Weaver and Willmoore Kendall.

DEMOCRACY AS A NEOCON TRICK

A useful clue to what might have been is provided by another intellectual child of *NR*, Ronald Reagan, who eventually was elected president in 1980. In fact, after his inauguration he asked his friend and mentor Buckley what position he would like in the Reagan administration, to which the witty writer replied, "Ventriloquist".[31] Reagan actually joined the Republican party as late as in 1962. Having been a unionist New Deal Democrat most of his life, he only began to inch towards the Right in the 1950s, under the initial influence of Chambers's book *Witness*.

Reagan came to Washington preaching such conservative goals as reducing government expenditure and slashing public debt. However, when he left eight years later the federal debt stood at roughly three times greater than he had found it. The size of government had also grown. Similarly, our own sainted Margaret Thatcher actually increased the size of the state, which she ostensibly was committed to rolling back. Neither politician can be blamed for this, at least not very strongly.

Unchecked democracy has its own ineluctable logic and leaves little room for true, Christendom-inspired conservatism in economics, politics, culture or social life. The conflict between the two is structural and eternal, which is why any original conservative intentions, even if sincerely held, will eventually go the way of all flesh once the politician finds himself in power.

---

31 Unlike his brother James who became a US senator, Buckley disdained practical politics. He did run for mayor of New York in 1965, but his aim was not to win but to find a public forum for enunciating the conservative position. When asked during the campaign what he would do if he won, Buckley famously replied, "Demand a recount."

Reality mugged by 'liberals'

1

The term 'neoconservatism' was only coined in 1973, but the underlying notion had at the time existed for at least a decade and probably closer to two. The socialist Michael Harrington, the inventor of the word, meant it as a putdown mainly describing Irving Kristol and Daniel Patrick Moynihan, but Kristol, credited by *Esquire* as 'the godfather of neoconservatism', picked the term up and ran with it.

Irving Kristol (1920–2009), a clever man and good writer, nonetheless reflected both in his work and his person the ungainly mess of American politics, particularly its Right end. "I regard myself as lucky to have been a young Trotskyist," wrote Kristol, making an inquisitive reader wonder if he would have counted himself equally lucky had the word Trotskyist been replaced with its exact equivalent: 'enthusiast for the murder of millions in pursuit of a hare-brained utopia'. Probably, considering how his legacy is interpreted by today's neocons.

Kristol proudly regarded his own political background as eclectic, though in fact it was not: "I have been a neo-Marxist, a neo-Trotskyist, a neosocialist, a neoliberal, and finally, a neoconservative." Kristol's emotional makeup made him unable to realise that all these 'neos' were different facets of the same thing: consistent rejection of the political heritage of Christendom with all its doctrinal, philosophical and cultural manifestations. In general, when a man's convictions resemble a weathervane over his lifetime, in most instances the body of his thought never changes – it just gets to wear different clothes.

Kristol's belated rebellion against communism and its

Trotskyist offshoots led him to what largely passed for conservatism in the United States at the time, but was in fact merely a rejection of the bloodier manifestations of modernity rather than of its anomic essence. In that he followed the path trodden by the *NR* staffers mentioned earlier and also by many intellectual communist apostates from other countries, such as Arthur Koestler, Ignazio Silone, Roger Garaudy, Malcolm Muggeridge *et al.*

The path thus lit up, Kristol's writing ability, organisational talent and bubbling personality led him to a successful career in journalism and publishing. In 1953 he co-founded (with Stephen Spender) the British magazine *Encounter*, which was for many years justly regarded as the world's most influential anticommunist publication. Eventually the hard-Left American magazine *Ramparts* blew the whistle on the CIA funding of *Encounter*, predictably ruining its reputation among the educated, which is to say predominantly leftwing, establishment. Said establishment could close its eyes to the sources of funding for *Ramparts* itself, a transparent Soviet front, but any association with Western intelligence was unforgivable.

When the Soviet Union 'collapsed' (the reasons for the quotation marks will be made clear later), *Encounter* was deprived of a *raison d'être*, or at least one that its backers considered worth pursuing. The magazine went out of business, and in a way the same may be said about the *faux* conservatism then prevalent in the West. Unlike true conservatism that is based on a clear understanding of what it is for, the *soi disant* conservatives were mostly defined by what they were against. Once the irritant was supposedly removed, so was their motivation. Or rather it was channelled into new areas consistent with the American religion but having little in common with conservatism.

From then on Kristol was associated with the American Enterprise Institute and devoted more time to writing his essays, many on politics but mostly on cultural and religious subjects. These were later put together in two collections, *Reflections of a Neoconservative: Looking Back, Looking Ahead* and *Neoconservatism: The Autobiography of an Idea*, which are still revered as scriptural texts by today's neocons.

It was Kristol who first defined neoconservatives as 'liberals mugged by reality', a spiffy phrase that, in common with many other epigrammatic aphorisms, sacrificed content for form. For every word in that definition, apart from the preposition 'by', is untrue. To begin with, the first generation of neocons, those who started and defined the movement more or less as it remains today, did not come from a liberal background. This irrespective of whether we use the term in its traditional meaning or in the perverse one currently favoured in America, where liberalism describes what in Europe is called social democracy, or socialism for short.

Instead the political minds and souls of the first neocons were weaned on the extreme extensions of socialism: Marxism and Bolshevism, especially Trotskyism. These have about as much in common with liberalism as cannibalism has with vegetarianism. Even social democrats, though they share many credal premises with Trotskyists and other communists, rightly regard them as bloodthirsty heretics. In their new incarnation the neocons were heretics too – to conservatism, which term they usurped, perverted and modified with a prefix. Just like the worst Christian heresies, the neocons presented a far greater menace to the original creed than any threat coming from those who overtly put themselves in opposition to it.

'Reality', in the sense in which Kristol used the word, did have something to do with the real world but it was only an infinitesimal part of it. It would be fairer to say that it was the neocons who mugged reality, not vice versa. Actually, a stress on a part at the expense of the whole is a good definition of heresy. The Greek word *hairesis* implies a choice, inclination towards one thing, which then forms a distinct view of the world. This can act as the starting point for a political party, religious sect or philosophical school.

In laying the foundations of his conservative heresy, Kristol followed a path well-trodden by other heretics, both religious and political. They do not reject the entirety of the doctrine from which they break away – they simply pervert it to death by picking out some of its aspects and relegating others either to the margins or to perdition. This inevitably destroys the balance on which the doctrine rests and, unless the heresy is defeated, the original faith dies.

The Arians, for example, called themselves Christians (not being as clever as Kristol they did not choose 'neo-Christians' instead) and indeed they accepted almost every Christian tenet with one tiny exception: the Incarnation and hence the essence of Christ as fully God and fully man. In this way they tried to rip the Trinitarian heart out of the religion, which could have had catastrophic consequences. Had Arius scored a victory at the Council of Nicaea in 325 AD, within a century at most Christianity would have ceased to exist as anything other than a small sect.

Islam, another Christian heresy, followed exactly the same route marked with many of the same signposts. It happily accepted some of the key postulates of Christianity: one omnipotent and omniscient God, God as the creator of the universe, God who loves mankind, personal immortality, the righteous being rewarded and the wicked punished in afterlife. Similarly to Arianism, Islam even enlisted Jesus Christ as a great prophet. What Islam denied was the divinity of Christ and therefore the key premise of the Christian civilisation. As a result it became the deadliest enemy Christendom has ever had, a capacity in which it continues with renewed vigour to this day.

Closer to my theme, Thomas Jefferson was a classic example of a heretic. He too called himself a Christian – with a minor exception or two: he loathed the mysteries, sacraments and miracles of Christianity, including the Virgin Birth, the Resurrection and the Eucharist. Jefferson's primitive rationalist mind refused to accept anything for which his senses could not provide forensic proof. He even went so far as to clip all the offensive passages out of the Gospels, converting it to his personal scripture. The same trick was later used on a larger scale by Leo Tolstoy, who took the trouble of rewriting all four Gospels and fusing them into one, in which nothing supernatural was retained.

Even closer to my theme, *mutatis mutandis* Bolshevism, Nazism and New Dealism were all socialist heresies, united in their common approach to the economy and their equally strong commitment to the primacy of a giant central state. Stalin's Five-Year Plan, Hitler's New Order and Roosevelt's New Deal bear such startling similarity to one another that one might think they were written by the same men. In fact the last two largely were.

One such transatlantic author was Gerard Swopes of General Electric, a company that distinguished itself by assisting both the Bolsheviks and the Nazis. Swopes more or less formulated Roosevelt's New Deal policy while sitting on the board of A.E.G., the German subsidiary of General Electric and a major backer of Hitler. Another busy programme designer was Paul Warburg of the Federal Reserve Bank of New York who was on the board of the American I. G. Farben, while his brother Max sat on the German board of the same company. And then there was Walter Teagle, also of the Federal Reserve Bank of New York, Chairman of Standard Oil of New Jersey, the company whose German subsidiary *Deutsche-Amerikanische Gesellschaft* had intimate links with the Nazis. This known Nazi sympathiser was one of the principal authors of FDR's New Deal package and also acted as economic consultant to the authors of Hitler's New Order.

Incidentally, Hitler readily acknowledged his indebtedness to Marxism in private, even as he attacked it in public. Hermann Rauschning, who renounced his Nazi Party membership in 1934 but until then had known Hitler well, recalls in his memoir *Hitler Speaks* the führer saying that "the whole of National Socialism" was based on Marx. "I have learned a great deal from Marx," conceded Hitler, "as I do not hesitate to admit."

What I describe as the rule by simulacrum is a classic stratagem of heretical practices. The heretics retain, or rather pretend to retain, some of the key doctrinal aspects and much of the terminology of the creed they in effect seek to undermine. However, they feign dismay over some unfortunate corruption of the original religion, which allegedly either compromises its purity or perhaps makes it unappealing to sufficiently high numbers. Thankfully the heretics are there to set things right.

The 'reality' by which Kristol claimed to have been 'mugged' was, in the good heretical tradition, carefully chosen. At the heart of it lay the basic New Deal assumptions largely informed by the statist economic theory of John Maynard Keynes. It could not have been otherwise in view of Kristol's global vision I quoted earlier: "The United States wishes to establish and sustain a world order that... encourages other nations... to mould their own social, political and economic institutions along lines that are at least not repugnant... to American values." Replace 'the United States' with 'the Soviet Union', 'American' with 'communist', and the formative influences on Kristol's thought shine through.

Only a powerful central state can undertake the mission of establishing and sustaining a world order of any kind, and the more powerful the central state the more likely it will be to succeed in the short term (any such attempt is doomed to failure in the long run). Keynes's economics, which his opponent Joseph Schumpeter described as "childish vision", is custom-made for such empowerment: it puts the nation's finances, including the personal wealth of its citizens, at the mercy of the state.

By manipulating the money supply as it sees fit and rejecting the notion of paying its own way at any time other than possibly during an economic glut, the state effectively determines the value of the money and property earned or owned by individuals. Coupled with confiscatory taxes inevitably extorted from the public by a Keynesian state, this gives the ruling elite total control over 'happiness', effectively the *raison d'être* of liberal democracy. This elite starts out worshipping at the altar of property consecrated by (St) John Locke and ends up befouling it – proving that its idol has been false all along.

While allowing the state to control 'happiness', such a *carte blanche* to extortion also has a vast potential for making 'happiness' considerably less happy, thereby undermining the state's own claim to legitimacy. That is why some democratic justification of dispossession is essential for a modern state committed to creating an illusion of governing, and hence expropriating, by public consent. The alternative simply would not work. When the state abandons even the veneer of consensual government and instead begins to rely on sheer violence so beloved of Lenin, Trotsky and Stalin, it reduces the whole population to the kind of hellhole penury that no modern philistine nation will countenance.

This was precisely the 'reality' that 'mugged' Kristol and his friends. They felt that, by spreading an American-style New Deal democracy, the utopian 'world order' they craved could be brought about more quickly and surely than by advancing the Trotskyist ideal they had espoused hitherto. They regarded as more promising a state operating Keynesian-democratic rather than Marxist-violent levers of control – in effect a state practising socialism minus the concentration camps. That is why for Kristol "...the democratic idea is the only legitimising political idea of our era." True enough, 'the democratic idea' can indeed legitimise anything. It did, for example, legitimise Hitler along with the post-war 'People's Democracies', but such minor glitches have never been allowed to interfere with the overall neocon vision.

Promiscuous government spending, which invariably accompanies the workings of a Keynesian state, is custom-made not only for the 'liberals' (overt socialists) but also for the neocons (crypto-socialists). On the one hand it vastly increases state power without the government having to rely on violent coercion. On the other hand it creates an illusion of 'happiness' by deferring the time when the penny drops with the force of a blockbuster and the whole pyramid scheme of state finances crashes down.

At this writing, as a direct result of her practising Keynesian economics for decades, the USA is bankrupt in the precise sense of the word: her liabilities exceed her assets. America's $16.7-trillion debt now stands at 73 percent of annual GDP, not counting internal debts, such as the depleted trust funds feeding Social Security and Medicare. According to the Congressional Budget Office, the debt is on course to reach 93 percent within 10 years and nearly 200 percent in 25 years. Only Weimar-style hyperinflation would then be able to manage the debt, but that treatment would be even worse than the disease.

The neocons do not mind. A payoff will come later, whereas they feel that their political aims can be achieved soon. This kind of mindset is boosted by their rejection of Christendom with its notion of an integral link tying together generations past, present and future. True conservatives will exercise fiscal prudence partly because they abhor the thought of saddling future generations with a ruinous debt. Neoconservatives do not even think in those terms – like all utopian ideologues they deem no sacrifice, present or future, too great to fast-forward the advent of what Kristol and a few nastier political thinkers called 'the new order'.

Hence the neocons' hostility to traditional conservatism, even in its rather diluted *NR* form. "The only existing conservative journal, the *National Review*," writes Kristol, "was not to our taste [for being] too stridently hostile to the course of American politics ever since 1932." That is, hostile to the New Deal. Kristol also talks with derision about "Goldwater's campaign against the New Deal, with which none of us had any sympathy." That is why "...in 1964, only a few neoconservatives supported Barry Goldwater while the rest of us went along with Hubert Humphrey." Kristol evidently saw no contradiction in professing what he tried to pass for conservative values while at the same time supporting socialist candidates for high political office.

The next generation of the neocons live off this legacy. Thus they supported Clinton against Bush ("On what I care about – human rights and promoting democracy... – Clinton is more amenable than Bush," wrote COLLENE) and elevated to secular sainthood Henry 'Scoop' Jackson, Democratic senator from Washington State. Jackson's voting record over a lifetime in Congress was consistently egalitarian and statist, which is to say socialist. However, Boeing was the biggest employer in the state whose interests it was Jackson's remit to serve. He thus had a hawkish attitude to military spending and, laudably, to the Soviet Union. As a sole qualification, this falls short of a claim to conservatism, but not to the 'neo' variety. Thus the neocon think tank in Britain proudly bears Jackson's name.

Irving Kristol also presaged Barack Obama, America's most socialist president, by advocating "some form of national health insurance", which he equated with progress. In fact, since some of Obama's reforms began to be applied, the cost of medical care in the United States predictably has risen by a third. No doubt Kristol would not let such minor incidentals cloud his vision had he lived to see the day. After all, nationalising healthcare, partly or wholly, means transferring more power to the state, which fits into the neocon ideology. Like all heretics, neither Kristol nor his followers would ever own up to their true aims. The neocons supposedly do not set out to supplant conservatism – their claim is that they only wish to extend its reach: "By enlarging the conservative vision to include moral philosophy, political philosophy and even religious thought, [neoconservatism] helped make it more politically sensible as well as politically appealing."

The underlying assumption is that until Irving Kristol accepted the burden of clarifying "the conservative vision" it had lacked any grounding in "moral philosophy, political philosophy and even religious thought". A reader not trained in the neocon lingo would be perplexed. A roll call of great conservative thinkers, some of whom I have mentioned quite a few times in these pages, would flash through his mind. How could Kristol say that? this reader would wonder.

For his benefit allow me to translate from neocon into English: true conservatism had refused to espouse rampant hedonism springing from totalitarian economism ("moral philosophy"), the primacy of the omnipotent central state ruling by fictional consent ("political philosophy") and aggressive atheism ("religious thought"). In other words, conservatism stubbornly insisted on staying conservative – something the neocons sought to correct by first destroying it and then gaining political victories in its name.

2

For someone who devoted much of his time to writing about religion and culture, Kristol had only a superficial grasp of both (which is still more than most of today's neocons possess). This is understandable, for these fields were clearly subordinate to the main interest of his life: hastening the advent of the neoconservative 'new order'.

Hence such annoying lapses as his referring to "...the Enlightenment dogma that 'the truth will make men free'." That he could not cite the actual source of the phrase chapter and verse (John 8: 32, as it happens) is forgivable in someone who as a child received a largely secular Jewish education.[32] What is unfortunate in a man writing extensively on religious subjects is that he was not even vaguely aware of the scriptural provenance of the phrase, nor had enough sense to realise how contrary to the spirit of the Enlightenment the phrase was. What was supposed to make men free according to Enlightenment demagoguery was not the truth coming from the omnipotent, omniscient, omnipresent God but action by the omnipotent, omniscient, omnipresent state.

But then Kristol does lament that "The New Left... comes more and more to resemble the Old Right, which never did accept the liberal-bourgeois revolutions of the 18th and 19th centuries." Presumably this is supposed to mean that, while true conservatives opposed the orgy of destruction, otherwise known as the Enlightenment, modern socialists do not feel this destruction went far enough. This, according to Kristol, makes them philosophical twins.

Go figure, as Americans say. The only thing that unites the New Left and the Old Right is that neither of them is neoconservative. Using Kristol's methodology, this makes them carbon copies not only of each other but also of Muslim fundamentalists, Taoists, vegans and most footballers. If such is the intellectual content of the rhetoric coming from the neocon leading lights, what can one expect from their mere epigones?

Kristol's interest in religion was largely defensive. After all, Christianity is innately opposed to everything the neocons hold dear, and a formidable opponent it can be too, especially at a

---

32 The part of his education that was not secular was eerie. For example, Kristol recalls how as a child he was taught to spit every time he passed by a church. This did not leave a lifelong mark, and in his mature years Kristol joined other clerical atheists, either Jewish or Gentile, in praising the social utility of the church – while of course still metaphorically spitting at its essence.

time when neocon dreams acquire a distinct nightmarish tint. Hence Kristol incessantly emphasised the outdated, obsolete nature of Christianity: "But bourgeois society is not interested in such transcendence, which at best it tolerates as a private affair..." And at worst, one would be tempted to add, it razes churches and massacres priests.

Commenting on the cultural tyranny of the Soviet state, Kristol remarked that "Sartre's Marxist writings have never been published in Russia, just as Brecht's plays have never been produced there, and just as Picasso's paintings have never been exhibited there." This was written in 1968, when I still lived in Moscow. Throughout the 1960s I spent many an hour at the Pushkin Museum of Fine Arts, often in front of *Old Jew with a Boy*, a powerful painting of Picasso's Blue Period. The Pushkin had a few other Picassos in its permanent exposition, while Leningrad's Hermitage had many more. Between them the two cities staged many of Brecht's plays, to which I can bear personal witness, having been in the audience on numerous occasions.

One should not judge a writer too harshly for such slipshod errors – and certainly another writer, not himself without sin, should not cast the first stone. In this instance, however, Kristol's cavalier treatment of religious and cultural facts betokens the widespread neocon contempt for the essence of Christendom and consequently the West. When writing about things they regard as vital, they tend to check their sources more zealously, hoping that this will add an air of verisimilitude to their pronouncements (which is not to say that even then they always get their facts straight).

An attentive reader, however, will not accept sound bytes as a substitute for sound thinking, and it is in this area that the neocons' failings are obvious. This is not to suggest that they did not in the past, nor do at present, possess the requisite mental faculties. Many of them, and certainly Irving Kristol, were highly intelligent men. Yet sound thinking is a necessary tool only for someone in pursuit of truth. Such a person will carefully hold up every thought he puts down on paper to the test of seeking the truth or, if he feels he has found it, communicating it properly. But someone who pursues not the truth but a specific political aim will invariably subject his writings to a different test: are they, or are they not, conducive to achieving his goal. This accounts for the essential dishonesty of all political propaganda, even when it dons, as in Kristol's case, the cloak of elegant style, erudite vocabulary and seemingly rational argument.

The word 'dishonesty' may appear too harsh, but it is accurate enough. A writer uttering mutually exclusive statements on consecutive pages because he does not realise they are mutually exclusive is either careless or not very clever. However, a writer who is bright enough to spot glaring contradictions in his prose and yet utters them all the same is dishonest. It is not that each time he is consciously telling lies: it is just that the difference between truth and falsehood is immaterial to him. What matters is the political El Dorado he sees in his mind's eye.

3

Kristol's fundamental dishonesty is revealed by his endless shifts from perceptive analysis to statements negating it. Political propagandists do not say what they think is true; they say what they think is useful. If the remarks they make are mutually exclusive, they are not unduly bothered by it. Thus in spite of his intelligence Kristol could do self-refutation with the best of them. For instance, he is perfectly correct when saying that "The family is, in our society, a vital economic institution. Welfare robs it of its economic function."

If true – and this *is* true – then surely a sound thinker enjoying access to a mass audience should spend every waking moment arguing against the welfare state. For robbing the family of its economic function will eventually rob it of most other functions as well: social, cultural, religious – any you care to name. As history has proved time and again, any institution no longer having a useful function to fulfil will eventually die out. When we are talking about the family, one of the most vital institutions of our civilisation, surely its disintegration will spell a catastrophe, one every man of influence should devote his life to preventing.

Yet throughout his neocon gospels Kristol tirelessly extols the virtues of 'a conservative welfare state'. "A welfare state, properly conceived, can be an integral part of a conservative society," he declares within two pages of his scathing castigation of the destructive nature of welfare. He then scolds his opponents for their "…futile protest against the principles of the welfare state, instead of trying a conservative welfare state."

Nor, as COLLENE puts it in a less direct fashion, should there be any limits on the size of the welfare state: "[We do not] believe, as some traditional conservatives do, that society should be minimalist in taking responsibility for the well-being of individuals."

To an unbiased observer 'a conservative welfare state' sounds like an oxymoron to end all oxymorons, but we must keep in mind that the neocons are after political expediency, not terminological precision. In this instance, Kristol co-opts to his cause a politician who could certainly serve as a useful role model for the neocons: "The idea of a welfare state is in itself perfectly consistent with a conservative political philosophy – as Bismarck knew, a hundred years ago."

Bismarck knew a few other things as well, such as how to start or provoke wars in pursuit of geopolitical domination, how to browbeat weaker neighbours into accepting Prussian supremacy, how to create an innately aggressive central state, how to rule through an unaccountable bureaucratic elite, how to use state socialism to bring the populace under his heel – in short, he was a proto-neocon *par excellence* and the very antithesis of conservatism. Yet Bismarck could indeed provide a useful lesson, other than the one on welfare that Kristol chose to heed: how neocon-like policies and philosophies can set the world up for a calamity.

It was Bismarck's policies, logically applied and developed, that led to the First World War and therefore to the Second. Hitler, if one went by his social, economic and geopolitical desiderata, rather than racial ones, was a larger-scale twentieth-century answer to Bismarck. Really, one wonders just how deeply Kristol pondered his understanding of conservatism – or indeed of modern history. My guess is that he did not ponder such things at all: he simply sought an intellectual mantle in which to drape his Trotskyist instincts and quest for a neocon 'world order'.

Meanwhile, as one reads through Kristol's prodigious output, the pile of contradictions keeps growing, as if tropistically reaching for the sun. For example, he spends half a page accepting that Tocqueville's prophesy on "public assistance and 'pauperdom' existing in a symbiotic relationship" has received ample empirical vindication in modern times. Indeed, every bit of research shows that the more lavishly a welfare programme is funded, the greater the number of people who will apply for it and do whatever they can to qualify. As Kristol must have seen some of the same research, he knew that welfare was a gift that keeps on giving.

And yet: "At this point, we are bound... to take our leave of Tocqueville. Such gloomy conclusions, derived from a less than benign view of human nature, do not recommend themselves... to the twentieth-century political imagination."

What does recommend itself to the twentieth-century political imagination is cold disregard for facts whenever they fail to substantiate an ideology. Tocqueville's "less than benign view of human nature" came from the echoes he still heard in his agnostic soul of Judaeo-Christian morality based on the doctrine of original sin. The example Kristol singled out as a point of disagreement with this morality, the mechanics of the welfare state, proves nothing other than that Tocqueville was right and Kristol was wrong.

But when an ideology is in full flow, facts are swept aside as irrelevancies – even when Kristol himself validates such facts: "In New York City today, as in many other large cities, welfare benefits not only compete with low wages; they outstrip them." Quite. And not just in American cities: in today's Britain someone receiving the full range of benefits would need to earn at least £50,000 a year to match them. Since most welfare recipients lack the necessary qualifications to earn such an income, their incentive to seek employment is not altogether powerful.

Such an arrangement is bound to encourage the less laudable aspects of human nature – if it did not, welfare rolls would be shrinking, which they do nowhere in the West. If human nature conformed to Kristol's 'benign' view of it, people would prefer the honour of honest toil to the indignity of handouts even if welfare offered greater material rewards. In fact, Kristol's view of human nature can be traced back to Rousseau's, and it was shared by other talented neocons, such as Allan Bloom. Verily I say unto you, chaps who nowadays include 'conservative' in their moniker do have peculiar antecedents.

As if dead-set to prove that 'neosocialism' would be a far more accurate term to describe his brainchild, Kristol equates socialism with civilisation: "…it is nothing short of a tragedy that anticapitalist dissent should now be liberated from a socialist tradition, which… had the function of civilising dissent…".

This lament is wrong not only philosophically but also factually: during Kristol's lifetime dissent against capitalism mostly proceeded precisely in accordance with 'the socialist tradition'. The civilising effects of this tradition included mass expropriations, wholesale massacres of those resisting, genocide, driving whole populations into labour camps, enslavement not just of certain groups but indeed of whole nations. In less carnivorous countries, expropriations and the concomitant growth in state power may have succeeded without resorting to violence, but they did succeed – all in strict compliance with the 'socialist tradition', as any reader of socialist classics will confirm. What exactly does this have to do with conservatism, even in its American meaning of economic liberalism?

4

In the generation following the publication of the Kristol canon, neoconservatism has swept all before it on the political Right. Neocon propagandists are well aware of this, and their triumphant noises can be heard all over the Western world. Since from now on I shall be relying on statements made by various neoconservative spokesmen of our generation, it is time to remind you yet again of the term I introduced at the beginning of this essay: Collective Neocon, COLLENE for short. The term is a useful timesaver: being deeply and loyally ideological, all neocons these days say the same things in the same voice. Individual attribution is therefore redundant.

It was not, for example, an individual thinker but COLLENE who explained that the neocons long ago "broke with traditional conservatives in the domestic-policy arena by making their peace with the welfare state, on which conservatives had waged war for decades."

In fact, like all successful heresies, neoconservatism did not just break with the original creed but supplanted it, rendering it at best impotent and at worst meaningless. Heresies do not reform; they deform. Because neoconservatism has much in common with the New Left and nothing at all with the Old Right, to use Kristol's nomenclature, it effectively invalidates both terms by marginalising the latter and incorporating the former. This linguistic consolidation, reflecting as it does an intellectual and moral muddle, first vanquished in America and is now proceeding apace in Britain and elsewhere. Its international spread resembles the shockwaves of an explosion: the closer to the American epicentre a country is politically, the more it will feel the effects.

Indirectly this success of neoconservatism supports my definition of true conservatism, the one based on its commitment to preserving the heritage of Christendom. Even though Christians (or, to be more exact, people who describe themselves as such) make up a third of the world's population, Christendom as a cultural, social and political entity no longer exists. In the West, Christian and any other religious beliefs have been relegated strictly to a matter of personal choice, antiquarian objects to which people pay a quaint tribute in their spare time. Any Christian who insists on manifesting or trying to uphold his faith in public runs the risk of mockery or, these days, even punishment.

Hence Western governments are nonchalant about the persecution of Christians in Asia and Africa, where militant fascistic groups and despotic governments go way beyond the simple marginalisation favoured in the West. Churches desecrated or burnt and Christians imprisoned, attacked or murdered are commonplace in today's world. Yet any sense that those persecuted Christians have anything to do with us is long since lost. In fact one detects a distinct lack of sympathy, an implicit shrug of the shoulders: if those people choose to stick to their obsolete faith where it is frowned upon, they have only themselves to blame. Who are they to go against the will of the majority? This is tantamount to taking issue with democratic principles, even in places where democracy is not yet practised.

Today's Western governments, some of them egged on by the neocons, are more likely to wage wars allegedly aimed at protecting Muslims from their own rulers than wars aimed at protecting Christians – often from the very same rulers. The West has gone aggressively secular, which effectively means anti-Christian.

In this atmosphere true conservatism is bound to suffocate. There seems to be less and less left for it to conserve; it has lost much of its sense of purpose. But the rule by simulacrum lives on, even as the real world is being crowded out by the virtual one. True conservatives have moved out of the house but they have left usable verbal furniture behind. The neocons have moved in, claimed squatting rights and taken possession of the words they found lying about. These they have picked up, dusted off and added to others already in their possession.

Hence we are served, among other egregious oxymorons, 'the conservative welfare state', which remains an article of faith with today's neocons. Never mind that such a hybrid cannot exist by any reasonable definition. To neocons, semantics is nothing; semiotics, everything. Some people, those who place themselves close to the right end of the political spectrum, will respond to the semiotic message and perk up. They will welcome the word 'conservative' and by transference will like the neocons. Others, those of the leftish persuasion, will respond to the signal sent by the word 'welfare' in much the same way. The two concepts, Right and Left, will come together in one amorphous blob, with neither term meaning much any longer. The slate has been wiped clean and the neocons can scribble any illogical, and typically mendacious, nonsense on it.

Having said all that, no political movement can succeed in a non-violent way unless it tugs on most people's heartstrings.

DEMOCRACY AS A NEOCON TRICK

From the very start American heartstrings have been plucked by the American religion, whose principal tenet is American exceptionalism. The more radical strata of the population tend to understand exceptionalism as supremacy, and it is to these strata that neoconservatism appeals most immediately. This is whence its natural support comes.

Yet at the same time neoconservatism manages to neutralise large segments of those who may be expected to be its natural opponents. Intuitive conservatives, those who have not yet related their instincts to a coherent political philosophy, may be tricked by the conservative-sounding words the neocons have purloined from the house vacated by the rightful owners. Such people would be inclined at least to give the neocons the benefit of the doubt, even if they do smell a rat somewhere in their political basement.

At the same time many of those whose instincts lead them towards the soft Left, people called 'liberals' in America and 'social democrats' in Europe, do not allow themselves to be sidetracked by the smokescreen of conservative verbiage laid by the neocons. Such people realise that the smokescreen is only there to hide real kinship, of the kind based not on a shared philosophy but on a shared DNA. They congratulate the neocons for such skilful subterfuge and support them implicitly.

Practically all the groups, Right, Left or Centre, have been trained to respond with Pavlovian alacrity to the word 'democracy', and the neocons are bright enough to have inscribed the word above all others on their political banner. The world, they preach, is no longer divided on the basis of such obsolete notions as religion, culture, nationality, geography, race, history. The only meaningful watershed is the one running between nations that are 'democratic' and those that are not.

The accolade 'democratic' is awarded on the purely formal criterion of elective politics. A state that allows a semblance of free elections is democratic and therefore virtuous. One that governs by any other expedient is non-democratic and therefore wicked. Since by now 'democracy' has become the principal dogma of the American religion, the lines are clearly drawn.

The neocons can now indulge the bellicose instincts coded into their DNA by their Enlightenment father and Trotskyist mother. They can now sell their war-mongering to the public as a sort of proselytism. The neocons are supposedly not out to punish or conquer other nations. They are to convert them to the only true, 'legitimising', political creed. For their own good those parts of the world that prove recalcitrant have to be treated as if they were naughty, disobedient children. While flogging them with laser-guided and unmanned canes, the neocons seem to be saying, "It hurts us more than it hurts you." Hence for example their nauseating weeping and wailing about the tragic loss of lives in the Middle East – in wars that broke out largely as a direct result of the neocons' agitation, both public and behind the scenes.

It is hard to say if there exist any neocons today who are smart enough or devious enough to pursue this strategy by deliberate design. Perhaps not. They all claim genuine attachment to the doomed mission of turning the world into a loose conglomerate of mini-Americas, and one has to believe them. After all, sustained, fervent propaganda has been known throughout history to be able to convince not only its targets but also the propagandists themselves, especially those – and they are always in the majority – who are incapable of independent thought.

Yet the proselytising American religion is false and therefore its exponents, witting or unwitting, will get things terribly wrong every time they act on their fideistic principles. No matter how honestly the neocons declare their beliefs and act on them, the beliefs themselves will remain dishonest. Every action based on them will therefore be practically disastrous and intellectually puny – this regardless of the particular neocons' academic attainments or IQ.

We have already seen that, in spite of Kristol's intelligence and erudition, his neoconservative prose is intellectually feeble. Paraphrasing Dr Johnson, one can say that his books are both brilliant and neoconservative. The trouble is that where they are brilliant they are not neoconservative, and where they are neoconservative they are not brilliant.

The present generation of neocons lack the fine qualities of their forebears, not only Kristol, but also Glazer, Kirkpatrick, Moynihan *et al*. So much more tragic it is then that this generation has had such a powerful influence on shaping the American, and generally Western, response to the two major developments of the last quarter-century: the 'collapse' of the Soviet Union and the rise of Islamic power. This response has been so ill-advised, and therefore potentially so disastrous, that it is worth considering in some detail over the next three chapters.

History ends, then restarts

1

If one believes Enlightenment and post-Enlightenment thinkers, history has ended several times in the last couple of centuries. The multiple nature of such cataclysmic events logically presupposes that each end has been followed by a re-start. History then would proceed apace for a while, only to come to yet another screeching halt when yet another fashionable theory rolled off the printing press. History, as depicted by the authors, resembles the Christian notion of death and resurrection – except that all those thinkers tend to be atheist in their work, and almost all of them in their personal lives as well.

The first such thinker was Hegel who was completing his *Phenomenology* in 1806, just as Napoleon was thrashing the Prussians in a battlefield sited next door to Hegel's employer, the University of Jena. The battle of Jena, according to Hegel, brought history to an end by effectively settling the political debate once and for all: every society on earth was now inexorably evolving towards the "universal homogeneous state". Such a state could only be based on the ideals of the French revolution adumbrated by Hegel's beloved Rousseau, encapsulated in the popular triad of *liberté, égalité, fraternité* (Hegel had a weakness for triads) and developed to a logical conclusion by another man he admired, Napoleon.

In never occurred to Hegel that the ideals of the French revolution were inseparable from its practices, such as the slaughter of whole social classes, the desecration and destruction of churches, the massacre of at least a million

Frenchmen during the Terror and the subsequent deaths of another two million during the Napoleonic wars. But even had Hegel pondered such unfortunate ramifications, he would have found a way of explaining them away dialectically. History, after all, was to Hegel a dialectical development of the Absolute Spirit[33] that had to know where it was going and why.

Schematically, Hegel's exegesis could have been as simple as truth itself. Thesis: the French revolution introduced most laudable notions to a world bereft of ideals (Christianity did not count as one such). Antithesis: alas, an attempt to hasten the advent of a society ruled by such ideals resulted in mass carnage and the worst tyranny Europe had hitherto known. Synthesis: by affirming affirmation, negating negation, converting quantity into quality or some such (hard to keep those things straight), a new world will ineluctably emerge in which no further debate will be possible. An ideal will have been attained.

In that sense history will have ended, even though people will still soldier on with their physical lives, solving their little quotidian problems. But the ultimate problem, that of perfect social and political organisation, will have been solved once and for all.

Both the teleological nature of Hegel's philosophy and its reliance on mock-Trinitarian methodology were among the most salient manifestations of what I call the rule by simulacrum. In Hegel's case such echoes of Christianity were 'dialectically' inevitable, for he himself was raised as a Lutheran, lapsing only in his mature years. Yet it is easy to understand how the 'Young Hegelians', such as Marx and Engels, could adapt Hegel's dialectics to their own warped, one-sided vision of the world. In fact the dialectical method, especially when wielded with a certain sleight of hand, can explain next to everything, which of course means that as often as not it explains next to nothing.

Be that as it may, by dispensing with Hegel's idealism and squeezing his whole dialectical philosophy into the straight-

---

33 The German word *Geist* is sometimes alternatively rendered as 'mind' in English.

HISTORY ENDS, THEN RESTARTS

jacket of economics, Marx became a heretic to Hegel in the same sense in which Hegel himself was a heretic to Christianity. Hegelianism finds a more comfortable niche within the liberal tradition, where it neatly slots into the continuum established by the proto-Enlighteners, such as Hobbes and Locke, the actual Enlighteners in France, Scotland and America, and the post-Enlighteners, among whom the neocons these days take pride of place.

That Hegel, who was pious as a youngster, could become such a seminal figure of the essentially atheistic Enlightenment may seem paradoxical, but not for long. In fact one could argue that the post-Enlightenment liberal ideology is a hybrid resulting from an interbreeding of Protestantism and secularism, both animated by revolutionary temperament. By declaring that 'every man is his own priest', Protestantism, especially in its Calvinist variants, jams the square peg of man into the round hole vacated first by the church and then eventually by God. At that point man becomes not just his own priest, but also his own God.

The rule by simulacrum dictates that man should usurp some of God's characteristics and prerogatives, particularly his promise to create an ideal life. The slight difference is that God's ideal is only attainable when earthly life ends, whereas the liberal ideal presupposes the possibility of creating paradise on earth. When the ideal seems to have been achieved, this may indeed create the impression that history has ended. The impression will last until empirical evidence proves yet again that the secular paradise is but a short-lived illusion, whereas the secular hell that succeeds it is very much a perennial reality.

At that point neo-Hegelians and other liberals will have to stop and catch their breath. It is not as if they will abandon their misguided beliefs – ideologues do not give up their cherished misapprehensions easily. Rather, the liberals will find some sort of dialectical explanation for what they will regard as a temporary setback. They will then do all they can to bring about some kind of social or political upheaval that would enable them to take their seemingly discredited ideology off the mothballs. The previous end of history, they will declare, was

251

but a false dawn. History did not end then but it has definitely ended now.

The neocons are all Hegelians whether they realise this or not, as most do not. Neither can they see that the mythical earthly Garden of Eden they seek is overgrown with moral and intellectual weeds. They firmly believe, or at least profess to believe, that a perfect synthesis will emerge from a clash between good (democracy) and evil (any other political method). In the long tradition of secular determinism they have to espouse an unshakeable faith in democracy eventually emerging victorious the world over, thereby ending any intellectual debate and consequently history.

All that is needed to add meat to the neocon hodgepodge stew is some tangible event providing justification, however flimsy, for their ideology. In that sense, the 'collapse of the Soviet Union' officially declared in 1991 was a godsend. At last virtue, as personified by American democracy, triumphed over evil, as embodied by Soviet totalitarianism.

Since until then the rest of the world had been struggling to choose one or the other (for simplicity's sake the neocon view of the world either did not allow any other options or ignored them when their existence was impossible to deny), the supposed triumph of liberal democracy settled the issue once and for all. The end was nigh and it was predetermined: the innate craving for universal suffrage residing in every man's heart could now be satisfied. It was only a matter of time, and not a particularly long time at that. History had effectively ended, and it was up to America and her allies to get this message across to those who were stubbornly refusing to see the obvious.

2

Such is the abbreviated gist of Francis Fukuyama's 1992 book *The End of History and the Last Man*, which remains the essential gospel in the neoconservative canon even though the author himself has since become an apostate to the creed.

"While earlier forms of government were characterised by grave defects and irrationalities that led to their eventual

HISTORY ENDS, THEN RESTARTS

collapse, liberal democracy was arguably free from such fundamental internal contradictions," explained Fukuyama. This echoed his neocon predecessors, such as Kristol with his democracy as the sole 'legitimising idea'. It also massaged the overblown egos of Fukuyama's neocon contemporaries, those to whom I refer as COLLENE. Believing that any political system can ever be free from 'grave defects', 'irrationalities' and 'internal contradictions' is only possible for someone who believes in nothing else. Because of man's Fall and subsequent fallibility, perfect societies cannot exist in this world. Nevertheless the belief that one is achievable through political action is among the fundamental tenets of the Enlightenment – whereas the demonstrable fact that such a society stubbornly refuses to emerge proves the fallacy of such tenets. Yet this particular one is essential for various Enlightenment offshoots, particularly Marxism. Fukuyama generously gives credit where it is due:

> "This understanding of History ... was made part of our daily intellectual atmosphere by Karl Marx, who borrowed this concept of History from Hegel, and is implicit in our use of words like 'primitive' or 'advanced', 'traditional' or 'modern', when referring to different types of human societies. For both of these thinkers, there was a coherent development of human societies from simple tribal ones based on slavery and subsistence agriculture, through various theocracies, monarchies, and feudal aristocracies, up through modern liberal democracy and technologically driven capitalism. This evolutionary process was neither random nor unintelligible, even if it did not proceed in a straight line, and even if it was possible to question whether man was happier or better off as a result of historical 'progress'."

And further:

> "Hegel believed that the 'contradiction' inherent in the relationship of lordship and bondage was finally overcome as a result of the French and, one would have to add, American

revolutions. These democratic revolutions abolished the distinction between master and slave by making the former slaves their own masters and by establishing the principles of popular sovereignty and the rule of law. The inherently unequal recognition of masters and slaves is replaced by universal and reciprocal recognition, where every citizen recognises the dignity and humanity of every other citizen, and where that dignity is recognised in turn by the state through the granting of *rights*."

One could argue that "the dignity and humanity of every other citizen" was upheld more effectively and sincerely in Christendom than "as a result of the French and American revolutions". The first order of the day in revolutionary France was to murder, torture and rob millions, demolish hundreds of priceless Romanesque and Gothic buildings, wreak devastation on the whole country and then on most of Europe. After their own revolution it took the Americans almost another century to declare an end to black slavery, and another century after that to grant equality to the blacks in all of the United States.

In this instance Fukuyama simply purloins a fundamental Christian belief and tries to pass it for uniquely American property, co-opting Hegel as an expert witness and declaring any conflicting *prima facie* evidence to be inadmissible. As a result, what was unadulterated demagoguery in the last quarter of the eighteenth century became demagoguery tinged with historical dishonesty towards the end of the twentieth.

Fukuyama would not let his views be affected even by the experience of his own family: his grandfather was among the 110,000 people of Japanese origin, 62 percent of whom were US citizens, interned in 1942 for the duration of the war. In 1988 Congress and President Reagan officially apologised for the internment on behalf of the US government. The legislation passed at the time admitted that government actions had been based on "race prejudice, war hysteria and a failure of political leadership". How did that jibe with 'the dignity and humanity of every other citizen', unless of course 'every other' was supposed to mean one in two?

HISTORY ENDS, THEN RESTARTS

To Fukuyama's credit, since his publishing triumph he has broken with the neocons, chiefly because of his opposition to the second, unprovoked attack on Iraq. In fact he correctly placed neoconservatism into the same territory as Leninism, though Trotskyism would have been even more accurate. Fukuyama was of course in an ideal position to peek underneath the verbiage and detect the emotional similarity between the neocons and the hard Left. All he had to do was to look into his own heart to realise that, though the chosen words were usually different, the underlying temperament and aspirations were the same.

His own apostasy added poignancy to his pen, as apostasy tends to do. The neocons, Fukuyama wrote, believe "that history can be pushed along with the right application of power and will. Leninism was a tragedy in its Bolshevik version, and it has returned as farce when practiced by the United States. Neoconservatism, as both a political symbol and a body of thought, has evolved into something I can no longer support."

It is interesting to see how, for all his desertion from neoconservatism, Fukuyama continues to cling to the Marxist jargon ("tragedy and farce"). He also continues to insist on the neoconservative belief in "the universality of human rights", which suggests that his view of the world, even if it has become more honest, has not become any more profound.

For a professional academic Fukuyama is also rather wobbly in his taxonomic vocabulary. What does "Leninism in its Bolshevik version" mean? What other versions are there? The Bolsheviks were Lenin's faction within the Russian Social Democratic Workers' Party (not to be confused with the National Socialist Workers' Party in Germany). There is no Leninism other than Bolshevism and no Bolshevism other than Leninism; they are full synonyms. Does Fukuyama mean that, if other versions of Leninism existed, they would be less tragic? Does he regard, say, Stalinism as one such? Still, one ought to welcome his belated conversion even if it did not make his thinking any more precise.

While decrying Fukuyama's change of mind, the neocons are still effusive about his masterpiece. As COLLENE puts it, "Fukuyama's thesis... provided a version of world history deeply appealing to those of a neoconservative persuasion." Moreover, "[Fukuyama's] view of history... [has] become part of the neoconservative DNA – that democracy is the desirable endpoint of all human societies, and that... it is the surest means of preventing nation-states waging war on each other."

People are entitled to their own opinion but they are not entitled to their own facts. Disregarding this simple truth, the neocons claim such entitlement among their inalienable rights. More fastidious observers would be tempted to point out that what the publisher Henry Luce referred to as 'the American [which is to say democratic] century', the twentieth, was by far the bloodiest hundred-year span in human history.

During that period 'nation-states waging war on each other' and also, let us not forget, on their own citizens killed anywhere between 300 and 500 million people. The number would seem to be sufficiently high at least to give pause to anyone praising the peaceful nature of modernity. The essential desideratum (as distinct from sloganeering) of democratic modernity is the *ad infinitum* empowerment and expansion of the central state. Such an overwhelming impulse cannot be contained within national borders for ever – sooner or later it has to spill over into other lands. This observation, and subsequent ratiocination, cannot possibly escape anyone searching for truth.

Yet we must always keep in mind that neoconservatism is not a system of thought but an ideology springing from a temperamental and moral aberration. Did not Thomas Jefferson postulate that any number of victims would be justified by the pursuit of a just cause? Of course the Founder, unfamiliar as he was with the upcoming delights of 'the American century', thought in terms of different orders of magnitude. However, numbers must not be allowed to affect the principle.

Lest an unsophisticated reader might confuse Fukuyama's 'end of history' with the Second Coming, COLLENE is on hand to provide a ready explanation: "Fukuyama was using the term [history] not in the sense of 'the end of worldly events', but in the Hegelian sense of 'the end of the evolution of human thought about... first principles'."

Aristotelian first principles, or 'absolute presuppositions' as Collingwood called them, are axiomatic assumptions acting as the foundation on which any subsequent intellectual structure can be built. To a mind able to probe beyond the political squabbles of today, no political system would measure up to the lofty perch of a first principle. Political systems are at best reflections of first principles (properly understood) and more commonly their denial. Even Hegel refrained from defining his 'end of history' in purely political terms, but the neocon mind, liberated from any necessity to think deeply, will accept no such restrictions. For a serious thinker, political philosophy is but a demonstration of how philosophy applies to politics. For a neocon, politics *is* the philosophy and vice versa.

In their maniacal insistence on this misguided historicism, the neocons are eager to co-opt anyone, including those who are not commonly regarded as fully paid-up members of their club. Later I shall comment on the widespread proliferation of neoconservative 'ideas' beyond their usual habitat, but suffice it to say for now that even leftist politicians in both America and Britain get into the spirit. There is no paradox there, for at heart they are driven by exactly the same spirit as that animating the neocons.

Thus COLLENE praises Labour's most successful election-winner: "[As] Tony Blair said in his famous 1999 Chicago speech, the familiar battles between left and right are over, with liberal democracy having emerged triumphant." In the next breath Tony Blair promised never to abandon his fight against 'the forces of conservatism', which undertaking goes some way towards refuting his previous statement. After all, if such wicked forces still need to be resisted, they have not yet been routed. Ergo the 'familiar battles between left and right' are not quite over yet – but hey, what is another silly inconsistency among friends?

The folly of neoconservatives can be best demonstrated by their woeful misreading of the event that inspired them to make loud triumphant noises. For the 'collapse of the Soviet Union' was nothing resembling the picture the neocons see in their mind's eye. It was many things, but 'the end of history' it most certainly was not.

Russia and the reign of error

1

The West's totemistic worship of democracy, exemplified at its extreme by the neocons, has led to a lamentable misreading of the events routinely described as the 'collapse of communism' in Russia. Like a panting dog at its master's feet, the West was happy to gnaw on the bone of democracy tossed to it by the Soviets. The actual meal stayed on the table, and its taste remained as revolting as ever.

The misjudgement came partly from ignorance, partly from intellectual dishonesty, but the main cause was wishful thinking. Just as Lincoln Steffens and other 'useful idiots' of yesteryear went to Lenin's Russia yearning to believe that the Potemkin villages put up by history's most awful regime were real, so were the neocons (and likeminded individuals) desperate to see their vision of the world vindicated. They were deceived because they were begging to be deceived.

Anyone whose knowledge of Russia did not come from newspaper editorials and the odd book knew from the word 'glasnost' that the whole thing was bogus. Since then a profusion of evidence has turned this intuitive understanding into a fact. Yet wishful thinking has taken such a firm hold on public opinion that this truth still remains unorthodox. Therefore, in order to fathom the full magnitude of neocon folly, it would be worth looking at the 'collapse of communism' in some detail.

The binary view of a world divided into democratic and non-democratic parts, with no gradations in between and no other opposite poles, is best described as neo-Manichaean rather than neoconservative. Those adhering to this view in earnest are either not very bright or not very observant. In the first instance they fail to sense that such a lack of nuance is counter-intuitive; in the second, they do not notice that geopolitical reality is infinitely more complex. Such primitive contrasting notions are always wrong even when they stay within the confines of theory. When they provide a springboard for a leap into policy, they are bound to lead to most unfortunate, and potentially catastrophic, errors of judgment.

A country should be judged on moral rather than political criteria. Morality is there to impose restrictions on man's natural instincts, which at any time since the Fall have been badly in need of restricting. In this narrow sense morality overlaps with civilisation, whose chief purpose is also to put brakes on wicked acts inspired by whatever comes naturally. This partial overlap makes moral criteria a reliable method of determining the extent to which a country is civilised.

Such criteria ought to be based on the country's proximity to virtue, rather than on the political method it adopts in governing its affairs. I shall spare you another long rota of vile regimes, such as Hitler's, ascending to power by democratic means, or yet another one of so-called 'absolute' monarchies of the past that were incomparably more virtuous than any of today's democracies – any reader is capable of compiling his own lists.

These are guaranteed to be extensive enough to show that "Is it democratic?" is a wrong question to ask when forming the judgment of a country, foreign or indeed one's own. Other questions are much more relevant, such as "Is it just?", "Is it oppressive?", "Does its government rule by law or arbitrary action?", "Is the state's power growing at the expense of the individual's?", "Does the state persecute in any way those who dissent in a peaceful manner?", "If Western, does it retain palpable links with Christendom?", "If it never was Christian in the first place, is it aggressive towards its neighbours, particularly our allies?" "Does it persecute those of Judaeo-Christian beliefs?", "Does it present a danger to us, our interests and our allies?" Anyone who believes that a democracy can always be relied upon to answer these questions is sleepwalking into a potential disaster.

The list of questions could grow much longer but, no matter how long it gets, it will only remain useful if probing into the essence of a society rather than its method of government. The ultimate question ought to run along these lines: "If we designate absolute evil (rare) as zero and absolute virtue (unattainable) as 10, where do we place this country on our imaginary scale of civilised virtue?"

As the starting point of foreign policy, such an approach would yield a more robust crop than the neocons' neo-Manichaeism ever can. Yet the neocons, and those attracted by their slogans, have reduced the entire complexity of nationhood to its political mechanisms rather than its essence. Worse still, for simplicity's sake they reduce the entire panoply of political phenomena to just one dichotomy: democracy or absence thereof. And even this dichotomy is further reduced to its formal shell.

This creates an opening for wicked regimes to pull a fast one by hiding behind a camouflage of democratic cardboard cutouts that cater to the foreign observers' wishful thinking. Such Potemkin villages do not have to be real or even realistic – those seeking a democracy fix will get just as high on a placebo. Thus, taking their cue from the People's Democracies of yesteryear, numerous Middle Eastern and African tyrannies have learned that if they scream 'democracy' with histrionic conviction the West will pay them in coin – and if they do not, the payment may come in the shape of drones and bombing raids.

Yet the very concept of a Potemkin village has a Russian provenance, and it was the Russians who showed how easily the neocons' binary primitivism could be manipulated for wicked purposes. Give the neocons and other gullible Westerners the thing they crave, a mirage of democracy, and they will not delve too zealously into things they do not understand, such as the reality of good and evil.

2

Understanding any phenomenon is impossible in the absence of a precise definition. And if a phenomenon is malignant, designating it with a misnomer can have lethal consequences. For example, many people use the words 'cold' and 'flu' interchangeably because the two conditions have similar symptoms. Yet a cold, if left untreated, will go away after a week. Influenza, if left untreated, can kill. Accurate terminology is just as vital in political science, except that it is harder to come by. Moreover, we are so used to loose definitions that we repeat them unthinkingly simply because others have repeated them often enough.

Thus our antennae do not twitch when journalists and academics keep yelping about the 'collapse of communism' in 1989, 1991 or whichever year they choose to designate as the point of no return. Had our minds not been numbed by such mantras, we would be tempted to ask awkward questions. Such as, what exactly has collapsed? Communism covers a multitude of sins, most of them of the deadly variety. It has many definitions, certainly many facets. Which of them lends itself to the assorted scribes, many but not all of them neocons, describing the events of those years as a 'collapse'? Some of them? All of them? Did the Soviet Union or its heirs shift the country the right way on the moral scale?

According to its theoreticians, 'communism' describes an ideal society wherein all property is held communally: from each according to his ability, to each according to his need, amen. But that society could not have collapsed for the simple reason that it never existed. Even pre-perestroika Soviet propagandists described their country as socialist, not communist. And if you look at any Western European country of today, with the possible exception of Switzerland, you will not get the impression that socialism has collapsed. At best it has not yet triumphed irreversibly.

If we take Marx's lead, socialism is tantamount to public ownership of the means of production, which is to say the economy. This arrangement is not only far from dead but is indeed in rude health. In Britain, for example, the government owns close to 50 percent of the economy; in France, over 60 percent. The corresponding figure for Stalin's Russia was 85 percent, still higher than in today's France but the gap is narrowing. And in today's communist China it is a mere 15 percent, which means China is not even socialist by Marxist criteria, never mind communist. This shows that the taxonomy based on Marxist assumptions has lost all meaning, if it ever had any in the first place. Applying a version of the moral scale I suggested earlier would allow a much more reliable classification.

Delving deeper, we shall see that even much of the economy residing in the West's private sector is not owned by the capitalist, Marx's bogeyman. Transferring ownership of giant corporations to the public through stock-market flotation has created a situation where ownership and control have gone their separate ways. The public may own a corporation, but it has next to no say in how it is run, even if it is being run into the ground.

The control rests in the hands of the directors, most of them coming from the professional managerial class whose advent Burnham prophesied with such remarkable foresight 70-odd years ago. 'Management' is now a popular academic discipline, and those who matriculate in it easily float not just from one company to the next, but also from one industry to the next – it does not matter whether they manage an oil company, a bank or an NHS trust. In an eerie sort of way this arrangement is not altogether different from that of the Soviet Union, where the public nominally owned the economy, but where all the kudos went to the *nomenklatura* having none of the ownership but exercising all of the control.

Interestingly, in the second half of the nineteenth century, when Marx's dreaded capitalism was at its peak, robber barons were at their most oppressive and, according to Freedom House, democracy did not exist, the average ratio of income earned by US corporate directors and their employees was 28:1. Yet in 2005, when history had ended, democracy was in full bloom and egalitarianism proudly reigned supreme, this ratio stood at 158:1 (a study jointly conduced by MIT and the Federal Reserve).

Therefore what separates today's managers from the employees is not merely an earning gap but an unbridgeable chasm. This is a clear-cut Soviet arrangement, except that in the Soviet Union this division, though as wide and deep as in today's West, was largely expressed in subtler ways than just cash on the nail.

'Communism' can also be used synonymously with 'Marxism', but we cannot in all honesty say communism, so defined, has collapsed. Nor will it ever tumble for as long as even 'conservative' politicians in the West, such as our former PM John Major, see a classless society as a desirable and achievable objective, for as long as mainstream European parties sing *The Internationale* or *Bandera Rossa* at their conferences and pick red as their colour, for as long as the entire complexity of the world is routinely reduced to the struggle between the haves and have-nots, and most Brits in particular accept the class view of society as a given.

'Communism' may also describe striving for the dictatorship of the proletariat, 'permanent revolution' and the universal demolition of the old order by violent means. This kind of communism indeed collapsed in Russia, but it did so not in 1989–1991 but in 1936–1938, when Stalin had most adherents of it shot or tortured to death for being stupid pests out of step with the real business at hand. The ice axe driven into Trotsky's brain by way of a full stop killed that insanity for ever – or at least until it came back in a different, neoconservative, incarnation, with 'democracy' replacing 'the dictatorship of the proletariat'.

Finally, 'communism' may also mean the Soviet Union's or Russia's policy aimed at dominating the world and gradually remaking it in her own image. Russia undoubtedly pursued such a policy under the Soviets, which made it a mortal threat to the West. However, what hard facts indicate that Russia no longer poses such a threat? None has ever been in evidence, and now less than ever. The language the Russians use these days is different from their erstwhile communist cant, but in any conflict in any part of the globe they still find themselves in confrontation with the West as unfailingly today as a generation ago.

Hence before we accept that communism has indeed collapsed, we must be satisfied that the entity that may have collapsed was indeed communism, tightly defined. As you can see, finding such a definition is no easy matter, and what reigns is not just error but downright confusion. Utterly befuddled, one turns to experts, in this case Richard Pipes, perhaps the most credible Western student of Russia over the last few decades. In his *Communism: A History*, the book he describes as an 'obituary of communism', his answer is: "The word *communism*... refers to three related but distinct phenomena: an ideal, a programme, and a regime set up to realise the ideal."

Tight it is not, but this is a definition of some sort. In fact, this tripartite description may well be the best we can do within the limitations of the traditional taxonomy. So which of the three phenomena of communism actually collapsed in 1991? Pipes goes on to draw parallels between communism and earlier attempts, from ancient Rome onwards, to force equality on an unsuspecting populace. So is egalitarianism the ideal? And is *The Communist Manifesto* the programme? Not really, according to Pipes. Leninism, he believes, had little to do with an honest attempt to bring Marx's ideals to life.

This points at the first cause of a typical taxonomic blunder in politics: Pipes is confusing ideals with slogans. True enough, the Bolsheviks never intended to act on Marx's *slogans*, those that had to do with eliminating poverty, liberating and uniting the working classes or correcting social injustice. But they did their level best to realise Marx's totalitarian *ideals*, those I have outlined earlier.

Lenin, according to Pipes, was "a fanatical revolutionary determined to destroy, root and branch, the existing social and political order." Rather than being motivated by "sympathy for the poor", this determination was "grounded in anger and driven by a craving for revenge... The principal feature of Lenin's personality was hatred". This is good knockabout stuff, and I can accept with open arms Pipes's correct characterisation of the motives animating the Bolshevik mayhem and its first ghastly perpetrator.

However, this brings the original question into sharper focus. What exactly collapsed in 1991 Russia? Hatred? Anger? Craving for revenge? Surely not. Such negative emotions are manifest in the ongoing cull of numerous opponents to the Putin regime – both domestically and internationally. In the latter case (London springs to mind) the regime's 'craving for revenge' may even be slaked with nuclear weapons, though so far thankfully of minuscule yield.

Having thus appealed to the experts, we have ended up no closer to understanding the true meaning of 'communism' or its 'collapse'. Quite the reverse: Pipes shows convincingly if perhaps unwittingly that the 'ideal', as he understands the word, had nothing to do with communism; the 'programme' had nothing to do with the ideal; and the 'regime' had nothing to do with the programme. What is left then? Whose obituary is he writing? To answer such questions, looking beneath the surface of history is clearly in order. Digging to a greater depth, we may find persuasive reasons to deride neocon triumphalism.

3

Shortly after the Bolsheviks grabbed Russia, and while still mopping up pockets of resistance within their own country at the end of the Civil War, they sent a vast army in the general direction of the Channel. Germany and France were the targets but, unfortunately for the impatient Soviet youngster, Poland lay in the way.

The West generally misunderstood the far-reaching ambitions behind the so-called Russo-Polish war. Even now historians sometimes describe it as a local conflict, ignoring the famous Order No.1423 issued by the Red Army commander Mikhail Tukhachevsky: "Soldiers of the proletarian revolution! Direct your eyes towards the west. It is in the west that the fate of the world revolution is being decided. *The way towards a world fire lies through the corpse of White Poland.* [My emphasis. AB] On our bayonets we are taking happiness and peace to workers of the world. Westwards – march!"

Thus Poland was a step along the way, not the final destination. Alas, the impetuous conquerors found the Polish army of 1920 to be quite a different proposition from the unarmed Russian peasants the Bolsheviks had been culling *en masse* and from the soft-handed 'contras' (i.e. aristocrats, priests, doctors, teachers, writers, scientists, administrators) they had been mutilating in all sorts of imaginative ways. But for the Poles' remarkable fight-back at Warsaw, the Soviets might indeed have gone all the way, as no viable military force existed to the west of Poland in the wake of the demob-happy pacifism in Germany, France and Britain.

Bolshevik rape attempts by proxy, namely in Hungary and Germany, were equally unsuccessful. The backlash was severe enough for the comrades to see the writing on the wall: the world was not quite ripe for a Bolshevik takeover. That the message was understood was due to Lenin and Stalin, who alone among the early Bolsheviks had enough of a realistic streak to mitigate their sanguinary impatience. Temporarily forced into a modicum of good behaviour, at least outside their own borders, the Soviets set out to consolidate their gains in Russia, while trying to subvert the West in ways less straightforward than a cavalry charge. Hence the first nihilist state since the French Revolution managed to survive, if only by the skin of its teeth.

Unlike Trotsky, the emotional inspiration of today's neocons, Lenin and Stalin represented the pragmatic strain of Bolshevism, which made them more dangerous in the long run. They were driven by evil more deep-seated than even the recess in which straightforward Marxism lurks. Their aim was to exterminate Christendom, pure and simple. Bolshevism, in a single country or worldwide, was for them the means, not the end.

They and their ideological heirs relied on Marxist verbiage for as long as it was useful. Internally, they used it to vindicate violence and deprivation; externally they used it to set the world up for the advent of more violence and deprivation. Being pragmatic rather than romantic monsters, they were at all times prepared to abandon communist rhetoric, or at least to temper its use if that would put them in a stronger strategic position. Shrewder men than the contemporaneous politicians in the West, Lenin and Stalin must have sensed that deep down the democratic West differed from the Soviets only in the means preferred to achieve the anti-Christendom ends, not in the ends themselves.

Few Westerners understood fully the mortal – and especially moral – threat that Bolshevism posed to the West. Even many of those who did were intuitively sympathetic to the idea of erasing the remnants of Christendom (a deletion otherwise known as progress), if not necessarily to the stomach-churning business of stuffing people alive into locomotive fireboxes. Lenin aptly described such Westerners as 'useful idiots', with the noun referring to their inability to understand the true nature of Bolshevism and the adjective pointing at numerous ways in which they could be made to serve the Soviets wittingly or unwittingly.

Sensing in the West a deep need to love the latest step in the march of progress, Lenin and Stalin responded to their adversaries' spoken and unspoken requests to make such love possible. To that end the Bolsheviks devised, over the mouth-frothing protests of Trotsky and his followers, a two-pronged policy that, with variations, Russia has been following ever since. The two prongs were at the time of their origination called Military Communism and the New Economic Policy (NEP). The former illustrated the difference between the means favoured by the Bolsheviks and the contemporaneous West; the latter hinted at the similarity of the ends.

The purpose of Military Communism was to rape first the country and then the world into submission; the chief objectives of NEP and its successors were to mitigate the effects of Military Communism, back-pedal, let some steam off and then set up the next round by attempting to present to the world a picture of 'change', 'liberalisation', Khrushchev's 'thaw', Brezhnev's 'détente', Andropov's 'communism with a human face', Gorbachev's 'glasnost', Yeltsyn's 'perestroika', Putin's 'reform' and so forth – with a repressive reaction to follow each time.

Sudden shifts in Russian policy can never surprise anyone who is familiar with this alternating pattern: the blood-thirsty collectivisation followed by Stalin's warning against 'vertigo from success'; the post-war witches' Sabbath followed by 'the thaw', which was bound to adumbrate Brezhnev's reaction, which in turn set the stage for the on-going NEP-like binge allied to garden-or-common criminality.

4

At the cutting edge of both prongs were different departments of the secret police, called the Cheka at the time of its founding. Since then the KGB, FSB or whatever this diabolical organisation calls itself now (it has had eight name changes, each hailed by 'useful idiots' as a sign of its evolution) has pervaded every pore of the Russian body politic. It not only executes but formulates Russia's foreign and domestic policy, its economic plans and, above all, its long-term strategy.

In the past it mostly worked behind the scenes but these days it has abandoned all pretence, which is understandable considering that many key members of the Russian government, starting with Col. Putin himself, are career KGB officers. The present tense is deliberate: it was Putin himself who once proudly declared, "There is no such thing as ex-KGB. This is for life."

From the very beginning it was assumed that the two-pronged policy had to be executed not just domestically but also worldwide. The Soviet state could not, and Russia still cannot, survive without the West's support, or at least acquiescence. Yet unswerving adherence to the cannibalistic 'War Communism' model was bound to give even well-disposed Westerners some second thoughts. Hence the sheep's clothing that the Soviet wolf has always had to don whenever possible, especially when going on foraging expeditions to the West. Thus disinformation and strategic deception do not just lie at the heart of Russia's foreign policy; they largely *are* Russia's foreign policy – and that is part of what makes the Cheka 'the essence of Bolshevism', in Lenin's phrase.

The history of the KGB (I am using the term generically, not to have to identify the precise nomenclature each time) is a continuous string of successful disinformation ops. An abbreviated list would include the post-war peace movement, as a result of which Western atomic scientists felt called upon to share their secrets with the Russians; the bogus anticommunist guerrilla movements in the forests of Lithuania, Latvia and the Ukraine in the late forties and early fifties, which neutered any real resistance; the détente and 'SALT process' of the seventies, during which the Soviets embarked on an unprecedented military build-up; the anti-nuke movement that largely succeeded in making the West overly reliant on hydrocarbons and so forth – all the way to the 'collapse' of the Soviet Union. The KGB's tactical flexibility always put it on a collision course with the rigid party apparatchiks calcified in their thinking. They correctly felt that the pragmatic approach favoured by the KGB was tinged with power-grabbing ambitions. That organisation, unlike the *nomenklatura*, was staffed with men of action. Useful as they might be in their place, they had to be kept at arm's length. Thus each purge of the Party perpetrated by the KGB was followed by a purge of the KGB perpetrated by the Party. Every secret police chief until 1954 was either executed or assassinated, including the most outstanding figure among them.

Lavrentiy Beria led that outfit, not always *de jure* but always *de facto*, from 1938 to 1953. Upon Stalin's death in March 1953, which Beria according to strong circumstantial evidence might have accelerated,[34] he proposed to his Politburo colleagues a bogus glasnost and perestroika programme. For the sake of verisimilitude Beria also suggested some real concessions. This anticipated Gorbachev in such details as acceptance of private enterprise, abolition of collective farms, withdrawal from Germany and her subsequent reunification, placing a greater accent on the production of consumer goods, granting more autonomy to the constituent republics and so forth.

The objective was all-familiar: presenting a human face to the West, luring it into disarmament and blackmailing it into a massive transfer of funds and technology, thereby gaining control first over Europe and then the rest of the world. Yet the more cautious Party hierarchy felt the professional Chekists were moving too fast. To slow them down Beria was killed,

---

34   In his 1956 'secret-session speech' Khrushchev inadvertently let the cat out of the bag by describing Stalin as a monster who found out the hard way that "tyrants who live by the axe will perish by the axe". Not only did Stalin's successor amusingly replace the Biblical sword with a more traditional Russian weapon, but he also hinted at the manner of Stalin's death.

reputedly in gangland style. In the honoured USSR tradition this was followed by a bloody purge of the KGB – the Party, assisted by the equally vindictive army, was taking revenge for 1936–1938, when KGB sadists had been torturing yesterday's deities to death. However, the KGB, in the decaying shape of Yuri Andropov, won the next round, and the Russian language made the most important contributions to the OED since 'disinformation': 'glasnost' and 'perestroika'.

When Andropov died in 1984, his protégé Gorbachev eventually took over, and it fell upon him to implement the KGB programme first designed by Beria, further developed by another KGB boss Shelepin and almost brought to fruition by Andropov. Already towards the end of Andropov's reign the Soviets began to abandon the hardnosed communist jargon in their communications aimed at foreign audiences. Instead they began to caress the ears of Western democracy junkies with mellifluous liberal words lifted from the pages of *The Guardian*, *Le Monde* and *The New York Times*. The West was clearly being prepared for the impending 'collapse', and it duly came in 1991 under Gorbachev's boozy successor Yeltsyn. The Soviet Union had to die so that the KGB may live on.

5

The 'collapse' came so suddenly and unexpectedly that no one in the West had time to think. Emotions, mostly triumphant ones, were so overwhelming that the critical faculty elevated to ultimate virtue by Descartes was put on hold. The most natural question under the circumstances, "Why did the Soviet Union collapse so suddenly?", was seldom asked and, when it was, the neocons had a field day with the answers.

Just as Marx believed that the proletariat was destined to be the grave digger of the bourgeoisie, the neocons believe that democracy is the grave digger of… well, anything other than democracy. They had always maintained that sooner or later democracy would vanquish all over the world, had they not? And had they not identified 'communism' as the only obstacle? Thus the 'collapse' happened because it was bound to happen; it was an historical inevitability. Neoconservative ideology, including its unwavering neo-Marxist determinism, was now amply vindicated. The USSR collapsed because the legs of the colossus had been made of clay all along. Now they had been cut off at the knee by the unbearable pressure of trying to contest an arms race against the USA. Hence the Soviets were no longer able to contain the Russians' ravenous quest for democracy, inexplicably muted as it might have been for the previous 1,000 years. QED. End of story. End of history.

Few stopped to ponder the unlikely neatness of it all. Just as the West, in particular its Anglophone part, was ready to buy the neocon vision of the world, and only the nagging presence of the Soviet obstacle was standing in the way, the obstacle was miraculously and spectacularly removed. Why? And why so suddenly? The rat of disinformation ran rampaging all over the world, yet practically no one managed to smell it – and those few who did were howled down and shamed into silence.

However, when all those glasnosts and perestroikas first came about under Andropov and Gorbachev, nothing at all pointed at the subsequent 'collapse' of the Soviet Union. The system remained stable, its monopoly on armed violence in the country absolute. None of the constituent republics had any kind of organisation capable of challenging the Soviet supremacy. The consumer economy was not doing well but then it never had; and if famines killing 10 million peasants in the 1930s had not toppled the Soviets, why would they roll over and play dead at a time when their country was, by comparison, prosperous and their hold on power firmer than ever?

Nor had any moral regeneration occurred within the ranks of the *nomenklatura* – under Gorbachev it was as capable of violence and mendacity as under Brezhnev. Witness the way it handled the 1986 nuclear disaster at Chernobyl, one of a long string of such events, both accidental and deliberate, going back to the 1950s.

For example, in 1957 an explosion at an underground nuclear facility in the Urals released 50 to 100 tonnes of high-level radioactive waste, contaminating a territory twice the size of Western Europe and killing tens of thousands. The Soviets kept the event under wraps and fumed with indignation whenever asked a direct question. Nor were they any more forthcoming about the monstrous tests designed to examine the lethal effect of nuclear weapons. One such test was conducted in 1954 at the Totsk testing ground, where a bomb with twice the yield of the one used in Hiroshima was dropped on army positions. Thousands died on the spot, and God only knows how many more by delayed action. That crime too was hushed up and remained classified for at least 50 years.

Building on this laudable tradition, Gorbachev immediately denied that anything untoward had happened in Chernobyl. Any suggestions of a nuclear accident anywhere in the Soviet Union, and certainly at Chernobyl, had to come from the CIA and other inveterate reptiles. State television was flooded with the Chernobyl footage of young mothers holding their happy, rosy-cheeked babies to camera and assuring interviewers that everyone was in perfect health. There were no TV crews about when those same babies (their total number remains classified to this day) began to die a few months later.

Had the West had less sophisticated detection equipment at its disposal, and had the winds not blown radioactive clouds towards Scandinavia and Scotland, the sainted Gorbachev would have got away with his lies. This goes to show that morally Soviet leaders remained rock-solid Bolsheviks – this regardless of whether they had ascended to power courtesy of the Party or the KGB.

As to the lost arms race being the last straw breaking communism's back, that argument does not cut much ice either. For by the mid-eighties the Soviets had already achieved at least parity with America in almost every strategic category. This is not a biased hawkish view but one enunciated by the dove of all doves, Eugene Rostow, Kennedy's and Johnson's foreign policy guru and Reagan's Director of the Arms Control and Disarmament Agency: "In 1985, the Soviet Union had a lead of more than 3.5 to one in the number of warheads on ICBMs and a lead of more than four to one in the throw weight of these weapons. Its sea-based and airborne nuclear forces have made comparable if slightly less spectacular gains. In addition, it

DEMOCRACY AS A NEOCON TRICK

had a near monopoly of advanced intermediate-range ground-based weapons threatening targets in Europe, Japan, China, and the Middle East." Fair enough. So why the instant 'collapse' just a few years later?

To quote Lenin, an authority on such matters, for a revolution to succeed the country must have a 'revolutionary situation' in place, thereby the rulers cannot enforce the old ways and the ruled will not accept them. Yet a dispassionate look at recent history reveals that no such situation existed in Russia at the time of 'collapse' in 1989 or indeed 1991.

Why then? It is not my purpose in this essay to analyse this complex development in detail, nor to suggest simplistically that all of it was merely an exercise in disinformation, although much of it undoubtedly was. But even if an attempt at exhaustive analysis were to be made, conjecture would still have to figure prominently. For the Soviet Union was ruled not by law, much less by the 'power of the people',[35] but by a small circle of men exercising total control. Thus a definitive answer to the question "Why did the Soviet Union suddenly collapse?" could only be found by peeking into the heads of those men, which is patently impossible.

Since at the time their control was as unchallenged and unchallengeable as it ever had been, then any 'collapse' could only have happened because they *decided* that it should happen. It was a matter of deliberate decision, and one should not confuse Gorbachev's or Yeltsyn's choice with Hobson's. They could have gone one way or the other. There was no historical inevitability involved, for no such thing exists in secular affairs. Materialistic determinism, so beloved of Marx, Lenin, Trotsky and the neocons, has been proved to be nonsensical so many times that it would be tedious to cite every instance here.

Therefore a conscious choice was made, and we can only guess why it was made. Some guesses however would be more educated than others, more firmly grounded in facts than the

---

35 A story making the rounds in the USSR involved a record-breaking collective farmer invited to attend a Kremlin reception. Upon his return to his village the lucky chap told his friends, "It's like they say: all power to the people. And I *saw* those people!"

RUSSIA AND THE REIGN OF ERROR

cock-and-bull story about the triumph of democracy sold to the world by the neocons and their followers. Moreover, many initial guesses, especially those based on the ancient *Cui bono?* principle, have since left the realm of conjecture to enter that of fact.

6

Some of these are based on what is fashionably called the human factor. I have mentioned earlier that Soviet leaders enjoyed a privileged life by comparison to the population they bullied. Yet this privilege was largely expressed through means other than just money.

In fact the upper reaches of the *nomenklatura* already lived under Marx's notion of communism in that their existence was demonetarised (money only became useful a few rungs below the top of the ladder). The state provided everything its leaders needed without any money changing hands: apartments, clothes, food, entertainment, country houses, Black Sea retreats – above all the ultimate high of unlimited power. There were several problems with that arrangement though. First, even though the lesser leaders did possess the kind of monetary wealth that to the downtrodden Russians seemed like a fairytale fortune, this was denominated in what those same Russians called 'wooden roubles', which is to say worthless currency.

Money in the Soviet Union had nothing to do with the amount of goods and services available (a situation our frenzied public spending financed by the printing press may soon duplicate here as well). Those were so scarce that at some point money became worthless – it could buy nothing beyond a certain level, not legally at any rate. Even those few privileged Soviets who were allowed to travel abroad could not spend their money there, for the rouble was not convertible. Thus the trusted comrades had to depend on the state's munificence, which tended to be rather fickle.

Stalin brutally enforced an arrangement under which the *nomenklatura*'s wealth and privilege were wholly contingent on the regime's good graces. Until the mid–1950s a fall from grace

275

usually meant a bullet in the back of the neck or a long spell in a concentration camp. But even thereafter, when deposed leaders were allowed to retire unmolested, they were reminded of the truth behind Thomas à Kempis's phrase "*Sic transit gloria mundi*". Their comparative penury in retirement inevitably came as an eye-opening shock, which any reader of Khrushchev's memoirs will confirm.

Another problem was old-fashioned envy. Privileged comrades could occasionally travel to the West, an ability that was in itself one of the greatest privileges. They therefore realised that the luxuries they enjoyed at home, such as flats in clean buildings, imported fixtures, electronic equipment, cars and so forth, were taken for granted by all middleclass Westerners, a large and expanding group. As to those residing in the higher reaches of Western society, the comrades could not even dream of their private jets, 300-foot Mediterranean yachts, residences all over the world.

How then could they privatise and monetarise their privilege, to make sure their wealth could compare with that of the well-to-do classes in the West, and also to have a sporting chance of keeping it after losing their *nomenklatura* posts? The reins had been loosened in the decades passing since Stalin's death, so this question could now be asked – and it could only be answered in one way.

The *nomenklatura* had to convert their privilege from 'wooden' roubles into paper dollars. However, this meant breaking the state's monopoly on the possession of foreign currency, which had been the holy of holies since Lenin's days. The monopoly was guarded more jealously than any other: about 250,000 Soviets were convicted for possessing dollars between 1953 and 1989. Many of them were sentenced to death.

The conclusion was obvious: if the nature of the Soviet regime made life hard for the *nomenklatura*, the regime had to change. After all, any gigantic bureaucratic structure, whatever its declared purpose, ultimately exists to serve the interests of those who run it. This also applies to such Leviathans as modern Western states or, say, our own dear NHS. It certainly applied in the USSR, where even token moral restraints did not apply. It was the country that served the *nomenklatura*, not the other way around. Thus the *nomenklatura* had to privatise, at least partially, the traditional sources of hard currency, such as the export of raw materials, precious metals, caviar, antiques, icons and so forth. Rivers of oil flowing to the West had to come back as streams of dollars, with many of them bypassing the state treasury. The privatised dollars could then be recycled into numbered accounts all over the world.

Here the *nomenklatura* was building on a rich pre-Stalin tradition. When Lenin and his gang of 'idealists' were torturing every ounce of gold out of the terrorised populace, the proceeds were not used to relieve murderous famines in the Volga area and elsewhere. Rather they went straight into the comrades' accounts at foreign banks, which occasionally led to international scandals.

For example, in 1921 *The New York Times* broke an earth-shattering story (remember to multiply the amounts mentioned by roughly 20 to get some idea of present value): "As we have found out, just in the past year the following amounts came into the accounts held by Bolshevik leaders: from Trotsky, $11 million in just one US bank, 90 million Swiss francs in the Banque de Suisse; from Zinoviev, 80 million Swiss francs in the Banque de Suisse... from Lenin, 75 million Swiss francs."

While the early unsophisticated comrades felt no need to launder the money first, the post-Stalin *nomenklatura* thought this would be advisable – one never knew how the West would react over time. In the early days, before the KGB professionals took over in earnest, the Party's bag of tricks was rather lean. Typically they relied on so called 'friendly firms', money-laundering setups under the guise of legitimate businesses. These were run by Westerners either sympathetic to the Soviets or even acting under their discipline. For example, Robert 'Cap'n Bob' Maxwell fell into one of these categories, and probably both.

Newly published archival data show that as early as the 1950s Maxwell was investigated by the FBI on suspicion of being a Soviet agent. The conclusion reached was that he was not, yet this conclusion was wrong. This should not surprise anyone:

both the FBI and MI5 were notoriously inept at flashing out Soviet spies. One of them, Kim Philby, almost became head of the British Intelligence Service; another, Aldrich Ames, ran the CIA Soviet desk for years; yet another, Robert Hanssen, was one of the FBI's top counterintelligence officers – this list can grow longer than anyone's arm.

The FBI spy catchers' ruling was probably correct technically: Maxwell did not "transfer technological and scientific information to the Soviets". He was much too valuable to risk on such trivial assignments. For Cap'n Bob was what the Soviets called an 'agent of influence', perhaps the most important one next to the American industrialist Armand Hammer. Said influence was exerted through politicians, journalists or 'friendly firms'. One such firm was Maxwell's Pergamon Press.

Maxwell, a retired captain in the British army, bought 75 percent of the company in 1951 and instantly made it an unlikely success. If the original investment miraculously did not come courtesy of the KGB, the overnight success definitely did. Maxwell signed a brother-in-law deal with the Soviet copyright agency VAAP (a KGB offshoot) and began publishing English translations of Soviet academic journals.

Making any kind of income, never mind millions, in that business would have been next to impossible. On the one hand, Soviet science at the time was hardly cutting-edge stuff, and those parts of it that were did not publish their findings in journals – they were (and still remain) classified. Interest in the Soviet academic press was therefore minimal, while the cost of translating and publishing it was immense.

Producing even academic periodicals originally written in English is a laborious and low-margin business requiring much specialised expertise. That is why it is usually undertaken by big and long-established firms, which Maxwell's start-up was not. Add to this the cost of translation and one really begins to wonder about the provenance of the riches on which he built his empire.

Subsequent intimate ties between Maxwell and the Soviets dispel any doubts. He became a frequent visitor to Moscow and a welcome guest in the Kremlin. Specifically, he met every Soviet leader from Khrushchev to Gorbachev, and they did not just chat about the weather. Maxwell was being told what line he was supposed to toe, and toe the line he did. For example, when an MP, Maxwell made a parliamentary speech defending the Soviet 1968 invasion of his native Czechoslovakia, bizarrely portraying the outrage as some kind of recompense for the country's betrayal at Munich.

In the 1970s Pergamon Press prospered by churning out such sure-fire bestsellers as books by Soviet leaders. On 4 March 1975, Maxwell signed, on his own terms, another contract with VAAP under which he published seven books by Soviet chieftains: five by Brezhnev, one by Chernenko and one by Andropov, then still head of the KGB. Under a 1978 contract he also brought out Brezhnev's immortal masterpiece *Peace Is the People's Priceless Treasure*, along with books by Grishin and Ponomarev, the former a Politburo member, the latter head of the Central Committee International Department.

All those books were published in huge runs and, considering the nonexistent demand for this genre, would have lost millions for any other publisher. But Maxwell was not just any old publisher and these were not just any old entrepreneurial ventures. The translation, publishing and printing were paid for by the Soviets at 100 times the actual cost, with the balance settling in numbered accounts.

In the 1980s Maxwell met Gorbachev three times, the last get-together also involving Vladimir Kryuchkov, the KGB boss. As a result Pergamon Press began publishing the English-language version of the Soviet Cultural Foundation magazine *Nashe Naslediye* (Our Heritage), along with the writings by both Gorbachev and his wife Raisa (Charles Dickens and Jane Austen they were not).

One objective pursued by the Soviets was propaganda, but this could have been achieved with less capital outlay and greater effect. The real purpose was the old Soviet pastime: money laundering and the looting of Russia in preparation for 'the collapse of the Soviet Union', which in effect was the transfer of power from the Party to the KGB. Pergamon Press played an important role in this enterprise, if a small one in the general scheme of things.

Between 1989 and 1991 the KGB transferred to the West eight metric tonnes of platinum, 60 metric tonnes of gold, carloads of diamonds and up to $50 billion in cash. The cash part was in roubles, officially not a convertible currency. But the Soviets made it convertible by setting a vast network of bogus holding companies and fake brassplates throughout the West. The key figures in the cash transfer were the KGB's financial wizard Col. Leonid Veselovsky, seconded to the Administration Department of the Central Committee, and Nikolai Kruchina, head of that department. Putin took a modest part in the looting of Russia as Deputy Mayor of Leningrad.

The focal point of that transfer activity in the West was Maxwell, the midwife overseeing the birth pains of the so-called Soviet oligarchy. We know little about the exact mechanics of this criminal scam, perhaps the biggest one in history. The actual operators knew too much, which could only mean they had to fall out with the designers. Specifically, in August 1991 Kruchina fell out of his office window. Two months later Maxwell fell overboard from his yacht. Veselovsky, who handled most of the leg work, managed to flee to Switzerland, where he became a highly paid consultant. He must have known quite a bit not only about his former employers but also about his new clients, which enhanced his earning potential.

Since the massive conversion of the *nomenklatura*'s wealth into dollars had to bypass official channels to a large extent, the Party and the KGB intermingled with the crime barons of the shadow economy. This created a new elite, where Party apparatchiks, KGB officers and gangsters fused into a cohesive group within which it became hard to distinguish among the principal constituents.

Perhaps the biggest influx of personnel into the new elite, especially its 'business' end, came from *komsomol*,[36] formally a youth extension of the Party that in fact had always had closer links with the KGB, acting as its breeding grounds. Thus three

---

36 *Kommunisticheskiy Soyuz Molodyozhi* – The Young Communist League (YCL).

RUSSIA AND THE REIGN OF ERROR

post-war KGB heads, Shelepin, Semichiastny and Andropov, came up through the ranks of *komsomol*. Incidentally, the same arrangement existed in Soviet satellites as well. Their equivalents of *komsomol* were just as tightly attached to their equivalents of the KGB. (This raises interesting questions about Angela Merkel who held a *nomenklatura* position in East Germany's *Kommunistischer Jugendverband Deutschlands*.)

It was from the ranks of *komsomol* that much of the freshly minted business elite was drawn. If you scratch most post-perestroika 'oligarchs', such as Khodorkovsky, Nevzlin, Abramovich, Berezovsky, you will uncover a former *komsomol* apparatchik or at least activist. The Russians refer to this group as 'appointed oligarchs', which is an accurate description. They were indeed appointed to act as guardians of the new elite's wealth, of which they were given a leasehold, not a freehold.

Their reward was the means to live high on the hog off the interest, even abroad if such was their wish. Their obligation was to remember they were the monkeys, not the organ grinders. When they forget this vital precondition, their memory is jogged in all sorts of ways, ranging from assassination to imprisonment. For example, Khodorkovsky, the richest 'appointed oligarch' and former *komsomol* head in one of the Moscow boroughs, spent 10 years in prison.

The top-to-bottom criminalisation of commercial activity in Russia guarantees state control not only of business but also of politics. Since no major transaction in the country can be conducted without some illicit money changing hands, the whole self-employed community is effectively held hostage to the government, indeed to Putin personally. One step away from the well-trodden path of obedience and sycophancy, and any 'businessman' can be imprisoned on ostensibly criminal, but in fact political, charges.

The European Court of Human Rights will then rule, as it did in Khodorkovsky's case, that the charges were not politically motivated. True enough, in any civilised country the prosecution would have won a similar criminal case on *prima facie* evidence alone. But in Russia the case would not even have been opened had Khodorkovsky not stepped out of political line. The lesson has been learned. Since even a parody of democratic politics requires heavy funding, and since no rich man is going to finance opposition parties on pain of imprisonment, no effective opposition to Putin can arise.

The new elite burgeoning under the aegis of the KGB took over Russia, which allowed it to combine business with pleasure. The pleasure part was now pursued all over the West, where members of this gigantic crime family are fêted as 'businessmen'. If that is indeed what they are, they must be the greatest entrepreneurs the world has ever known – it took most of them but a few months to turn from small-time crooks into billionaires.

"Pecunia non olet" (money does not stink), quipped the Roman emperor Vespasian when questioned about his tax on the urine sold to tanners by public lavatories. As Vespasian was crude even by the standards of Roman emperors, he can be forgiven for his soldierly directness. What is upsetting is that after two millennia of subsequent civilisation we still have not outlived the principle enunciated by Vespasian. Except that we couch it in legal cant based on property rights, a subject dear to every conservative heart. However, society has a superseding right to protect its moral health, and it is this right that is jeopardised by the presence of freshly minted Russian billionaires.

Ever since the 'collapse' of the Soviet Union, they have been arriving in England, first in a trickle, lately in a stream. Their money arrives with them and we welcome it. The Brits cannot afford to buy £80-million houses; good job someone can. Who cares how that £80 million was earned? On occasion KGB assassins arrive in the oligarchs' wake, to chastise them when they misbehave and forget who is boss. Even though this makes London look like Chicago *circa* 1925, we accept it as the inevitable cost of doing business. *Pecunia non olet.*

Everyone knows, or ought to know, that it is impossible become a billionaire in today's Russia without engaging in activities that in any civilised country would land their perpetrator in prison. Since the KGB mafia fronted by Putin controls Russia's economy completely, no one can become a billionaire

RUSSIA AND THE REIGN OF ERROR

there without active cooperation with organised crime, if only by paying protection kickbacks. And since the mafia is criminal, every Russian billionaire is, as a minimum, its accessory.[37] They all, possibly with one or two exceptions, have a criminal mentality, and they bring it to London along with their money. We close our eyes on the former because we like the latter. *Pecunia non olet.*

However, the Russians' pursuit of happiness does not mean they ignore the traditional business at hand: exercising control over a good part of the world.

7

The Soviet economy was configured as a Moscow-centred network. In practical terms that made it virtually impossible for the constituent republics to break away from Russia in any other than a purely formal way. Most republics were irrevocably attached to Moscow, with the oil pipe acting as the umbilical chord.

The ruling elites in the republics were linked with Moscow even more closely – they were the flesh of its flesh. Thus when power at the centre passed from the Party over to the secret police, exactly the same thing happened at the periphery. Secret police generals, such as Shevardnadze in Georgia and Aliev in Azerbaijan, took over and declared formal independence from Russia, while remaining her lifelong agents.

Only in the three Baltic republics did the Soviet Union collapse for real, if not necessarily straight away. In 1990 Lithuania was the first to declare her independence,[38] with Prof. Vytautas Landsbergis becoming her first head of state. Within a few months, however, he was ousted by a Moscow-controlled

---

37 The sainted Gorbachev is now running his own foundation originally capitalised at $8 billion. Considering that his highest salary was an equivalent of $600 a month, he must have saved a fair amount by taking bag lunches.

38 Gorbachev response was typical of all Soviet chieftains: he sent commandos to Vilnus to quell the trouble. His subsequent claim to secular sainthood is based on the fact that his hit squad murdered merely hundreds, not the hundreds of thousands that would been exterminated under Stalin.

junta. When asked who in the new government was KGB, Landsbergis ruefully replied, "They all are."

Since then the Baltic republics seem to have re-established their independence, but they are the only three that have. All others are still being *de facto* run out of Moscow, paying tribute to their masters out of their own ill-gotten gains. Georgia, incidentally, was well on the way to becoming independent under President Saakashvili. However, after an aggressive five-day war in 2008 the Russians brought Georgia back into the fold, eventually ousting Saakashvili in 2012 and replacing him with their own puppet. And when the Ukraine ousted the Russian puppet Yanukovych in 2014, Putin's reaction was equally violent.

As to their Eastern European satellites, the Russians had to loosen their stronghold there for tactical reasons. Yet loosening is not the same as abandoning, and it would be naïve not to realise that the Russians have not relinquished their control altogether. It is simply exerted by means more subtle than tank thrusts and commando raids. The conduits through which power is transmitted are mainly army and secret-police officers, most of whom were trained in Russia and many of whom remain loyal to her. Largely due to the triumphant noises the neocons bullhorned all over the world at the time of the 'collapse', many of such KGB puppets have since gained sensitive positions in NATO and the EU.

For example, in early 2008 the Hungarian Sandor Laborc was appointed head of the NATO Committee for Security and Intelligence whose function is to coordinate the intelligence efforts of 28 countries. Gen. Laborc is an honours graduate of the KGB Dzierjinsky Academy in Moscow, which was obviously deemed to be the perfect educational qualification for the job. This is tantamount to Anjem Choudary being appointed to head an anti-terrorist task force, or else Dr Shipman being put in charge of care for the elderly.

In order to study at the Dzierjinsky Academy in the eighties (1983–1989 in Laborc's case), the aspirant had to demonstrate not only the requisite ability but also the kind of loyalty to the Soviet cause that could not have been faked. After all, the examiners at that academic institution have enough experience in interrogation to tell heartfelt from feigned devotion. Gen. Laborc, in other words, sold his soul to the devil, and this kind of transaction can never be reversed. Such was the man who acquired unrestricted access to NATO secrets, and he was not the only one.

It is also obvious from heaps of circumstantial evidence that the Russians have long-term plans involving the European Union. Thus in his 1994 Nobel lecture Gorbachev spoke of "... the European space from the Atlantic to the Urals...". "Since it includes the Soviet Union," he said, "which reaches the Pacific, it extends over the nominal geographic borders..."

But every child, especially one of neocon parents, knows the Soviet Union had collapsed and no longer existed at that time. If such a child has studied geography, he also knows that the area of the former Soviet Union that lies between the Urals and the Pacific is in Asia, not in the 'European space'. What every child does not know, and neither do the grown-ups who formulate our foreign policy, is that 'geographic borders' have become 'nominal'. In other words, 'Europe' is not a geographical but an *ideological* concept. As far as the Russians are concerned, it has always been exactly that.

Before the 'collapse', Russia's control of the world was structured as a four-circle Inferno. The first circle was the Soviet republics, over which the Russians had absolute control both *de facto* and *de jure*. The second circle was comprised of the 'People's Democracies' in Eastern Europe and elsewhere, over which the control was almost as tight *de facto*. The third circle included Finland, to some extent Austria and various third-world and non-allied countries, many of which were under the Soviets' control while remaining technically independent. The fourth circle was the West proper, wherein the Soviet influence, while by no means negligible, was too sporadic for their comfort.

As a result of the 'collapse', the circles were shifted. Erstwhile Soviet republics were upgraded to a status not dissimilar to that formerly enjoyed by the quasi-independent 'People's Democracies', and the latter were elevated to the status of Finland *circa* 1960. The Russians shifted the first two cicles for one reason only: to produce a shift in the opposite direction in the third and fourth circles, especially the West. They abandoned the control mechanisms of the past probably because they felt others would be more promising in the future. In the Russians' eyes the European Union offered greater geopolitical opportunities than the Soviet Union.

Their judgment is good: just imagine a European Union that includes Russia and all her satellites, which it eventually will if it survives long enough. Who is going to run such a newfangled empire? Surely the country that possesses the continent's greatest military muscle by far, not to mention the greatest energy reserves. Empires are always dominated by their power centres, which is why they used to be called Roman (not Etruscan), British (not Indian), Russian (not Polish) and Austro-Hungarian (not Bohemian).

Whether the Russians planned to take advantage of European federalism all along or simply reacted to it opportunistically is an interesting but moot question. What matters is that they have both the means and the motive to emerge as a major beneficiary of it.

8

Such, in most schematic terms, was the process that led to an outburst of triumphant enthusiasm all over the West, but particularly among the neocons. With the sleight of hand that comes naturally to ideologues, they portrayed the 'collapse' as a resounding victory for their cherished liberal democracy. Today, barely two decades later, anyone with any grasp of current affairs knows that today's Russia is as far from either liberalism or democracy as it was at any time since 1917. Surprisingly, such knowledge has only slightly muted the noises emanating from the neocons. Against all evidence they insist on portraying the nakedly authoritarian rule of Putin's transparently criminal elite as merely a temporary setback, one that will soon be reversed.

There are various reasons for this onset of myopia. First, a Russia growing more openly hostile to the West by the day delivers a welcome source of global tension. The neocons' congenital bellicosity demands a major standoff providing a focal point for their ambitions. If before they clamoured for the introduction of democracy in Russia, they can now agitate for its return. Any historical evidence showing that the 'collapse' might have been a sham from the beginning is being swept under the carpet.

Then of course the neocons detect in Russia the same aggressive internationalism that is their own stock in trade. That sense of emotional kinship may trump any potential clash of national and geopolitical interests. This also explains why, like their idol Woodrow Wilson, the neocons are great champions of multinational organisations, ideally a world government.

The concept lacks even novelty appeal. For example, in his *Life of Alexander* Plutarch talks about his subject's quest "to make all men citizens of one single state under one single government," and, "to make universal peace, to reign in unity and concord, and to secure the communication of all men with each other." What was a utopia almost two millennia ago remains just as utopian now, but no one can accuse the neocons of suffering from a surfeit of common sense.

This time-tested craving for world government, further strengthened by Marx and his followers, such as Antonio Gramsci and the Frankfurt school, explains the affection for the European Union that most neocons share with Russia. This is a seeming paradox because on the face of it the EU clashes with the demands of the American religion. The European Union was, after all, put together partly for the explicit purpose of offsetting America's economic power on the continent and around the world. To that end the EU has effectively turned itself into a protectionist bloc, with multiple tariffs being imposed on American imports. The Americans retaliate in kind, trade suffers and so especially do consumers on both sides, who ultimately pay for all those levies at the tills of their local shops.

Nevertheless every US administration since Wilson's has been ecstatic about the idea of a pan-European state even when it was still in an embryonic state. Why? Are the Americans out to cut off their economic nose to spite their face? Of course not. We must remember that the USA has been pursuing global imperial ambitions for over a century now. It is reasonably clear from all available evidence that the American establishment, especially the neocon part of it, sees the EU, for all its protectionist churlishness, as a facilitator of such ambitions. They seem to believe that, tariffs or no tariffs, the EU will sooner or later fall under their control. The belief is not wholly groundless.

For one thing, in their desperate attempts to keep this moribund concoction afloat for a while longer, the eurocrats are steadily reducing defence budgets in all European countries, this in spite of an extremely precarious geopolitical situation. Consequently they will have to depend on American protection as much as in the past, particularly when Russia begins to tighten the screws.

In American public bars one often hears laments about their country having to spend a fortune on defence because European countries refuse to pull their weight. But the neocons, and those in Washington who have bought into their vision, are not complaining. The situation, as far as they are concerned, resembles the protection racket: retailers pay off the mob to keep smaller criminals at bay. Before long the charges become unaffordable and the gangsters take over the business. The comparison to organised crime is more metaphorical with the neocons than with the Russians, but the underlying animus is similar.

Thus COLLENE: "I believe that the European Union more accurately reflects what the world will look like at the end of history than the contemporary United States. The EU's attempt to transcend sovereignty and traditional power politics by establishing a transnational rule of law is much more in line with a 'post-historical' world than the Americans' continuing belief in God, national sovereignty, and their military."

The presumptive triad of the outdated beliefs the Americans are still lamentably supposed to hold seems odd, but only at first glance. Underneath it all one detects a neocon soul craving for a world where Christianity would no longer exist as a viable force, while the American religion, along with its democracy-based scriptural canon, would conquer the world and keep it conquered without having to rely exclusively on US armed forces.

Meanwhile, just like the Soviets who spouted Marxist phraseology when it was useful and then abandoned it when it no longer was, the neocons are preparing to replace their jingoist jargon with a set of internationalist shibboleths. Their natural bellicosity demands wars, but not simply those serving American national interests. Thus whenever an opportunity presents itself to export Democracy to other regions, particularly the Middle East, the neocons' eyes light up.

Not that they necessarily feel that there exists any contradiction between the American religion and global expansionism. In fact COLLENE comments that it is impressive "how often promoting democracy has actually advanced other American interests." "American interests as the neocons see them" would have been an important qualifier. But it was never uttered.

2001 and all that

1

The neocons had little to do with the 'collapse' of the Soviet Union and neither did they set up the tragedy of 11 September, 2001. However, they showed both the perspicacity to detect a chance for advancing their cause and the resolve to grab the opportunity with both hands when it presented itself.

From the neocons' standpoint, the world's most famous terrorist act could not have happened at a better time. Something like that was desperately needed for them to translate their bellicose instincts into belligerent policy. Russia may have been reverting to her pre-collapse self, but it was going to take her years to qualify as a potential flashpoint able to rally the West to the neocon cause. It would take even longer for the neocons to realise they had misread the situation in Russia, and longer still to admit their mistake. Well, not a mistake, really, for ideologues are never wrong. The neocons had been right all along. It is just that the dastardly Russians conspired to grab the defeat of democracy out of the jaws of the neocons' victory. They ought to be rebuked for being so uncooperative, but there is no need for any adjustments to the ideology.

The airliners that al-Qaeda flew into those tall New York buildings were a godsend, except that God supposedly played no role there at all. According to the neocons, the terrorists and those who inspired them acted out of political, rather than religious, convictions. Religious faith stands for little in the neocon vision of the world – they divide people along strictly political lines or, to be exact, along the watershed separating democracy from any other method of government.

The picture painted by the neocons is charming in its simplicity, if ever so slightly off-putting in its crudeness: the al-Qaeda murderers flew those planes into the Twin Towers because they wished to eradicate the architectural symbol of democracy and free enterprise. By doing so they went against the innermost aspirations of the whole world, emphatically including its Muslim part. There is nothing wrong with Islam or, for that matter, any other religion. They are all equally good, which is to say equally irrelevant. Tolerance is the prime virtue, is it not? Locke was right about that.

Therefore the terrorists had acted not as Muslims but as... what then? Mercifully, the neocons' knack for coining neologisms came to the rescue. The terrorists were not any old Muslims. They were Islamists. Or better still, Islamofascists. They represented an infinitesimal minority in the Muslim world, where most people are at heart politically moderate seekers of democracy, just like everyone is everywhere in the world. It therefore behoves the West, ideally with the neocons at the helm, to satisfy the cravings of all those moderate Muslims by bringing democracy to the Middle East, thereby isolating and eventually eliminating the Islamists among them.

COLLENE's reading of one conflict in the Middle East is characteristic: "Israel, a democratic country whose existence had been approved at the UN, was being assailed by totalitarian enemies..." One would be more inclined to say that a Western country was being assailed by Muslim enemies, but this slight change in wording would entail a cardinal shift in the whole neocon philosophy. Note also the use of the UN as a vindicator of Israel's existence. It is hard to avoid the impression that the United Nations exists solely for the purpose of providing support to either side of any argument. It did indeed vote for the partition of Palestine in 1947: score one for the good side. But then the bad side could even the score by citing the 1975 General Assembly Resolution 3379 that "determine[d] that Zionism is a form of racism and racial discrimination".

This is yet another example of the neocons' woeful ignorance of history and of religion as its driver. This lacuna in their education invariably leads to a misunderstanding of current events, which in turn produces ill-advised policies. For there is no such thing as Islamism. There is only Islam, a doctrinally aggressive religion that has inspired a demonstrably aggressive civilisation. Neither is there any such animal as a moderate Muslim, not in the Western understanding of moderation at any rate. There are only Muslims or non-Muslims. The neocons assumed – or at least claimed to have assumed – that, once the ghastly tyrants were out of the way, moderate Muslims would take over. Rather than killing one another and anyone else they disliked they would then vote in democratic elections and live happily thereafter. This assumption has been proved as gloriously wrong as it was bound to be, and as intelligent people untainted by ideology knew it would be all along. But even the sight of thousands of Muslims dancing in the streets all over the world to celebrate the 11 September atrocity did not broaden the neocons' vision.

Some cursory familiarity with the sacred texts by which Muslims live would have helped, but ideologues tend to overlook facts that might interfere with their lapidary convictions. Otherwise they would have discovered many interesting Koran verses, such as these:

"Slay them [unbelievers] wherever ye find them..." (2:91); "We shall cast terror into the hearts of those who disbelieve." (3:151); "Take them [unbelievers] and kill them wherever ye find them. Against such We have given you clear warrant." (4:91); "The unbelievers are an open enemy to you." (4:101); "As for thief, both male and female, cut off their hands." (5:38); "Take not the Jews and the Christians for friends..." (5:51); "Slay the idolaters wherever ye find them, and take them captive, and besiege them, and prepare for them each ambush" (9:5); "Whoso fighteth in the way of Allah, be he slain or be he victorious, on him We shall bestow a vast reward." (4:74); "...If they turn renegades, seize them and slay them wherever ye find them..." (4:89)

There are 107 such verses in the Koran, conservatively counted, plus 41 calling for jihad. Unlike the violent passages in the Old

Testament, all of these are open-ended, not tied into a particular situation or historical context. This should suffice to show that Islam, for all its sterling qualities,[39] cannot be automatically presumed to foster moderation in its adherents. This is not to say that all Muslims are avid killers of infidels and apostates. Far from it. Some of them are Muslims in the same sense in which Leon Trotsky was a Jew or Richard Dawkins is a Christian. They were born to a faith whose practices they do not really follow and whose dictates they do not necessarily obey. Such Muslims may indeed be really moderate – what they are not is real Muslims.

The argument that violently proselytising Muslim zealots constitute only a minority does not quite wash either, even though it may well be technically true. Every outburst of mass aggression has always been led by a small cadre of impassioned elite. The elite would then either persuade or coerce the inert masses to come along. This holds true for the American Founders who professed to be acting on behalf of the people, whereas most of the people were either indifferent or even hostile to their cause. It was also the case with the French and Russian revolutionaries who then proceeded to annihilate millions of those in whose name they were allegedly acting. It is also true of 'Islamism', which is the neocon for Islam.

There is nothing new about this comment, heretical as it may sound to modern ears half-deafened by the neocons' propaganda helped along by the newly hatched PC orthodoxy. A few decades ago even schoolchildren would have shared the common perception of Islam, as enunciated, among many others, by Winston Churchill: "No stronger retrograde force exists in the world. Far from being moribund, Mohammedanism is a militant and proselytising faith."

The 1,400 years that have passed since Muslim horsemen first swept out of the red-hot Arabian sands have witnessed

---

39   There are many things in Islam that conservatives might envy. Respect for one's elders and the tradition they embody, the importance of family, widespread religious worship, contempt for drunkenness, drugs and pornography – all these are admirable, taken one by one. Taken all together, however, and then mixed with less admirable features, they add up to a civilisation that is incompatible with our own.

an incessant fight to the death between Christendom and the Islamic world. The pendulum has swung back and forth within a wide amplitude, but its swings have never been actuated by a desire for reconciliation. The sides' success or failure solely depended on the intensity of passion injected into their civilisations at each historical moment, and also on their relative muscle mass. When the strength in one overlapped with the weakness in the other, the former gained the upper hand – until the pendulum swung the other way and the power ratio changed. For instance the initial success of the Crusades testified to the greater might of Christendom at that historical instant; their ultimate failure showed that the tables were then turned. Similarly the Muslim invasion of southern Europe occurred at a time Christendom was in retreat, retaining enough strength for rearguard action only.

As they were conquering the Iberian Peninsula, the Arabs pushed into Gaul, and only Charles Martel's victory in the 732 Battle of Tours (also called the Battle of Poitiers) stopped them from taking over most of Europe. That period was marked by an impassioned Islamic world waging war on an enfeebled Christendom still reeling from the fall of the Western Roman Empire. Hence Martel's victory against the Arabs came against the run of play, and a welcome victory it was too. Nonetheless, in the two centuries after Mohammed's death, Islam managed to conquer half of what used to be the Roman Empire. No neonatal civilisation has ever been quite so precocious.

Rather than being specifically Arab, this propensity for aggression has religious roots. After all, if the founder of the West's formative faith was a martyr, the founder of Islam was a brigand and a military leader. His lifetime fame came not just from the book he dictated, but also from the caravans he raided and the cities he sacked. *De Imitatione Mohammedi* would not quite have the same ring as *De Imitatione Christi*, but all believers regardless of their faith see the founder of their religion as an example to follow. Anyway, unlike Christianity, Islam could not have been spread by peaceful sermons: its theological content was too weak to claim a meaningful number of converts merely by persuasion.

Mohammed, who had spent several years in Nestorian monasteries, concocted his doctrine as a patchwork quilt of rags torn out of schismatic Christianity, Judaism, Zoroastrianism or whatever other religions were active in the region. Devout practitioners of those faiths were bound to see Mohammed's Abrahamic revelations as heretical, derivative or disingenuous. Consequently, for his fiery word to conquer it always had to be propped up by cold steel.

When passion in the Arab world waned and Islam's sword hand went limp, the freed energy was re-injected into the Ottoman Turks who went on to wage non-stop wars from the thirteenth century onwards. In the process they conquered Byzantium, Albania, much of what later became Yugoslavia, a great portion of the Habsburg Empire, some of Poland, Sicily, Cyprus and other Mediterranean islands. The tempo of their aggressive expansion was eventually slowed down in 1683, when they were defeated at the gates of Vienna by Jan Sobiesky, king of the Polish-Lithuanian Commonwealth. (Coincidentally, that battle was fought on 11 September.) One could say that Martel and Sobiesky were among the early opponents of multiculturalism.

From then onwards Europe managed to keep Islamic aggression at bay, thanks largely to the scientific and technological advances owing their existence to the sound metaphysical base whence they sprang. The Turks availed themselves of the military technology their own civilisation could not produce, but of necessity they had to lag several steps behind. Having suffered martial setbacks throughout the nineteenth and twentieth centuries, Islam had to lie low until such time when geopolitical confrontations were no longer settled merely by the more sophisticated killing kit.

2

Just as the weakness of the Roman Empire first in the West and then in the East set up the subsequent Islamic conquests, the *coup de grâce* delivered to Christendom by the two great 'American-century' wars began to shift the power ratio towards the

Muslim world. This became possible because in the new order emerging after the Second World War the nature of global politics changed. Political power no longer grew out of the barrel of a gun, as Mao postulated. To a large extent it now grew out of the barrel of oil.

Having explored and developed the Middle Eastern oil fields, Western powers transferred them to the local governments, thereby loading the gun aimed at the heart of the West.[40] The gun began firing after the Second World War, in ever longer bursts. Many factors came into play there, such as the worldwide propaganda against colonialism and imperialism expertly whipped up by the Soviets and indulgently endorsed by the Americans. Neither of them was opposed to the imperial idea as such – it was only the traditional empires that were the burrs under their blankets. As both the Americans and the Soviets were seeking empires of their own, any guilt they could implant into the psyche of their historical adversaries would advance their own neo-imperialistic goals.

In due course, the Soviets, this time acting on their own, launched a worldwide propaganda offensive against nuclear power, which alone can provide a reliable and safe alternative to hydrocarbons on the scale required by the West. The corollary to that was the growing strength of the Arab world that could now use the West's dependence on oil as a blackmail weapon. This did not unduly bother the Soviets because they laboured under the misapprehension that the influence they enjoyed in the Middle East at the time would last for ever.

The Soviets managed to gather and unite under their anti-nuke banner the entire spectrum of the Left, with hues ranging from reddish to greenish to brownish. The focus of the campaign was not just nuclear weapons but also nuclear energy – both were being linked to the ghastly umbrellas drawn with varying mastery by cartoonists the world over. Since the uranium used to produce electricity is way short of the purity

---

40   Ibn-Saud, who modestly named his country after himself, was personally making over \$100 million a year from oil back in the 1930s, when this was serious money.

required in the uranium used to produce devastation, the allusions were as scientifically illiterate as they were politically effective. Meanwhile few Western 'liberals' stopped to think why, for example, the ruling communist party of East Germany was cranking out nuclear power stations like hotcakes, while its West German branch was organising marches against such stations west of the border.

That campaign has outlived the Soviet Union, though of course not the KGB. Except that these days it is augmented by the similarly inspired drive against 'fracking', the production of shale gas. American companies have made huge advances in developing safe and economically feasible techniques of extracting shale gas, whose reserves are for all practical purposes unlimited. Hydraulic fracturing has already enabled the United States to cut both its energy costs and its dependence on Arab oil, which is exactly the outcome to which assorted 'liberals' are opposed.

That the Left still holds tremendous power even after 'the end of history' is evident in the German government's decision to phase out all nuclear power stations. France, which relies on nuclear power to produce 85 percent of her electricity (and a good portion of ours), is also planning a rollback, while in parallel refusing to develop shale gas. The inevitable result will be that both nations, and hence the EU, will have to submit to the eagerly awaiting embrace of both Russian and Middle Eastern hydrocarbon producers, which is bound to tilt Europe's foreign policy towards the Muslim world.

The neocons too have a vested interest in maintaining the power of Islam in the Middle East, even though this ostensibly clashes with their much-touted commitment to the security of Israel. Such conflicting pieties are impossible to avoid when one proceeds not from reason and morality but from a pernicious ideology, which is to say an ideology. Anyone wishing to challenge this assertion must be prepared to explain, for example, how it is possible to reconcile fashionable feminism with the equally trendy multi-culti support for vigorous Islamic immigration, jam-packed as it comes with antediluvian attitudes to women.

3

When a strategic balance shifts, the beneficiary experiences an upsurge of energy. Its radical elite becomes more shrill, its populace more receptive. All that is required for the passion to burst out is a catalyst, some sort of point around which the newly radicalised elite can rally. The 1948 creation of the State of Israel acted as one such catalyst for the Islamic world.

In due course this event provided the same service for the neocons. There it was at last, a reliable and eternal fault line ready to turn into a fissure at any time. The neocons did not even have to draw the battle lines – these came pre-drawn, complete with attendant propaganda. Israel was an oasis of democracy in a non-democratic desert. Islamists, not to say Islamofascists, wanted to drive Israel into the sea not because she was Jewish but because she was democratic. Hence the only way to put an end to hostilities in the Middle East would be to expand the oasis by bringing democracy to the whole region. That would create lasting peace since any religious or ethnic antagonism professed by the Islamists is but a pretext masking their compulsion to fight democracy tooth and nail.

Hence the neocons have put the defence of Israel at the top of their propagandistic catechism: a permanent turmoil in the region provides a perpetual pretext for aggressive wars waged in the name of democracy. As long as the neocons keep the real reason for their love of Israel under wraps, they find their task easy. After all, every decent Westerner favours Israel over her enemies, though of course for different reasons.

Strategically inclined and historically literate individuals realise that Israel is the West's bulwark in its historical confrontation with Islam. Should lava erupt again out of the volcano that is the Muslim world, Israel would be the West's only reliable ally in the region. Those whose thinking goes beyond geopolitics remember that Israel and Christendom share much of their canon. Israel also acts as guardian of the sites held as sacred by Christians, and it takes little imagination to predict the devastation of such sites should the Muslims vanquish.

Then again, while the creation of Israel undoubtedly

provided some inspiration for Islamic forces spoiling for a fight, it is wrong to place the blame for the impassioned Muslim resurgence solely on that historical event. In fact, the briefest of looks at some of the world's flashpoints over the last 20 years will show that most of those involved Muslims and had nothing to do with Israel.

Specifically one could mention the conflicts between Bosnian Muslims and Christians, Côte d'Ivoire Muslims and Christians, Cyprus Muslims and Christians, East Timor Muslims and Christians, Indonesian Muslims and Christians in Ambon island, Kashmir Muslims and Hindus, Kosovo Muslims and Christians, Macedonian Muslims and Christians, Nigeria Muslims and both Christians and Animists, Sunni and Shi'ite Muslims throughout the Islamic world, Muslims and Christians in the Philippines, Chechen Muslims and Russians, Azeri Muslims and Armenian Christians, Sri Lanka Tamils and Buddhists, Thailand's Muslims and Buddhists in the Pattani province, Muslim Bengalis and Buddhists in Bangladesh, Muslims and Protestant, Chaldean Catholic and Assyrian Orthodox Christians in Kurdistan. The impression is hard to avoid that Islam sooner or later finds itself at war with any neighbours it happens to have.

Interestingly, both the neocons and the 'paleoconservatives', their American opponents on the Right, tend to overplay Israel's role in igniting hostilities featuring Muslims. The motives of both sides are fairly transparent if not always laudable. I have already mentioned the role Israel plays in funnelling and concentrating neocon aggressiveness. In their turn, the paleoconservatives refuse to put the defence of Israel at the top of their agenda, but they do not just do so on merit or out of contrariness. Nor do they necessarily place the issue in its historical or religious context. Instead the paleos often resort to the lowly polemic trick of accusing the neocons of either dual loyalties or even of 'Israel first' sympathies. Such point-scoring accusations spring from an actuarial calculation of the proportion of Jews among the neocons.

Neocons counter by accusing paleoconservatives of anti-Semitism, and in a few isolated instances both sides may have a point. No doubt some Jewish neoconservatives support

Israel out of ethnic solidarity, and no doubt some paleoconservatives are suspicious of Israel because they dislike Jews. But any analysis based solely on such factors is too primitive for words. The real demarcation runs between the hermetic and proselytising strains in the American religion of exceptionalism. In the past these strains were called interventionists and isolationists; in vogue now are the terms neoconservatives and paleoconservatives. Nothing but the terminology has changed.

The paleos, who are close to my definition of conservatism without fitting it fully, are more capable of sound analysis than the neocons. Yet they put this ability on hold when, for example, supporting their anti-Israel position by arguing that until 1948, the year Israel was founded, the Muslims had committed no major terrorist acts on US territory. That is true, but the first such act came 53 years after the partition of Palestine, and the next one after that, the 2013 bombing of the Boston marathon, another 12 years later. If the Muslims indeed see the USA as the terrorists' Target No. 1 because of her support of Israel, then one must commend them for their extraordinary patience. Compared, say, to the IRA 1969–1997 bombing campaign in Britain, such infrequency of action is nothing short of unprecedented in the annals of terrorism.

The neocons ascribe the low-key terrorist activity in the USA to the aggressive war the country has been waging in the Middle East since 2003. The Muslims, they say, are quaking in their boots. This brings to mind the old story of a man waving his hands about in an underground station. When asked why he is doing that, he replies that he is chasing crocodiles away. "But there are no crocodiles here," he is told. "Yes," he says, "this is why." Such non sequiturs are characteristic of neocon thinking – and the paleos' thinking is no more nuanced when they ascribe the necons' support of Israel solely to their Jewish origins.

It is true that many neocons have Jewish roots, although such founders of the movement as Jeane Kirkpatrick and Daniel Patrick Moynihan were not manifestly Hebraic. But relying on actuarial techniques in political analysis is neither grownup nor clever. Americans, being as they are a genuine melting pot of a nation, are obsessed with calculating proportions of various ethnic groups, for example those serving in Congress or sitting on the Supreme Court. It is as if the 27 current amendments to the US Constitution have been augmented by a Twenty-Eighth: "The demographic composition of every political institution shall faithfully reflect that of the nation at large."

Amazingly the neocons agree to think along the same lines. Thus Irving Kristol: "...a disproportionate number of neoconservatives are Jews." The word 'disproportionate' suggests some transgression against the Twenty-Eighth Amendment, yet unwritten. By using this word, Kristol, himself of Jewish origin, regurgitated the old anti-Semitic arguments used against pernicious cabals, such as Russian revolutionaries, to name one. These arguments are usually unsound even on the crude level at which they are pitched. For example, the proportion of Jews in the first Soviet governments, while higher than in the whole country, was roughly the same as the proportion of Jews in the urban (in other words literate) population – and actually lower than the proportion of people with secondary education or higher. It was these groups whence most Bolsheviks, either Gentile or Jewish, came.

Moreover, most neocons are secular Jews who are as indifferent to Judaism as they are to Christianity. They are not neocons because they are Jews – it would be nearer to the truth to say they are Jews because they are neocons. In fact one could cite a few examples of neoconservatives who began to accentuate, or indeed to remember, their Jewishness only after they became neoconservatives. One wonders how their self-perception would change if they had to rally their cause around the defence of, say, Thailand. The secure bet is that they would then develop an inordinate affection for Buddhism.

4

The greatest calamities in the world occur when major countries undergo mind-altering crises at a time when they are led by weak, misguided or simplistic men. The destruction of the

World Trade Centre on 11 September, 2001, triggered off such a crisis; George W. Bush was such a man.

Until then Bush's personal inclinations had been staunchly paleoconservative. Yet at the time he became president, real conservatism, even in its American, republican incarnation, had fallen by the wayside as a viable political force. The Right had been taken over by its neoconservative simulacrum, and Bush's immediate entourage did not number a single conservative among the lot.

Not being a man of independent mind and strong will, Bush allowed himself to be swayed by his advisors' entreaties. As a result he responded to the tragedy of 11 September in a stock neocon way, by instantly turning into a crusader for forcing democracy on the kicking and screaming world. Without giving the matter much thought or studying it at depth he instantly knew that Islam had nothing to do with the outrage. "Islam is peace," he declared six days after the attack, proceeding on the historical and theological evidence that must have been vouchsafed only to him and the neocons in strict confidence.

"...President Bush underwent a change," rejoices COLLENE. "September 11 made him, as Norman Podhoretz put it, 'politically born again as a passionate democratic idealist'." A neocon, in other words. In his born-again capacity Bush instantly lost whatever common sense he had hitherto possessed. According to his neonatal neocon faith, America was no longer just out to punish the perpetrators of the evil deed and forestall its repetition. Her aim now had to be to reshape in her own image all culpable nations, along with any others that got in the way.

As COLLENE explains, "...corollaries of erasing tyrannies and spreading democracy [are] interventionalism, nation-building, and many of the other difficulties... [that] long concerned traditional conservatives." Contextually neocons had no such concerns, which they went on to prove in short order, using Bush as the puppet whose wires they could pull. Their task was clear: "America has two jobs to do...: the elimination of hostile terrorist groups and the toppling of governments that harboured them."

303

Under the influence of the neocons Bush began to make not only geopolitical but also philosophical pronouncements, a role for which he was demonstrably unsuited. In the immediate aftermath of the tragedy he declared that "Moral truth is the same in every culture, in every time, and in every place…" This Kantian belief in the innate universality of the moral law is somewhat compromised by the stoning of adulterers and the crippling of thieves, both regarded as moral in some quarters but not in others. But Bush's inference that 'every culture, in every time and in every place' ought to have the same political system was pure neocon folly liberally laced with demagoguery.

Parenthetically, the neocons love dragging philosophy, appropriately distorted to suit their purposes, into debates about policy. Thus COLLENE justifies America's military crusade for democracy by appealing to the unsuspecting Königsberg hermit long since safely dead: "Kant's precepts… make it plain that, for a system of perpetual peace, every constituent nation must be 'republican' (that is a liberal democracy) and 'the law of nations should be founded on a federation of *free* states.'"

When writing his *Perpetual Peace*, poor Immanuel never suspected how his ideas would be used in our time. Yet this particular idea strikes a chord with the neocons, and conservatives too sometimes fail to detect its discordant nature. However, even Irving Kristol, never mind the Founders and certainly Kant, was aware of the difference between republicanism and liberal democracy. Obviously such knowledge is not transmitted either dynastically or osmotically.

Do let us accept at face value the defensible idea that "the elimination of hostile terrorist groups and the toppling of governments that harboured them" was a legitimate response to 11 September. How did it then follow that the United States should launch an unprovoked aggression against Iraq? It was known all along that Iraq had nothing to do with the attack on the World Trade Centre, and neither did it harbour those who had prepared it. In fact, COLLENE admits as much: "Secretary of State George Schultz insisted that 'Iraq has effectively disassociated itself from international terrorism.'" Yet, with the characteristic neocon knack for self-refutation, the same book says just a few pages later, "The president explained why Iraq was indeed a threat like no other, and how September 11 has demonstrated the urgent need to confront it."

Ideologues, regardless of what their ideology might be, will say anything that suits their purpose. Neither logic nor veracity comes into it. Thus COLLENE justifies aggression against Iraq by saying that "Perhaps the most convincing evidence of Iraq's involvement in terrorism is that it harbours well-known terrorists. The death... of the notorious terrorist Abu Nidal in Baghdad provided a useful reminder that Iraq has become a state of last resort for the pariahs of the international terror community." Actually the death of Abu Nidal 'provided a useful reminder' of exactly the opposite, considering that he was riddled with bullets by Saddam's hit squad, probably on his direct orders. Some harbouring. Some last resort.

Neither did Iraq possess any weapons of mass destruction, a possibility used as the second spurious *casus belli*, once it became no longer possible to insist on Iraq's complicity in 11 September. If any Middle Eastern country was implicated, it was not Iraq but Saudi Arabia, whence came most of the perpetrators, their chieftain Osama bin Laden, many other al-Qaeda leaders and much of their financing. But the world's biggest oil producer had to stay off-limits for even criticism, never mind military chastisement.

To their credit, the neocons were refreshingly honest about the real motives behind the invasion of Iraq and its link to 11 September. In a word, there was no link. The terrorist attack conveniently provided a pretext for the democracy crusade, which in itself was at least partly a pretext for the neocons' urge to express their pent-up pugnacity. Iraq was chosen not because it had anything to do with 11 September but because after the 1991 Operation Desert Shield the US military knew the Iraqi army was a soft touch. Though one of the largest standing armies in the world, it was poorly trained, suffered from low morale and was no match for the American invasion force.

As COLLENE puts it, "One of the countries that was seen as ripe for democracy was Iraq, and on that neocons and their friends in Washington began to agree." It was this unfortunate meeting of minds that led to Operation Desert Storm. In addition, according to the neocons, the invasion of Iraq pursued not just retributive or strategic goals, but also metaphysical ones. In fact, they ascribed to it a role roughly similar to that of the incarnation of Jesus Christ who came into this world to redeem its sins and ultimately defeat evil.

"As the events of 9/11 remind us, evil exists in this world, and it has its consequences," rues COLLENE. "Fortunately evil can be defeated. Just as Ronald Reagan's assault on the 'evil empire' was key to toppling Soviet communism, so has President Bush's response to the evil of September 11 exacted a steep price from the terrorists who orchestrated that horrible day."

This statement is mendacious on so many levels that simply listing them would take up a full page. Suffice it to say that, as I argued in the previous chapter, Ronald Reagan had little to do with toppling Soviet communism. Neither did Bush's response exact a steep price from the orchestrators of 11 September. Nor can evil ever be defeated by military means.

What the neocons and those under their sway saw in their sights was not just Iraq and not even the whole of the Middle East. They defined their task as conducting a Trotsky-style international 'permanent revolution' until America explicitly and the neocons implicitly have become the dominant global force. COLLENE concurs: "The United States should... consider itself as at once a European power, an Asian power and, of course, a Middle Eastern power." Africans and Australians must feel slighted by their continents having been left out. Nothing short of discriminatory, this.

And further: "President Bush speaks of engaging Iraq in accord with American principles... This may strike many as a tall order – but not nearly as tall as the president's insistence on engaging *the world* in accord with American principles. ... The Bush administration hopes to accomplish this happy end." The Bush administration, as we know with the 20/20 acuity of hindsight, did not manage to accomplish this happy end. The neocons have their work cut out for them: it will take a much greater effort to do to the whole world what America has done to Iraq, with Britain's able assistance.

5

Let us for the sake of argument accept the neocons' assurances at face value. Let us allow that they have no ulterior motives and all they really want is making America and her allies more secure by turning the whole Middle East into a functioning democracy. If that is indeed their goal, it is woefully misguided. For neither American strategic interests nor Israel's security can be served by promoting democracy in the region.

To understand this the neocons would have to abandon some of their core assumptions, those they share with the unapologetic Left. Specifically they would have to accept the argument that the real adversary of the West is not Islamism, Islamofascism or even Islamic terrorism. It is Islam. The neocons fail to acknowledge this because they make the typical philistine mistake of believing that everyone is, or is anxious to be, just like them. They themselves ignore religion and usually regard it as an annoying irrelevance – therefore they assume that Muslims are roughly similar. But this assumption is wrong.

The levels of piety vary throughout the Middle East but nowhere do they drop down to the level of the West's indifferent agnosticism. That is why the green banner of Islam still boasts a greater unifying power than any other modern institutional symbol. And history shows that Islam has always been hostile to the West, both doctrinally and viscerally. In the past it was supposedly so because the West espoused a wrong religion; at present, it is presumably because the West espouses none. One way or the other, such hostility has seldom been allowed to seethe under the surface – typically it splashes out as violent action, of which 11 September is only one small example. The conclusion is straightforward: the more devoutly Muslim a state is, the greater danger it presents to America, Israel and the West in general. Therefore it is in the West's interest to support the most secular Muslim regimes, while isolating or trying to undermine those run by proselytising theocracies.

In practice this means supporting the most undemocratic regimes, for Muslims, unlike most Christians and Jews, tend to be active practitioners of their creed. A democratic election is therefore likely to bring to power an Islamic regime – and this is exactly what happened in Iran, Turkey, Egypt and so forth. Alas, this strategic conclusion escapes American purveyors of democracy, particularly those of the neocon persuasion. Rather than encouraging more or less secular, which is to say undemocratic, regimes in the Middle East, the Americans have gone out of their way to help them on their way out.

Iran is one example. Since the 1979 Islamic revolution Iran's hostility to the West has been remarkable even by Muslim standards. By comparison, the Shah with his torturing secret police begins to look like a humanitarian Westerniser. At least he never threatened to develop nuclear weapons and blow up half the world. Unfortunately his commitment to universal suffrage was less unequivocal than America's, the only country this side of the erstwhile Soviet Union that knows exactly how the whole world should govern itself.

The Shah did not meet such exacting standards and was ousted with American acquiescence and possibly direct complicity. He was replaced by Ayatollah Khomeini who did not mind government by consent, provided he was the one who consented. Since then the Ayatollah, first Khomeini, then after his death in 1989 Sayyed Ali Khamenei, has held the title of Supreme Leader, not a traditional democratic nomenclature. Still, there is no doubt that Iran has become more democratic than it was under the Shah. It has also become a factor of lethal danger not only to Israel but also to the West in general.

As a rule, the army is the principal force for secularisation in Muslim lands. It was not by popular uprisings that most secular or quasi-secular regimes have ever taken over there. It was by military coups. This has been the case in Turkey, Pakistan, Egypt, Iraq, Iran, Syria, Lybia – indeed in every place where variously unpleasant but generally secular regimes were installed. Of course democratic demagoguery would not wear it: democracy *über alles* has to be its battle cry.

Yet anyone with elementary knowledge of modern history will know that an Ayatollah is the only realistic alternative to the Shah, the Muslim Brotherhood to Mubarak, tribal cannibals to the Ba'athist regimes in Iraq and Syria, Erdogan to a secular government beholden to the army. A Hilary Clinton or a Nick Clegg or especially a Norman Podhoretz is not an option in any of those places.

For example, Kemal Atatürk (d. 1938) secularised Turkey not by democratic politicking but by brute force. It was by that expedient that the predominantly Islamic Turks were made to confine their religious fervour to peaceful worship. Then, in the last decade or so, the West got into the act, spearheaded by the EU but with the Americans bringing up the rear. Turkey, they proclaimed, is at heart a European country – after all, as much as five percent of her territory is in Europe. As we all know, every European country must either belong to the EU or perish (one wonders how they had managed for centuries before the EU came into being) and Turkey is no exception. But the EU being a staunch champion of democracy, it could not possibly countenance the army exercising any serious influence in any of its member states.

Since at the time Turkey unwisely wanted to join the EU, the army was shunted aside, and the country became sufficiently democratic to satisfy the refined tastes of the EU and the USA. As a result it predictably became 'Islamist'. Which of course it had been all along at the grassroots – but, thanks be to Allah, not politically.

Forgetting that their own state was born with the midwifery of a military insurgency, the Americans and the whole 'free world' they supposedly lead decry military coups on form, while ignoring their content. One interesting example of this compulsive formalism was the reaction of both Britain and the USA to the 1999 coup in Pakistan. Both countries felt called upon to pronounce a verdict on that development, Britain because a Commonwealth country was involved, America because she feels compelled to make sanctimonious comments on everything.

The politicians of the two countries acknowledged that the overturned government was corrupt, tyrannical and unpopular; that the military coup brought in a relatively secular government that was none of the above; that the abrupt change of government may have averted a nuclear shootout between

India and Pakistan. To any sane person these reasons would have sufficed if not to welcome the new regime with open arms then at least to give it the benefit of the doubt. But to our purveyors of democracy any arguments against their tyrannical formalism are taboo. Hence the American and British leaders had to rebuke the new regime for being undemocratic irrespective of anything else.

Even before 2001 the Americans' adoration of abstract democratic principles had struck a significant blow for the growth of Islamic power, that time in Europe. During the 1998–1999 Kosovo War, NATO (a euphemism for the USA) conducted a two-month bombing campaign against Serbian targets including Belgrade, all in the name of democracy and self-determination. That Wilsonian convulsion was accompanied by a propaganda offensive where, in the tradition of this genre, the scale of Serbian atrocities was exaggerated by two orders of magnitude. As a result the nasty but potentially Christian Serbian regime had to accept the autonomy of Kosovo, which in 2008 went on to become an independent republic. Thereby Europe was rewarded with yet another Muslim state in its traditionally volatile region (in addition to Albania and to some extent Bosnia).

Getting back to the Middle East, towards the end of 2010 American seekers of democracy largely instigated 'The Arab Spring', a wave of mainly violent unrest throughout the region. With American blessing rulers have been forced from power in Tunisia, Egypt (twice), Libya and Yemen; uprisings have erupted in Bahrain and Syria; major protests accompanied by violence have broken out in Algeria, Iraq, Jordan, Kuwait, Morocco and Sudan; minor unrest has occurred in Mauritania, Oman, Saudi Arabia, Djibouti and Western Sahara.

Thousands of people were killed in Egypt in 2013 by the army reclaiming power it had lost to the radical Muslim Brotherhood in 2011. Back then, to the accompaniment of the neocons' cheers, the democratically elected Brotherhood immediately began to undo what it saw as dangerous secularism. Under its new leadership Egypt yet again was being turned into the flag bearer of Islamic extremism aiming

2001 AND ALL THAT

to unite all anti-Israeli forces in the Muslim world.

Somewhat illogically the Brotherhood fanatics and their likeminded co-religionists elsewhere immediately began to murder Christians and burn down not just synagogues but also churches of every denomination, from Coptic to Catholic to Protestant. Yet, as with most other revolutions, destruction proved to be easier than creation. It did not take Egyptians long to realise that the triumph of the only true faith came packaged with the demise of any half-decent standard of living. Riots came back, this time aimed against the Brotherhood. In time-honoured tradition the army stepped in to restore the status quo. Thus the only result of American meddling was replacing one set of generals with another – while thousands of victims swelled the collateral-damage rubric of the ledger.

6

If the West still remained Western in any other than the purely geographic sense, the proper thinking after 11 September would have followed a straight and clearly signposted path:

For 14 centuries Islam has been at war with the West. As proved by 11 September and also by the nature of most armed conflicts in today's world, Islamic energy is at its peak. So must be the West's vigilance and resolve: the Muslims must be prevented from harming the West and its allies. The reason they can parlay their impassioned energy into action with relative impunity is that they hold the oil-dripping sword of Damocles over the West's head. Therefore this sword must be take away from them.

Thus the proper course of action is to declare that any act of Islamic terrorism against the West will henceforth be regarded as an act of war – waged not by one country against another but by one civilisation against another. The aggressors may be as stateless as the neocons claim, but their support certainly is not. There is *prima facie* evidence that the support comes from Saudi Arabia, Iran and other wealthy Middle Eastern oil producers.

Since what enables them to provide this support is their vast reserves of hydrocarbons, the West (be that the US or

311

NATO or some *ad hoc* alliance) will take over the oil fields in those countries and hold them indefinitely. It will then keep the oil prices way below their present extortionate levels and use the revenues to bolster the real economies of those countries, rather than the purloined wealth of their kleptocratic rulers. If that measure still fails to stop international Islamic terrorism, the West will reserve the right to retaliate in any manner it deemed appropriate – including tactical nuclear strikes.

Notice that there is not a single word there about introducing democracy to the Middle East (impractical and undesirable), global war on tyranny (futile), securing UN support (disingenuous), or about alleviating the plight of women and homosexuals in Islamic lands (neocon policies at their most utopian and hypocritical). Nor is there any incontinent outpouring of soupy sentimentality masked by empty phrases about 'nation building', the neocons' favourite buzzword. An external power can only destroy nations, not build them. Nations either build themselves or perish long before the foundations have been laid. As to equating nation building with a proliferation of voting booths, this folly does not even qualify as clever demagoguery.

This is one illustration of the difference between conservative and neocon thinking – and of the likely course of action if real conservatism, rather than its neocon perversion, could be possible in a modern West. But since it is the neocons who set the terms of the foreign-policy debate, what have we actually achieved instead?

The West and Israel are more vulnerable to Islamic terrorism than ever before. Iran is about to acquire a nuclear capability – and possibly use it. Iraq has effectively lost its statehood and is priming herself for a massive bloodbath the second the Americans leave (full dress rehearsals are being staged even while the Americans are still there). This may well plunge the whole region into the kind of war of all against all the results of which are always unpredictable and uncontrollable. Turkey (a NATO member) is likely to be drawn into a conflict over the Kurds. Egypt has been turned into a cauldron of bubbling blood. Syria is being torn apart by civil war – any regular reader of newspapers could extend this list, made longer by every subsequent morning issue.

Islamic fanatics, those belonging to the Muslim Brotherhood and similar organisations, realise they may suffer temporary setbacks, such as the one in 2013. Yet they believe that ultimately Islam will vanquish. After all, by accepting the neocon vision of the world, the West is effectively disarming itself philosophically, politically and morally.

Our enemies' tactics become crystal-clear: the Brotherhood *et al* must scream the emollient word 'democracy' as loudly and frequently as American ears demand. At the same time their real strategic objective may be divulged only for internal consumption, since their own people need to hear something different. This was made explicit by one of the Brotherhood's guiding lights Mohamed Akram in *An Explanatory Memorandum on the General Strategic Goal for the Group in North America.*

The strategic objective is to dismantle American institutions and turn the USA, along with her allies, into a Muslim nation. As a first step, the Brotherhood must convince Muslims "that their work in America is a kind of grand Jihad in eliminating and destroying the Western civilization from within and 'sabotaging' its miserable house by their hands... so that... God's religion is made victorious over all other religions." Kamal El-Helbawi, the Brotherhood's former press secretary was even more specific: "Our ideal is a global Islamic state. Why can't we create a country called 'The United States of Islam?'"

Reading neocon propaganda or, which is more reliable, looking at the West's actions inspired by the propaganda, one may get the impression that the neocons too aim at the Islamisation of the world, or of the Middle East to begin with. Their secondary goal seems to be putting an end to 2,000 years of Christianity in the Middle East. This is of course not the case and no collusion to that effect exists. But history shows that the greatest calamities are hardly ever caused by conspiracies. It is folly that is the deadlier culprit, and the neocons may yet succeed in creating a disaster beyond our imagination.

7

The proof of the pudding may be in the eating, but applying this principle to policy affecting millions of people is always ill-advised and often criminal. Human lives are not a proper arena for experimentation, nor for trying out various ideologies or political philosophies to see what comes out in the wash. People are not material to be used to some end; they are an end in themselves. Before any serious action is taken, internally or externally, its initiators are duty-bound to weigh the likely consequences in the balance. The weighing exercise is always complicated but never impossible. It does however take some deep and nuanced thought, which is an edifice that can only ever be erected on firm intellectual, moral and spiritual foundations.

However, the foundations on which the neocons, and those receptive to their agitprop, build their ratiocination are termite-ridden. Being possessed men of frantic action, they press ahead with the construction project regardless, only to see the building come tumbling down like the walls of Jericho. Unfortunately it is not just bad ideas, such as the neocon notion of internationalism, but also good people who get buried under the rubble.

"What does... American internationalism mean?" asks COLLENE rhetorically. "First, it clearly follows from 'American exceptionalism' – a belief in the uniqueness and the virtue of the American political system that, when translated into foreign policy terms, offers the United States as a model for the world."

This and the previous chapters show what dire consequences the neocon-inspired democracy crusade can have for the world. The pudding has been shoved down our throats and found to be rancid. In due course it may also prove to be poisonous.

An epilogue without an end

1

It is useless to complain, as many Christians do, that Christianity is marginalised and increasingly suppressed in modern democracies. This is like complaining that cannibals marginalise vegetarians and suppress vegans. Modern democracy and Christendom cannot coexist; they are mutually exclusive. Some modern parties may call themselves Christian Democratic, but in reality they are usually not the second and certainly not the first. For every political, economic, social, moral and philosophical premise of modern democracy starts from denying Christendom and the religion that begat it.

This dichotomy has grievously harmed the West's public affairs and indeed public morality. In the process it has damaged even more the ability to contemplate public affairs and public morality. After all, it is impossible to understand a complex entity by studying only its small details, rather than the overall design. When a giant machine begins to sputter and malfunction, it is often not a mechanic but a design engineer who needs to get his house in order. Experience shows that a political mechanism usually breaks down not because it is not run properly but because it is poorly designed. In a society too one cannot gain a reliable understanding of quotidian details if one is forever mired in their midst. Achieving such an understanding requires a bird's eye view of the whole picture, which is impossible when one is actually in the picture.

There is no doubt that neither science nor history nor even philosophy can even approach religion in providing this panoramic vision – they cannot enable one to see the whole picture, to perceive how all its elements fit together. Thus an analytical methodology based on the founding principles of our civilisation will always achieve better results than empiricism that is so beloved of the modern Western mind.

Our society is ill, and no temporary relief of the symptoms will cure the disease unless we diagnose it accurately and understand its aetiology. That is why analysis from metaphysics is intellectually more sound and productive than that from politics, economics or political economics. The underlying disease has afflicted the spirit of the West – its physical maladies are merely symptoms.

2

"In a revolution, as in a novel, the most difficult part to invent is the end," wrote Tocqueville. Predicting the dénouement is so much harder for someone who neither wrote the novel nor abetted the revolution. The best such an outside observer can hope to achieve is a dispassionate scrutiny of the plot, accompanied by an analysis of the principal characters and the narrative strands.

Thus it is impossible to predict how the democratic revolution will end. What is indisputable, however, is that it was truly a revolution. And though we may not be able to predict the exact finale, we can rest assured that at some time it will indeed end. Everything ends sooner or later.

Like any other revolution, the democratic one seeks to replace old certitudes with new mythology. If a revolution is successful, the mythology eventually turns into orthodoxy and in due course it itself becomes a certitude. At least that is how it is usually perceived by most people. Those few who are capable of recognising make-believe for what it is are usually either too lazy or else too fearful to share their understanding with others. While there is no excuse for laziness, they do have a reason to be afraid. Orthodoxies, especially those of recent provenance, do not like being contradicted and they hate being mocked.

The democratic revolution, like any other, attempted to erect the new on the ruins of the old. That presupposed the necessity of turning the old into ruins, and so it has transpired. Courtesy of Joseph Schumpeter we these days feel at ease with the idea of creative destruction, and in many areas the term has much validity. In order to create modern neuroscience it was necessary to destroy Aristotle's belief that the heart is the neurological centre of man. To create his own theory of the universe, Newton had to destroy Ptolemy's. To build a new centre of Paris, Baron Haussmann had to wipe out the houses adorning the old centre. The invention of three-field rotation consigned slash-and-burn agriculture to distant memory.

Yet some destruction is just that, destruction, and no Phoenix rises from the ashes. When Cromwell's Puritans or French Huguenots were smashing religious statues, the destruction was pure and simple. When post-war British councils were pulling down Georgian terraces to replace them with modern monstrosities, they destroyed without creating. The French who, according to Régine Pernoud, one of the country's greatest mediaevalists, demolished 80 percent of their Romanesque and Gothic buildings in the century following the revolution, replaced them with little of value.

What about the democratic revolution then? Was the destruction it wreaked creative or merely destructive? It was both, and the only way of seeing which end outweighs the other is to put the revolution on some scales whose precision we trust. The balance will then tip one way or the other and we shall have our answer. This is of course a metaphor, for real scales, properly zeroed and calibrated, leave no room for interpretation. They are as objective as only inanimate machines can ever be. People, however, are animate and sapient. This means they are subjective, and those who claim they are not usually tend to be even more so.

This essay has been one such weighing exercise, and the results are as unequivocal to me as they would be to anyone else proceeding from the same starting point and using the same analytical methodology. The democratic revolution has destroyed infinitely, excruciatingly more than it has created. Moreover, its successes mostly fall into the purely material domain, while its failures have undermined the realm of the spirit – something on which the edifice of our civilisation rests.

Modern people find it easy to ignore this realm for as long as they can be certain of their physical well-being. Offered the sublime gifts of freedom, wisdom and moral heroism, they have flung them back into the donor's face. Instead they demand 'happiness', however nebulous, however defined – as long as it is defined in strictly material terms. Keep the supply of variously ingenious trinkets coming, and today's people will be happy to restrict their spiritual pursuits to whatever such trinkets provide. It is of little concern to them that the avalanche of I-Pads, DVD players and tweeted inanities is burying under the rubble all that historically made the West Western.

"But seek ye first the kingdom of God, and his right-eousness; and all these things shall be added unto you," was the key promise – and premise – of our civilisation. Yet today's men have stood it on its head. They seek 'all those things' first and last, hoping that somehow the kingdom of God will come free of charge with the last batch. And if it does not, that is fine too. Who needs it? Everyone, is the answer to that, and today's people are beginning to sense this, as they are suffering from the gaping emptiness of their lives.

We are seeing today that matters are not quite so straight-forward as they are fancied by modern imagination. In the beginning was the Word, and when it is no longer heard everything that comes thereafter will suffer, including the supply of material happiness. We are observing today declining standards of living across most of the West, and the ongoing economic crisis is a harbinger of things to come. The materi-alist, egalitarian premise on which modernity was built is proving grossly inadequate to keep it upright. Our society is becoming more unequal, not less; its material wealth is dimin-ishing, not growing; its democracy is delivering increasingly less liberty and even less freedom.

Modernity is ruled not by reason, as it claims, but by a compendium of scattered, unconnected and generally meaningless slogans, put forth without much thought and then discarded at a kaleidoscopic speed. The one that has endured longest is the one with the greatest destructive potential:

equality of everything. This slogan was hoisted up on the mast of modernity as it was heading for the rocks. Everything was supposed to be equal: all beliefs and disbeliefs, all opinions and judgments, all social and economic conditions and – germane to my theme here – all political rights.

Yet equality of everything presupposes belief in nothing, and man cannot live without believing. Hence the macabre hopelessness of what today passes for philosophy: an existential hole cannot be filled with I-Pads. It can only be lined with despair. The thought that life has no meaning other than life itself is as unbearable spiritually as it is unsound logically. Pursuing happiness in their meaningless existence, people only succeed in finding misery. Rather than being rewarded for their materialism they are being punished for their soullessness. Paradoxically some of the punishment is meted out in the very material sphere they worship with such abandon.

3

Unchecked democracy is the political expression of egalitarian materialism, just as unchecked free enterprise is its economic expression. Yet no manifestation of a corrupt idea will thrive, certainly not for ever and, historically speaking, not even for a particularly long time. A bad idea will rig self-refutation time bombs to all its offshoots.

The bombs are going off one by one. Hence we are seeing today that modern liberal democracy, whatever the initial intention behind it, has turned into a modern tyranny. This comes complete with a direct and ever more forceful attack on every founding tenet of liberalism, including especially free speech. Newspapers everywhere are censored and, even worse, self-censored. The censorship is not yet as draconian as in the totalitarian regimes of yesteryear, but only a blind man will fail to see that the diktats of political correctness are inexorably pushing it that way. Political correctness is fascism that gets its way without having – yet – to resort to much violence.

Just as the political gap between all modern regimes is narrowing, so is the economic gap. The more widely democratic egalitarianism is cloned into the economic arena, the more the economy begins to resemble a huge, and hugely corrupt, socialist corporation – and the less equal it becomes. More and more modern states begin to run their business as megalomaniac Ponzi schemes, with predictable results. States sink into insolvency and their citizens are only half a step behind. The only people who benefit are the elite that either runs the state or is in cahoots with those who do. The chasm separating the haves from the have-nots grows, and resentment grows *pari passu*. The spiritual depths needed to accept inequality of condition with indifference are no longer being plumbed.

Even worse, since politics is the fulcrum around which everything in the modern West revolves, and since Democracy (always implicitly capitalised) is the fulcrum of modern politics, the same process is observable in areas not traditionally seen as demonstrably political. Unable to deliver equality of condition, modernity insists on presupposing and trying to enforce the equality of everything else: taste, wisdom, morality, 'rights'. The only judgment people are encouraged to make is that no judgment must be made. They are all useless, presumably because, being all equally valid, they cancel one another out. 'Judgmental' and 'opinionated' are now among the worst putdowns in America and increasingly in Britain.

Democracy, in its modern, unchecked incarnation, has become part of what I call the rule by simulacrum. It pretends to be what it is not and insists on make-believe being accepted as real. But as it is not real the only way to enforce the rule by simulacrum is either to coerce or to brainwash people into compliant docility.

4

Sooner or later most revolutions turn into a Saturn devouring his own children, and the more radical the upheaval the more and the sooner will its perpetrators suffer. The French and Russian revolutions were more radical than the English and American ones, which is why before long they both slaughtered the revolutionaries. But ultimately even the more vegetarian revolutions will turn carnivorous, and the democratic one is no exception. Like all modern revolutions it was perpetrated by the middle classes, albeit acting in the name of 'the people'. And it is the middle classes that are being crushed by the juggernaut of Democracy.

Hilaire Belloc presciently wrote in his 1912 book *The Servile State* that when egalitarian principles are applied to a supposedly free economy, it will sooner or later become redistributive and therefore servile. Though the remedies Belloc proposed had more to do with romantic fantasy than with economic policy, his crystal ball was in working order. We can see with a naked eye how, by forcing socialist distribution down the throat of capitalist production, modern governments take a wrecking ball to property, that cornerstone of middle-class security and liberty.

As a result, economies in the Western world begin to resemble those in the third world, where a small elite towers above a great wad of dispossessed and déclassé humanity. A small minority of the erstwhile middle classes move up to join the elite, while the rest sink into the morass of servile proletarianism – not only in their economic condition but, more important, also in their tastes, beliefs and general mores.

The amenities of civilised existence, such as above all home ownership, are increasingly moving outside the middle classes' reach. Modern states can only survive by expropriatory zeal, and it is the middle classes that the states are zealously expropriating. Direct taxation is the most visible but not the most devastating stratagem of accelerating confiscation. Even more damaging is the steady debauchment of currency, making a mockery of fiscal prudence, that traditional bourgeois virtue, especially when informed by Protestantism. If the last 50 years of the 'American' twentieth century produced an inflation of 2,000 percent in Britain, then the traditional frugality of the middle classes cannot survive: as their capital is shrinking, even those who by nature are neither wastrels nor gamblers have to spend all they earn (and often much more than they earn) or else take silly risks with investments, usually in property.

In Britain this tendency has produced asset inflation that

outstrips the money inflation by a factor of seven, effectively pricing the middle classes out of the neighbourhoods in which the middle classes have traditionally lived. Instead they are forced to move out and intermingle with the lower classes, or rather increasingly with the underclass thoroughly corrupted by the welfare state. Since the state in its munificence has also destroyed public education, that traditional social and economic hoist, before long the middle classes intermingle with the underclass not only in physical location but also in tastes and values. That is to say the middle classes cease to exist. The pipeline through which economic, artistic and political talent used to flow into society is shut down, and the new, increasingly brutalised and internationalised elite reigns unchallenged.

5

Exactly the same trend, and for all the same reasons, is observable in the politics of the West. All Western countries are these days ruled by a political class that is further separated from the masses than it ever was in any monarchy. The rule of the new elite is absolute and it can only be sustained by systematic destruction of everything standing in its way. Its greatest, if diminishing, obstacles are survivals of Christendom, not only Christianity itself but also its inherent tradition of decentralising both political and economic power. Just as modern businesses gravitate towards megalomaniac expansion, so do modern governments grow into gigantic puppet masters pulling the wires of the populace from the secure distance of national, or increasingly more often international, centres of power.

Democracy is the mendacious slogan used by this elite to self-vindicate and self-perpetuate. The concept has been divested of all serious meaning in exactly the same way as the notion of 'socialism' was desemanticised in the Soviet Union. There the commissars would put on stern expressions and admonish a doubter by saying, "If you are against [starvation wages, Dickensian warrens of communal flats, concentration camps, deficit of everything from food to books], you are against socialism." No further argument was necessary, especially since this one had the implicit weight of a bullet behind it. Similarly, today's Western ruling elites say, "If you are against [the ruinous welfare state, moron-spewing education, states refusing to pay their way, the general proletarisation of culture, homosexual marriage, expropriation through draconian taxation], you are against democracy." Nothing more needs saying, a smug QED smile is deemed to be well justified.

Neither higher reason nor even elementary logic need apply. Once Democracy is run up the flagpole all are supposed to snap to attention and salute. The massive brainwashing effort that goes by the name of modern education has rendered people incapable of asking even the most obvious questions. Democracy will not be challenged and therefore it will not be checked. Human nature being what it is, democracy will then turn into the rule of a distinctly mediocre but aggressively self-serving elite. As democracy's ability to govern is no longer tested, it dies away.

If by enforcing its deified status Democracy happens to destroy constitutional arrangements that have passed the test of centuries, no one is unduly bothered. Witness, for example, the systematic destruction of the upper house of our Parliament, whose historical function has been to act as a gasket between the unelected power of the monarch and the elected power of the Commons. To act in that capacity effectively and credibly, members of the House of Lords must be free from political pressures; under no circumstances must they be beholden to any political party. Their lordships' judgment must be based on their conscience, their understanding of the country's best interests and their disinterested desire to serve those interests. When this is the case, the Lords can act as an essential, vital check on democracy, which is to say on the power of the ruling political elite that is not always guided by the noblest of principles.

Unlike old monarchies, new democracies tolerate no competition. So it stands to reason that the ruling elite either has to eliminate the upper House altogether or, if this ideal solution is still not practicable, to reduce it to a travesty of its former self. Like most modern perversions this worthy fight has to be joined under the banner of Democracy. Our intellectually challenged modernity is encouraged to put into effect yet another simple, and simply ignorant, syllogism. Democracy is good; the House of Lords is not democratic; ergo, the House of Lords, in its traditional form, is not good. Conclusion: members of the Lords must be either appointed by the political elite whose favour they curry or, ideally, they ought to be elected in the same meaningless and fundamentally dishonest manner the political elite itself is elected.

In other words, just as the US Senate at its founding used to be a simulacrum of the Lords, the House of Lords must now become a simulacrum of the US Senate. In fact, one hears calls all over the print and broadcast media for renaming our upper house the Senate. And why not? We already have our own mock-American Supreme Court that has usurped the judicial functions traditionally exercised by the House of Lords and the Judicial Committee of the Privy Council. We are about to get our own FBI, which flies in the face of traditional law enforcement practices in Britain. Before long we are going to write down some sort of constitution complete with a zillion amendments that will supersede the English Common Law. So why not convert the Lords into a Senate and effectively an extension of the Commons? No reason at all.

Try saying to a modern politico that yes, the House of Lords is not democratic and so it must remain because but that is its whole point. He will contort his features in genuine, or more likely put-on, bemusement. Are you against democracy then? he will ask. Implicitly, you will thereby declare yourself to be a fierce opponent of Goodness, Virtue and Rule by Simulacrum. Off with your head – at this point in a manner of speaking only, but watch this space. It takes rare independence of mind and strength of conviction not to fall for this well-practised trick.

Whether this stratagem naturally developed out of the *Zeitgeist* or it is indeed a neocon trick, is hard to say. A bit of both, is the likeliest scenario. The *Zeitgeist* doubtless is pulling in that direction but, no matter how powerful it is, it never acts on its own. There is always an impassioned group working to convert it into action. American, and increasingly British, neoconservatives are perhaps the most vociferous and pernicious of such groups, but they are not the only ones. These days Democracy has proved its destructive credentials to such an extent that it is readily deployed even by undisguised socialists or even communists (for example in China), whose genesis is manifestly undemocratic.

This alone would be sufficient to show that Democracy is but an empty cavity that can be filled with any wickedness modernity can concoct. The neocons, along with their predecessors, followers and acolytes, have succeeded in perching Democracy on top of a totem pole high enough to keep it a safe distance away from any decortication or criticism. It is treated as a god, except that this deity will neither forgive nor save. As it has proved over the last century, the pagan god of Democracy is mythological in its goodness but very real in its wickedness. It is a wrathful demiurge whose thirst for blood must continue to be quenched. The neocons, self-appointed apostles of this deity, act in the spirit their secular religion imposes. In this they are nothing short of consistent.

Here ends the epilogue of this essay. How the epilogue of the democratic revolution will end is hard to predict. One thing is for sure: if it is the neocons who write it, God save us all.

A very brief bibliography

John Adams *Adams-Jefferson Letters, Papers of John Adams*
Thomas Aquinas *Summa Theologiae, On Kingship*
Aristotle *The Politics*
Augustine of Hippo *The City of God*
Hilaire Belloc *The Servile State*
Jeremy Bentham *Introduction to Principles of Morals and Legislation*
Sergo Beria *Beria My Father*
Alan Bloom *The Closing of the American Mind*
James Boswell *The Life of Samuel Johnson*
William F. Buckley *God and Man at Yale, Did You Ever See a Dream Walking?*
Edmund Burke *Reflections on the Revolution in France, Thoughts on the Present Discontents, Speeches*
Alexander Boot *How the West Was Lost, The Crisis Behind Our Crisis, God and Man According to Tolstoy*
James Burnham *The Managerial Revolution, Suicide of the West*
Whittaker Chambers *Witness*
François-René de Chateaubriand *Memoirs from Beyond the Tomb*
G.K. Chesterton *Delphi Complete Works*
Samuel Taylor Coleridge *Essays on the Principles of Method*
COLLENE (See Introduction)
R.G. Collingwood *An Essay on Metaphysics, The Principles of Art*
The Constitution of the United States of America
The Federalist Papers Alexander Hamilton, John Jay and James Madison
Johann Fichte *Foundations of Natural Right*
Milton Friedman *Free to Choose*
Francis Fukuyama *The End of History and the Last Man*
Friedrich Hayek *The Road to Serfdom, The Constitution of Liberty*

GWF Hegel *Phenomenology of Spirit*

Thomas Hobbes *Leviathan, Behemoth, De Corpore Politico*

David Hume *Essays, An Enquiry Concerning Human Understanding*

Thomas Jefferson *Writings, Autobiography, Notes on the State of Virginia and Private Papers, Addresses, Letters*

Dr Samuel Johnson *The Works of Samuel Johnson*

Immanuel Kant *Critique of Practical Reason, Towards Perpetual Peace*

Russell Kirk *The Conservative Mind: From Burke to Eliot, The Politics of Prudence*

Irving Kristol *Reflections of a Neoconservative: Looking Back, Looking Ahead, Neoconservatism: The Autobiography of an Idea*

Stephen M. Lee *George Canning and Liberal Toryism, 1801-27*

Walter Lippmann *The Cold War*

David Lloyd George *War Memoirs*

John Locke *An Essay Concerning Human Understanding, A Letter Concerning Toleration, Two Treatises of Government, Political Essays*

Bruce Lockhart *Memoirs of a British Agent*

Niccolò Machiavelli *The Prince, The Discourses on Livy*

Joseph de Maistre *Considerations on France, The Generative Principles of Political Constitutions, Letters on the Spanish Inquisition, On God and Society, On the Pope*

Karl Marx *The Communist Manifesto*

Sergei Melgunov *The Red Terror*

John Stuart Mill *On Liberty and Other Essays, Utilitarianism*

Ludwig von Mises *Socialism*

Baron de Montesquieu *The Spirit of the Laws*

Michael Oakeshott *On Human Conduct, On History and Other Essay*

José Ortega y Gasset *Revolt of the Masses*

Thomas Paine *Right of Man, Common Sense and Other Political Writings*

St Paul *Epistles*

Richard Pipes *Communism: A History*

Plato *Dialogues* (especially *The Republic, Timaeus, Critias* and *Laws*)

Plutarch *Life of Alexander*

Ayn Rand *Atlas Shrugged*

Hermann Rauschning *Hitler Speaks*

BIBLIOGRAPHY

Friedrich Reck-Malleczewen *Diary of a Man in Despair*

Vasily Rozanov *The Apocalypse of Our Time*

Jean-Jacques Rousseau *Discourse on the Origin of Inequality, On the Social Contract*

George Santayana *The Life of Reason*

Leopold Schwarzschild *The Red Prussian*

Adam Smith *An Inquiry into the Nature and Causes of the Wealth of Nations, The Theory of Moral Sentiments*

Oswald Spengler *Decline of the West*

Leo Strauss *Natural Right and History*

Anthony C. Sutton *Western Technology and Soviet Economic Development*

Alexis de Tocqueville *Democracy in America, Ancien Regime and the Revolution*

Eric Voegelin *The New Science of Politics*

Voltaire *Letters on England*

George Watson *The Lost Literature of Socialism*

Peter Witonski *The Wisdom of Conservatism*

Index

Abélard, Peter, 56
Abramovich, Roman, 281
Acton, John Dalberg, Lord, 118, 119, 123
Adams, John, 70, 86, 90, 155
Adams, John Quincy, 98, 105, 106
Adams, Samuel, 85
Ahmadinejad, Mahmoud, 154
Akram, Mohamed, 313
Albert the Great, 56
Alcibiades, 154
Aliev, Gaidar, 283
Allende, Salvatore, 200
Ames, Aldrich, 278
Ames, Fisher, 71
Andropov, Yuri, 268, 271, 272, 279-281
Anselm, St, 55
Aquinas, Thomas, St, 17, 49, 56, 147
Aristotle, 17, 21-23, 25, 27, 28, 44, 45, 40, 88, 118, 145, 154, 163, 174, 317
Arius, 232
Ashbrook, John M, 224
Atatürk, Kemal, 309
Auden, WH, 210
Augustine of Hippo, St, 17, 37, 43, 55, 60

Bagehot, Walter, 53
Bancroft, George, 123
Beethoven, Ludwig van, 57
Belloc, Hilaire, 321
Bellow, Saul, 211
Bentham, Jeremy, 18
Berezovsky, Boris, 281
Beria, Lavrentiy, 270
Beria, Sergo, 198
Bismarck, Otto von, 241
Blair, Tony, 189, 257
Bloom, Alan, 18, 211, 243
Bozell, Brent, 210
Brahms, Johannes, 57
Brecht, Bertolt, 239
Brezhnev, Leonid, 268, 272, 279
Buckley, James, 228
Buckley, William F, 209-212, 215, 220, 224, 228
Bukharin, Nikolai, 214
Bullitt, William, 183, 184
Burke, Edmund, 6, 17, 49-51, 65-68, 81, 99, 100, 118, 148, 151, 205, 206, 227
Burnham, James, 17, 210, 212, 213, 215, 216, 218-220, 263
Bush, George HW, 236
Bush, George W, 210, 303, 304, 306
Bush, Prescott, 210

331

Caesar, Julius, 28, 37
Calvin, John, 167, 192
Canning, George, 17
Caracalla, Emperor, 77
Carlyle, Thomas, 205
Cary, Lucius, Viscount Falkland, 148
Castro, Fidel, 199
Chambers, Whittaker, 210, 212-216, 218-220
Chaplin, Charlie, 198
Charles, Prince of Wales, 115 (n)
Chateaubriand, François-René de, 17
Che Guevara, 32, 117
Chernenko, Konstantin, 279
Chesterton, Gilbert Keith, 59
Choudary, Anjem, 284
Christie, Walter J, 180
Churchill, Winston, 126, 146, 147, 183-186, 294
Clegg, Nick, 309
Cleisthene, 26
Clémenceau, Georges, 135
Clementi, Muzio, 57
Clinton, Bill, 236
Clinton, Hilary, 309
Coleridge, Samuel Taylor, 17, 67, 205
Collingwood, Robert George, 17, 44, 163, 205, 257
Condé, 'the Great', 120
Condorcet, Marie Jean de, 71
Conquest, Robert, 210
Constantine, Emperor, 31
Copernicus, Nicolaus, 63, 64
Creel, George, 135, 136, 141
Cromwell, Oliver, 317
Crozier, Brian, 210, 212

Danton, Georges, 157
Davis, Jefferson, 90
Dawkins, Richard, 195, 294
Decter, Midge, 193
Denikin, Anton, 141
Derrida, Jacques, 112 (n)
Descartes, René, 43, 64, 271
Diderot, Denis, 66, 227
Dos Passos, John, 79, 210, 212

Eastman, Max, 210, 212
Eisenhower, Dwight, 196, 224
El-Helbawi, Kamal, 313
Eliot, Thomas Stearns, 103, 196, 205
Engels, Friedrich, 216, 217, 250
Erdogan, Recep Tayyip, 308
Eybler, Joseph Leopold, 57

Fermi, Enrico, 198
Feuerbach, Ludwig, 225 (n)
Fichte, Johann Gottlieb, 18
Ford, Henry, 180-182
Foucault, Michel, 112 (n)
Franco, Francisco, 181
Franklin, Benjamin, 66, 71
Friedman, Milton, 77, 160, 161, 168, 210
Fuchs, Klaus, 198
Fukuyama, Francis, 18, 19, 252-256

Galileo, Galilei, 63
Garaudy, Roger, 230
George III, 69, 70, 77, 120
Gibbon, Edward, 77
Gilder, George, 160, 161, 168
Glazer, Nathan, 18, 248
Godwinson, Harold, King, 45
Goldwater, Barry, 224, 225,

INDEX

227, 236
Gorbachev, Mikhail, 268, 270-274, 279, 283 (n), 285
Gramsci, Antonio, 287
Grant, Ulysses, 89
Grayling, Anthony C, 195
Greenglass, David, 198
Greenspan, Alan, 208
Gregory the Great, 60
Grishin, Victor, 279

Haag, Ernest van den, 210
Hailsham, Quintin Hogg, Lord, 190, 191, 215, 222, 223, 225
Hamilton, Alexander, 76, 86
Hammer, Armand, 278
Hammett, Dashiell, 199
Hanssen, Robert, 278
Harrington, Michael, 229
Harris, Arthur, Sir, 181
Hart, Jeffery, 210
Haussmann, Georges-Eugène, 317
Hayek, Friedrich, 17, 168, 207
Hegel, Georg Wilhelm Friedrich, 17, 227, 249-251, 253, 257
Hellman, Lillian, 198
Helvétius, Claude Adrien, 66, 71
Henry, Patrick, 85
Henry VIII, 51
Herostratus, 11
Hiss, Alger, 186 (n), 197, 214
Hitler, Adolf, 91 (n), 154, 177, 178, 180, 181, 183, 209, 217, 233, 260
Hobbes, Thomas, 17, 64, 66, 119-122, 251
Hooker, Richard, 205

Hume, David, 18, 60, 71, 115, 166-169, 227
Hummel, Johann Nepomuk, 57
Humphrey, Hubert, 236
Haydn, Joseph, 57

Ibn-Saud, 297 (n)
Irving, David, 212

Jackson, Henry, 236
Jaffa, Harry, 224-227
Jay, John, 86
Jefferson, Thomas, 66, 71, 72, 78, 80-82, 86, 88, 90, 91 (n), 96, 98, 99, 112, 119, 121, 123, 155, 165, 225, 226 (n), 232, 256
Jesus Christ, 32, 34, 35, 75, 90, 95, 117, 162, 169, 196, 232
Johnson, Samuel, Dr, 21, 22, 81, 100, 170, 205, 247
John XII, Pope, 60
Joyce, William, 120
Julian, the Apostate, 33, 34

Kamenev, Lev, 214
Kant, Immanuel, 18, 147, 227, 304
Kempis, Thomas à, 276
Kendall, Willmoore, 210, 227
Kennedy, John Fitzgerald, 96, 105-107
Kennedy, Robert, 198
Kerry, John, 210
Keynes, John Maynard, 234
Khamenei, Ayatollah, 308
Khodorkovsky, Mikhail, 281
Khomeini, Ayatollah, 308
Khrushchev, Nikita, 268, 270 (n), 276, 279

Kirk, Russell, 17, 205-211, 222, 221, 223, 225, 227
Kirkpatrick, Jeanne, 18, 157, 248, 301
Knox, Dudley Wright, 178
Koestler, Arthur, 230
Kristol, Irving, 18, 19, 22, 106, 137, 210, 212, 222, 223, 225, 226, 229-232, 235-244, 247, 248, 302, 304
Kruchina, Nikolai, 280
Kuehnellt-Leddith, Erik, von, 210

Laborc, Sandor, 284, 285
Lafayette, Marquis de, 226 (n)
Landsbergis, Vytautas, 283, 284
Lattimore, Owen, 199
Lee, Robert E, 89, 90
Leibniz, Gottfried Wilhelm von, 63
Lenin, Vladimir, 11, 18, 91 (n), 98, 100, 122, 138, 140, 141, 177, 209, 213, 216, 217, 235, 255, 267, 268, 274, 276, 277
Liebknecht, Karl, 134 (n)
Lincoln, Abraham, 89, 98, 99, 127, 128, 224
Lippmann, Walter, 186
Lloyd George, David, 138-141
Locke, John, 17, 26, 50, 64, 66, 68, 71, 72, 76-78, 80, 82, 85, 90, 115, 119-122, 234, 251, 292
Lockhart, Bruce, 140
Lombard, Peter, 56
Louis XIV, 58, 120, 156
Luce, Henry, 157, 256
Lukashenko, Alexander, 154

Luther, Martin, 114
Lycurgus, 30

Machiavelli, Niccolò, 17, 111
Madison, James, 80, 81 (n), 86, 88, 155, 181
Maistre, Joseph de, 17, 49, 50, 83, 121
Major, John, 193
Mann, Thomas, 22
Mansfield, William Murray, Lord, 81
Mao Zedong, 186, 199, 297
Martel, Charles, 295
Marx, Groucho, 147, 264
Marx, Karl, 18, 39, 160, 216, 217, 233, 250, 251, 253, 263, 265, 271, 274, 275, 287
Maxwell, Robert, 277-280
McCarthy, Joseph, 199
McClellan, George B, 89
McCollum, Arthur H, 178
McLuhan, Marshall, 16
Melgunov, Sergei, 219
Merkel, Angela, 281
Meyer, Frank, 210, 212, 215, 219, 220
Michelangelo, 24
Mill, John Stuart, 18, 123, 124
Mises, Ludwig von, 17, 168, 210
Mohammed, 295, 296
Monroe, James, 85, 129, 130, 132
Montesquieu, Charles-Louis de, 18, 66, 123
Morgan, John Pierpont, 181, 182
Moynihan, Daniel Patrick, 18, 229, 248, 301

INDEX

Mozart, Wolfgang Amadeus, 57
Mubarak, Hosni, 308
Mugabe, Robert, 154
Muggeridge, Malcolm, 219, 230
Mussolini, Benito, 89, 209

Napoleon I, 129, 249
Napoleon III, 129
Neuhaus, Richard, 210, 211
Nevzlin, Leonid, 281
Newman, John Henry, 205, 211
Newton, Isaac, 63, 64, 317
Nguema, Francisco Macías, 154
Nidal, Abu, 305
Nisbet, Robert, 210
Nixon, Richard, 197, 198, 224

Oakeshott, Michael, 17, 210
Obama, Barack, 236, 237
Olney, Richard, 130
Oppenheimer, Robert, 198
Ortega y Gasset, José, 17
Orwell, George, 169
Osama bin Laden, 305
O'Sullivan, John, 210
O'Sullivan, John L, 97

Paine, Thomas, 72, 73, 99, 100, 225-227
Paul, St, 6, 37, 38, 49, 109, 126, 127
Pericles, 28, 107
Pernoud, Régine, 317
Perón, Juan Domingo, 154
Pershing, John J, 134
Philby, Kim, 278
Picasso, Pablo, 239
Picchini, Niccolò, 57
Pipes, Richard, 265, 266
Pitt the Younger, William, 149

Pius IX, Pope, 47 (n)
Pius XI, 171
Plato, 17, 18, 25-27, 29, 45, 88, 107, 119, 145, 154, 161, 163, 174, 217, 224
Plutarch, 287
Podhoretz, Norman, 18, 303, 309
Ponomarev, Boris, 279
Pontecorvo, Bruno, 198
Praxiteles, 24, 107
Ptolomy, 317
Pushkin, Alexander, 217
Putin, Vladimir, 154, 266, 268, 269, 280-282, 284, 286

Rand, Ayn, 207-209
Rauschning, Hermann, 233
Reagan, Ronald, 96, 215, 224, 228, 254, 306
Reck-Malleczewen, Friedrich Percival, 221 (n)
Reilly, Sidney, 139, 140
Renan, Ernest, 112
Robeson, Paul, 198
Robespierre, Maximilien de, 11, 91 (n), 157
Roosevelt, Theodore, 98
Roosevelt, Franklin Delano, 176-179, 182-185, 233
Rosenberg, Ethel, 198
Rosenberg, Julius, 198
Rostow, Eugene, 273
Rousseau, Jean-Jacques, 17, 26, 73, 121, 127, 243, 249
Rozanov, Vasily, 186

Saakashvili, Mikheil, 284
Saddam, Hussein, 305
Salieri, Antonio, 57

335

Santayana, George, 13, 17
Sartre, Jean-Paul, 239
Schlamm, William, 212
Schubert, Franz, 57
Schumpeter, Joseph, 57, 234, 317
Semichiastny, Vladimir, 281
Shelepin, Alexander, 271, 281
Shevardnadze, Eduard, 283
Silone, Ignazio, 230
Smith, Adam, 18, 64, 71, 115, 166-169, 227
Sobell, Morton, 198
Sobiesky, Jan, 296
Sobran, Joseph, 210, 212
Socrates, 27, 58, 145, 154
Solon, 30
Sophocles, 107
Spender, Stephen, 230
Stalin, Josef, 166, 179-183, 185, 187, 196, 209, 216, 217, 221, 233, 235, 264, 267, 268, 283 (n)
Stamitz, Johann, 57
Steffens, Lincoln, 259
Strauss, Leo, 18, 72
Süssmayr, Franz Xaver, 57
Sutton, Anthony C, 184 (n)
Swopes, Gerard, 233
Szilard, Leo, 198

Teagle, Walter, 233
Thatcher, Margaret, 228
Thurmond, Strom, 196
Tiberius, Emperor, 42, 192
Tocqueville, Alexis de, 84, 97, 109-128, 133, 149, 155, 170, 222, 242, 316

Tolstoy, Leo, 232
Trotsky, Leon, 18, 100, 138, 141, 187, 213, 221, 222, 235, 264, 267, 274, 277, 294, 306
Trumbo, Dalton, 199
Tukhachevsky, Mikhail, 266
Turenne, Henri de La Tour, Vicomte de, 120
Turgot, Anne-Robert-Jacques, 71

Veselovsky, Leonid, 280
Vespasian, Emperor, 282
Voegelin, Eric, 17, 210
Voltaire, 17, 66, 112, 227

Wallace, Henry, 111
Warburg, Max, 233
Warburg, Paul, 233
Washington, George, 80, 88, 90, 98, 99
Waugh, Evelyn, 198, 210
Weaver, Richard, 227
Weber, Max, 167
Welles, Orson, 198
William of Champeaux, 56
Wilde, Oscar, 147
Wilson, Woodrow, 134-141, 176, 177, 287
Winthrop, John, 95, 96
Wolfe, Tom, 210
Wrangel, Pyotr, 141

Yanukovych, Viktor, 154, 284
Yeltsin, Boris, 268, 271, 274
Yudenich, Nikolai, 141

Zinoviev, Grigory, 214, 277